George T. Wolz
St. Charles College
December 20, 1965

Diligently Compared

The Revised Standard Version and the King James Version of the Old Testament

by

MILLAR BURROWS

. . . and with the former Translations diligently compared and revised . . .

(Preface, King James Version)

THOMAS NELSON & SONS

London *New York* *Toronto*

to the memory of

GEORGE DAHL

devoted, conscientious scholar,
faithful and beloved friend,
profoundly devout Christian

Library of Congress Catalog Card Number: 64-25281

Printed in the United States of America

PREFACE

Conceived originally as a "Companion" to the Revised Standard Version of the Old Testament, this book has turned out to be something quite different. Most of the topics that would ordinarily be treated in a Companion, as that term is commonly used, are now admirably covered by the annotated editions of the Revised Standard Version, Bible Dictionaries, and introductory articles in commentaries. A few basic questions, however, still require elucidation. Why was a revision of the English Bible necessary in the first place? What presuppositions and principles governed the making of the Revised Standard Version? To what extent and in what ways, if any, is it an improvement on the King James Version, the Revised Version, and the American Standard Version? For most readers of the English Bible this means simply: How does the Revised Standard Version differ from the King James Version, and why? To answer these questions as specifically and fully as possible within the limits of a single volume of moderate size is the purpose of this book.

To achieve that purpose, not only general statements but a good deal of illustrative material must be presented. The various kinds of changes made in the revision of the older translations and the reasons for making them can be made clear only by citing specific instances. To assemble the material for such an exposition I have gone through the whole Old Testament verse by verse, comparing the Revised Standard Version in detail not only with the King James Version but also with the Revised Version, the American Standard Version, the Hebrew text, and the ancient Versions. The enormous mass of data thus accumulated had to be classified, and only a fraction of it could be used. Enough instances had to be chosen to make each point clear, without giving so many that the reader would be unable to "see the woods for the trees." Even so, it proved extremely difficult to keep the result within reasonable limits.

The rigid selection and drastic condensation thus imposed could not be expected to produce a smooth, readable text. This book will not be found easy to read. It was not easy to write. It is intended for serious students of the English Bible, who may know nothing of Hebrew or Aramaic but have enough general education and enough power of concentration to follow such a close-knit exposition. Probably the book will be more useful for reference than for consecutive reading. At the same time, the arrangement will, it is hoped, facilitate "skimming" to get the main points without examining all the illustrative data.

The Revised Standard Version is here cited in the form approved by the Standard Bible Committee in 1959, incorporating some changes in detail as compared with previous printings. For the King James Version several editions have been consulted on occasion, but I have used mainly "The American New Self-Pronouncing Sunday-School Teacher's Bible" copyrighted by A. J. Holman & Co., Ltd., and published by the American Bible Warehouse at Philadelphia.

It is a pleasant duty to acknowledge here my obligation to my wife for her help in reporting statistical studies, and above and beyond that for her sympathetic encouragement during the preparation of this book. Such acknowledgments are not uncommon in prefaces, but in this case I have more than the usual grounds for gratitude in view of the extremely trying circumstances under which she helped me far more than she knew. To Dr. Luther A. Weigle, Chairman of the Standard Bible Committee of the National Council of Churches, I am indebted for the initial suggestion that I undertake this project, and for much valuable counsel along the way. I must express also my thanks to the National Council of Churches for making possible the preparation and publication of the book, and to the editorial staff of Thomas Nelson & Sons for their conscientious and efficient attention to the problems of production.

MILLAR BURROWS

Winter Park, Florida
June 9, 1964

CONTENTS

Preface iii
Abbreviations vii
Note on the Transliteration of Hebrew and Aramaic Words ix
Introduction 1

PART ONE

CHANGES IN ENGLISH WITHOUT CHANGE IN MEANING

Chapter
I Form and Procedure 9
II The Elimination of Archaic Language 16
III Changes in the Meaning, Associations, or Use of Words 21
IV Simplified Style, Condensation and Omission 26
V Additions 30
VI Changes in the Order of Words 35
VII Free vs. Literal Translation 38

PART TWO

DIFFERENCES OF INTERPRETATION

VIII New Understanding of the Meanings of Words 55
IX Proper Names 61

Chapter

X	Divine Beings	66
XI	Man: Physiological and Psychological Terms	74
XII	Ethnic and Social Relationships	79
XIII	Legal Terminology	83
XIV	Sin and Salvation	88
XV	Salvation	92
XVI	Public Worship	95
XVII	Geographical and Biological Terms	104
XVIII	Miscellaneous Words	109
XIX	Conjunctions	117
XX	Prepositions	122
XXI	Pronouns and Suffixes, the Definite Article, Particles	134
XXII	Grammatical Forms: Person, Number, and Gender	142
XXIII	The Cases	151
XXIV	Verb Forms: The Stems; Active and Passive	162
XXV	Tenses	168
XXVI	Infinitive, Participle, and Imperative	178
XXVII	Sentence Structure and Connection of Ideas	190

PART THREE

THE HEBREW AND ARAMAIC TEXT

XXVIII	Textual Changes without Footnotes	199
XXIX	Textual Changes with Footnotes	210
	Conclusion	224
	Index of Subjects	227
	Index of Old Testament References	230
	Index of Hebrew and Aramaic Words	271

ABBREVIATIONS

A	*The American Standard Version* (1901)
BWB	*The Bible Word Book,* by Ronald Bridges and Luther A. Weigle (Thomas Nelson & Sons, 1960)
cp	Compare
E	*The Revised Version* (1881–5)
EA	Both E and A
e.g.	For example
f	The following verse or chapter
ff	The following verses or chapters
IB	*The Interpreter's Bible,* 12 volumes (Abingdon Press, 1951–7)
IDB	*The Interpreter's Dictionary of the Bible* (Abingdon Press, 1962)
Introd RSVOT	*An Introduction to the Revised Standard Version of the Old Testament* (Thomas Nelson & Sons, 1952)
J	*The King James Version* (1611)
JR	Both J and R
lit.	Literally
mg	Margin, i.e., marginal note or footnote
OT	Old Testament
R	*The Revised Standard Version* (OT 1952)
v.	Verse
vv.	Verses

NOTE: For the books of the Bible, the Versions, etc., the same abbreviations are used as in the Revised Standard Version.

NOTE ON THE TRANSLITERATION OF HEBREW AND ARAMAIC WORDS

For the identification of Hebrew and Aramaic words a simplified system of transliteration has been adopted. For verbs the simple root-form is given in capitals without vowels. Other words are transcribed in small letters, with long vowels marked; short vowels are not marked, and half-vowels are omitted. The vowels are spelled as in Latin etc.: *ā*=English *ah; ē*=English *ay; ī*=English *ee*. Hard and soft sounds of consonants are not distinguished (following a vowel, except when doubled, *b* is pronounced as *v*, *g* like no sound in English but slightly aspirated, *d* as *th* in "this," *k* like German *ch* in "Ach," *p* as *f*, and *t* as *th* in "thing"). The apostrophe (ʼ) stands for א, the reversed apostrophe (ʻ) for ע, *ḥ* for ח, *ṭ* for ט, *ś* for ס, *q* for ק, *ṣ* for צ, *s* for שׁ, and *ś* for שׂ. When used as vowel-letters ו and י are indicated only by the long vowel, except that in "hollow" verbs they are transcribed to distinguish ע״ו from ע״י roots.

INTRODUCTION

§1 The King James Version of the Bible has been honored and loved for three and a half centuries wherever the English language is spoken. Familiarity with it from childhood has given it such sacred associations that for many people any change in it is repugnant and alarming. For a century and more, however, the need for a new translation, or at least a revision of the old one, has been felt more and more. Why is this so? Many people who love the hallowed Bible of their fathers still wonder what was wrong with it that we should need a new one. This book endeavors to answer that question and to explain how the Revised Standard Version meets the need in the Old Testament.

First of all, one point must be emphasized. The Revised Standard Version is not a new Bible. It is not even a new translation, but a revision of the old one. The King James Version did not need to be replaced by another Bible because it was teaching false doctrine or a wrong way of life. Many false inferences have been drawn from it, even in matters of great importance, but not because of serious errors in translation. Only by misinterpretation, for which the translation is not to be blamed, can wrong ideas of what God is like, or of what he requires of man, be derived from the King James Version; and any translation can be misinterpreted.

Yet the King James Version does need revision, for reasons to be explained later (§§ 3–4). Its faults are matters of detail, most of them of little importance or interest in themselves; yet the more we honor and revere the Bible, the more concerned we should be to know exactly what it says and what it means. The more we look to it for guidance in faith and practice, the more must we seek to make sure that we get from it what it was meant to convey even in the smallest details, and that its message is not distorted or obscured by the translation but made clear.

§ 2 The Revised Standard Version is the latest in a series of officially authorized revisions of the King James Version.[1] The Revised Version, published in England in 1881–5, and the American Standard Version, published in 1901, had attempted to provide the necessary revision. Neither of them, however, took the place of the King James Version in church and home. Students and ministers found them useful, but the demand for a more thorough and adequate revision persisted, and new discoveries made it still more imperative. The Revised Standard Version was therefore undertaken to supply what was still needed.

The copyright of the American Standard Version had been acquired in 1928 by the International Council of Religious Education, now the Division of Christian Education of the National Council of the Churches of Christ in the United States of America. In 1937 the Council decided that a revision was needed. The task of making it was entrusted to a committee, now known as the Standard Bible Committee. It was composed of scholars chosen on the basis of individual competence, not denominational representation. The cooperating denominations were officially represented by an Advisory Board which reviewed the Committee's work.

The Committee was divided into two sections, for the revision of the Old and New Testaments respectively. All changes, however, had to be approved by two thirds of the whole Committee.

Each book of the Bible was assigned for revision to one or more of the members of the Committee, whose preliminary draft was discussed in detail and thoroughly amended by the whole section concerned. It was then further studied and again discussed and amended, sometimes two or three times. Particular problems were sometimes assigned to members for investigation and recommendation, and minor editorial tasks were entrusted to a subcommittee; but every word and every punctuation mark had to

[1] For a brief history of English translations of the Bible see the Introduction to *The New Testament Octapla,* edited by Luther A. Weigle (Thomas Nelson & Sons, 1962).

be approved by vote of the Committee before final adoption. In this the Revised Standard Version differs widely from the King James Version, in which many important decisions were made by a small editorial committee. Another notable difference between the Revised Standard Version and any of its predecessors is that the Standard Bible Committee continues in existence, charged with the oversight and, if found necessary, further revision of the translation.

To make clear the relationship between the Revised Standard Version and its predecessors it will be necessary to quote a great many specific examples. In order to keep to a minimum the amount of space required by these citations, each version will be designated by a single letter, as follows: J, the King James Version; E, the English Revised Version; A, the American Standard Version; R, the Revised Standard Version.

As has been said, R is a revision, not of J directly, but of A. A great many of the differences between R and J, therefore, had already appeared in A and E; others were suggested in their marginal notes (EA mg). Most readers of R, however, wish to know, not where and how it departs from A, but why it differs in this verse or that from the Bible they know, which is J. Only rarely, therefore, will changes previously made by EA or by A alone, and retained by R, be distinguished here from those first introduced by R. All changes, old and new alike, will be treated merely as differences between R and J.

At not a few points, as a matter of fact, R discards changes made by its "basic text," A, and returns to the reading of J. The most conspicuous example is A's use of "Jehovah" as the name of God, where both J and E use "Lord," as R does also (see § 44). E and A went too far, moreover, in their effort to use uniform renderings of Hebrew words, which often have different meanings in different connections. Here too, R returns now and then to J.

§ 3 The necessity of revising J arises largely from the fact that it was made so long ago. It cannot serve our time as it served the generation of the Pilgrim Fathers. Men still find in it the Word of God, but not as easily as in former days, partly because the English language is not what it was 350 years ago. Many old words are no longer used or understood; others are misunderstood because their meanings have changed. Antique grammatical forms and ways of expressing ideas come between the text and the reader. For all its beauty and power, the language of J is often unnatural, unreal, and even unintelligible for modern readers. Anything that detracts from the clarity of the sacred text weakens its impact on our generation, and no generation ever needed it more than ours.

The English of J is not, in fact, impeccable; it occasionally slips into forms of speech not considered correct now, however they may have been regarded in the time of James I. In spite of such occasional infelicities, however, it is still "a standard of grave and reverent speech." The task entrusted to the Standard Bible Committee was to prepare a revision which would "embody the best results of modern scholarship as to the meaning of the Scriptures, and express this meaning in English diction which is designed for use in public and private worship and preserves those qualities which have given to the King James Version a supreme place in English literature." By that standard R must be judged, so far as its use of the English language is concerned.

§ 4 Revising the English of the translation, however, was not the only thing needed, or even the most important. An adequate translation for our day must "embody the best results of modern scholarship as to the meaning of the Scriptures." Thanks to much research and many discoveries, we can now understand the original languages of Scripture better than the most learned scholars could understand them three centuries ago. Thousands of texts in languages whose very existence was then unknown have been unearthed, enormously increasing our ability to interpret correctly the Hebrew and Aramaic of the OT.

Back of the translation, moreover, and the interpretation it conveys, lies the difficult task of establishing a correct text. The Bible, like all ancient writings, was handed down in handwritten copies for many centuries before the invention of printing. As a result of inevitable mistakes in copying, our surviving manuscripts differ among themselves at many points. Which of two or more forms is correct, or most nearly correct, is not always easy to tell. Here too, however, we now have resources only partly available, if at all, to the earlier translators.

Our explanation of the differences between J and R will thus fall under three heads: (1) changes in English, (2) different interpretations of the text, (3) more correct readings of the text itself. In practice of course, these must be dealt with in the opposite order: the best text in each verse must be determined first, then its meaning, and, finally, the best way to express that meaning in English. For our purpose here, however, it is most convenient to proceed as in an archeological excavation, examining the uppermost and latest level before digging down into the earlier levels beneath it.

In order to save space, a fairly uniform procedure has been adopted for comparing J and R in the following chapters. J's rendering is quoted first, preceded by a small superscript J and followed by a dash; then, with a small superscript R, comes the rendering of R. References to chapters and verses follow in parentheses. The marginal notes of J and R, if any, are given in square brackets. E.g., ^{J}talent [Or, *weighty piece*]—^{R}cover (Zech 5.7); i.e., J reads in Zech 5.7 "talent," with a marginal note, "Or, *weighty piece*"; R reads "cover."

Part One

Changes in English Without Change of Meaning

Chapter I

FORM AND PROCEDURE

§ 5 Following EA, R arranges prose passages in paragraphs, instead of printing each verse as a separate paragraph as J does. Poetry is printed as poetry. When J was made, the understanding of the metrical structure of ancient Hebrew poetry had been lost for centuries. Poetry was still written in Hebrew during the Middle Ages, but it was cast in the forms of European poetry.

The form of ancient Hebrew poetry has two major characteristics, accentual meter and parallelism of thought. The meter is accentual in the sense that each line contains a certain number of accents or beats, with no regularity in the number of unaccented syllables, instead of having a specific number of syllables or a succession of long and short or accented and unaccented syllables in a definite pattern. The accentual meter makes it comparatively easy to reproduce in translation the rhythm of the Hebrew verse, and R endeavors to do this wherever it can be done without affecting the meaning. Naturally a change in J's wording or word-order is sometimes required to achieve this end.

Parallelism, the other distinctive mark of classical Hebrew verse, is the arrangement of lines in couplets or triplets, with a close relationship in meaning between the lines. Sometimes the successive lines express the same meaning in different words; sometimes they are contrasted; sometimes the second supplements and completes the meaning of the first. A typical example is the ancient Song of Lamech in Gen 4.23–4:

"Adah and Zillah, hear my voice;
  you wives of Lamech, hearken to what I say:
I have slain a man for wounding me,
  a young man for striking me.

If Cain is avenged sevenfold,
truly Lamech seventy-sevenfold."

Less obvious and more complicated is the division of poems into stanzas. Here there is no regularity. Recurring catchwords or phrases and metrical patterns afford some clues, but often the only safe guide is the meaning. Some attempt is made by R to divide long poems into stanzas, but it cannot yet be carried through consistently. The matter still requires further study.

Poetry is printed as such in EA in Job, Psalms, Proverbs, the Song of Solomon, and Lamentations, and in many of the short poems scattered through the legal and historical books. R recognizes still other bits of poetry: Gen 2.23; 3.14–19; 14.19–20; 48.15–16, 20; 2 Sam 20.1; 2 Kings 19.21–28 (=Is 37.22–29); 1 Chron 12.18; 2 Chron 10.16; Ezra 3.11; Eccles 1.2–11, 15, 18; 3.2–9; 7.1–13; 8.1; 10.1–4, 8–20; 11.1–4. In the prophetic books EA did not distinguish poetry from prose. The transition from rhythmic prose to verse and back is in fact so smooth in these books that the line between poetry and prose is sometimes hard to draw. R attempts to draw it, however, retaining the prose form in doubtful instances.

A characteristic form of poetic composition in the OT is the alphabetical acrostic, in which successive lines or groups of lines begin with the successive letters of the Hebrew alphabet. The most elaborate example is Ps 119; here even J marks the structure by headings. Elsewhere the acrostic form is ignored by J, even where it is as clear as it is in Ps 119. The Book of Lamentations, for instance, consists of five acrostic poems. R separates the stanzas in each poem but omits the Hebrew letters, which mean nothing to the English reader unacquainted with Hebrew.

Recognition of the metrical form has consequences for the translation, affecting word-order (Chap. VI), sentence structure (Chap. XXVII), and sometimes even the meaning of a word, which is clarified by the parallelism of thought.

§ 6 In keeping with contemporary practice, R punctuates much more lightly than J. Only very rarely is a heavier punctuation used. Sometimes an exclamation point takes the place of a period. Hyphens, introduced often by E and even more by A, are sometimes kept in R (e.g., first-born); sometimes where J has two words, which EA combine with a hyphen, R has one word (e.g., ^{J}to day—^{EA}to-day—^{R}today; ^{J}hoar frost—^{EA}hoar-frost—^{R}hoarfrost). R's usage in all such matters follows Webster's International Dictionary.

Parentheses are introduced by R in some places to make clear the connections between verses or parts of verses (e.g., Gen 25.17; Lev 21.3; Is 7.8; Nahum 2.2; cp § 123). Dashes occasionally serve the same purpose (e.g., Ex 4.4; Is 20.2).

An innovation in R is the use of quotation marks, which are sometimes an important aid for understanding. In Ex 4.26, for example, they show that the words "because of the circumcision" are not part of what Zipporah says but explain why she calls Moses "a bridegroom of blood." So in Ps 81 R makes it clear that vv. 6–16 are a quotation of what the voice mentioned in v. 5 said to the Psalmist.

The use of quotation marks in the OT is not without difficulty, especially when there are quotations within quotations, as often in Jeremiah. Where three or more quotations are nested within one another, R marks the outermost by double quotes, the second by single quotes, but to avoid undue awkwardness gives no indication beyond that (see, e.g., Jer 32.3–5). There are a few exceptions to this treatment (e.g., v. 25).

In this connection J's use of italics to indicate words inserted by the translators may be mentioned. R abandons this practice, regarding words inserted to complete or clarify the meaning as an essential part of the translation. J's italics will be ignored from here on, except where the subject of added words is under discussion (§§ 20–23).

§ 7 The use of capital letters presents many problems. J begins every verse with a capital letter, even in the middle of a sentence (e.g., Gen 1.18); R, grouping the verses in paragraphs, discards this practice. Like J, R does not capitalize the personal pronoun of the third person masculine singular when it refers to God. The only exception is that R introduces the capital H when the pronoun is used, in effect, as a divine name: "I am He" (Is 41.4; 43.10, 13, 25; 46.4; 48.12).

In Dan 7.9 where J reads "the Ancient of days," the original does not have the "determinate" form which in Aramaic takes the place of a definite article; R therefore reads "one that was ancient of days." In vv. 13 and 22 the Aramaic does have the determinate form; J again reads "the Ancient of days," R "the Ancient of Days." R reads "Father" (Is 63.16; 64.8) and "Redeemer" (43.14; 44.6, 24; 47.4; 63.16), where J has "father" and "redeemer" (both read "Redeemer" in 49.7, 26; 54.5, 8).

Neither J nor R is entirely consistent in the use of a capital with the word "Saviour" (R "Savior"). The choice depends in part upon the presence or absence of the definite article. Both J and R have a small *s* in 2 Sam 22.3 and Jer 14.8, but a capital in Is 43.3; 45.15, 21; 49.26; 63.8. In Ps 106.21 J reads "saviour," R "Savior."

A similar lack of uniformity appears in the title "King" when applied to God: ^{JR}king (Ps 20.9); ^{JR}King (Ps 47.6; 95.3); ^{J}king—^{R}King (Jer 8.19; 10.10); ^{J}King—^{R}king (Ps 10.16; 47.2, 7; 84.3). In Ps 20.9 there is a textual problem; the reading adopted by R makes the word "king" refer to the human ruler (see R mg).

The use of "LORD" in capitals for the Hebrew divine name, where A has "Jehovah," has been mentioned (§ 2; see also § 44). Where the word does not stand for the sacred name but for a common noun used as a divine title, only the initial L is capitalized. Since the same noun is used also for human lords, the use or non-use of an initial capital may involve a question of interpretation, as ^{J}Lord—^{R}lord in Ps 45.11; so also ^{J}shepherd—^{R}Shepherd in Eccles 12.11 and ^{J}teacher—^{R}Teacher in Is 30.20.

In the spelling of "spirit" with or without a capital *S* when it refers to the Spirit of God our English versions vary. Neither J nor R is entirely consistent: e.g., ^{J}spirit—^{R}Spirit (Is 11.2); ^{JR}spirit (59.21); ^{J}Spirit—^{R}spirit (63.10); ^{JR}Spirit (63.11).

Designations of the Messiah often have an initial capital in R as in J where the Messianic reference is clear; where it is uncertain, improbable, or clearly not intended R uses a small letter. Examples of such terms are Branch (see § 92); ^{J}The Prince of

Peace—[R]Prince of Peace (Is 9.6), [JR]Prince (Dan 8.25), [J]prince—[R]Prince (8.11); [J]Star . . . Sceptre—[R]star . . . scepter (Num 24.17); [J]the Son of God—[R]a son of the gods (Dan 3.25); [J]the Son of man—[R]a son of man (7.13), [J]O Son of man—[R]O son of man (8.17); [J]the Sun of righteousness—[R]the sun of righteousness (Mal 4.2). Here again the translation may or may not imply a particular interpretation.

The use of capitals in designations of angels presents a similar problem: e.g., [J]the Angel of the LORD—[R]the angel of the LORD (Gen 22.11, 15; even the definite article is questionable here); [J]an angel of God—[R]the angel of God (2 Sam 14.17, 20; 19.27; cp 1 Sam 29.9, [JR]an angel of God); [J]the prince of the host—[R]the Prince of the host (Dan 8.11).

There are other differences in the use of capitals in special connections: e.g., [J]Priests . . . Ministers—[R]priests . . . ministers (Is 61.6); [J]shewbread—[R]bread of the Presence (Ex 25.30 etc.; see § 68); [J]Sanctuary—[R]sanctuary (Ex 15.17; so J elsewhere); [J]HOLINESS UNTO THE LORD—[R]Holy to the LORD (Zech 14.20); [J]the pit—[R]the Pit (designating the realm of the dead, Job 33.18; Ps 88.6; Is 51.14); [J]the grave—[R]the Pit (with the same Hebrew noun, Job 33.22; cp Lam 3.53, with a different word but the same meaning, [J]dungeon—[R]pit).

Geographical and topographical names are spelled with initial capitals in R; e.g., [J]The valley of slaughter—[R]the valley of Slaughter (Jer 19.6; see Chap. IX for other examples).

§ 8 J has an elaborate apparatus of marginal notes (unfortunately omitted in some editions), giving alternative or more literal renderings. Similar notes appear in R as footnotes at the bottom of the page. R reduces such notes to a minimum, however, and therefore omits many of those given in the previous versions. On the other hand, a good many new notes appear in R. Where, for example, the numbering of the verses in our English translations differs from that of the Hebrew text, a note points this out (e.g., 1 Sam 20.42).

Notes giving the literal meaning where a somewhat free rendering has been adopted are much less frequent in R than in J but are used where they seem necessary, with the abbreviation "Heb," much as in J; e.g., [J]a nail [Or, *a pin:* i.e., *a constant and sure abode:* So Is 22.23]—[R]a secure hold [Heb *nail* or *tent-pin*] (Ezra 9.8); [J]a wall—[R]protection [Heb *a wall*] (v. 9).

Where the meaning of the Hebrew is somewhat uncertain, and another interpretation seems almost equally probable, R gives an alternative rendering in a note, usually introduced by "Or," as in J. The first such note in R is on the first clause of Gen 1.1: In the beginning God created [Or *When God began to create*].

An "Or" note may give merely an alternative English rendering with no different meaning; e.g., [J]tabernacles—[R]booths [Or *tabernacles*] (Lev 23.34). Here the note merely connects the word used in the text with the familiar traditional designation of the annual festival (see § 67).

Since J's use of italics is abandoned (§ 6), added words (§§ 42–52) are sometimes indicated in R by a note, "Heb lacks . . ." (e.g., Ps 84.5). Less frequently words in the Hebrew text are omitted by R, and a note, "Heb adds . . . ," is given, sometimes with a brief explanation (e.g., 2 Kings 15.25; Dan 2.4).

At a good many places in the OT a translator can only do his best with a difficult text and admit that he cannot be sure of its meaning. At such points R often has a note, "Heb obscure," or occasionally "The Hebrew of this verse is obscure" (1 Sam 13.21; Prov 30.1; Is 23.13; cp Job 34.33; Ps 68.30; 141.7; Prov 12.12). Sometimes the note reads "Heb uncertain" (e.g., 1 Sam 20.15; Job 12.6; Ps 49.14), meaning that either the interpretation of the Hebrew or the text itself is uncertain; more exact is the formula, "The meaning of the Hebrew is uncertain" (e.g., Job 41.11; Prov 4.8; 30.31; Song 3.10; Hos 11.7), "The meaning of the Hebrew word is uncertain" (Deut 33.2; Judg 5.10 and often), or "The meaning of this verse is uncertain" (Job 19.26). Occasionally it is necessary to say that the meaning of a word is unknown (e.g., 2 Sam 23.20; 1 Chron 26.18).

Footnotes of other kinds are used as occasion demands. In 2 Chron 7.19, where the Hebrew shifts from the singular to the plural ([J]if ye . . .), R adds a note, "The word you is plural here." Proper names (§ 42) are sometimes interpreted in footnotes, as in J (e.g., 2 Chron 20.26; Ezek 20.29). The play on words in Amos 8.1f is indicated by notes: summer fruit [*qayits*] . . . end [*qets*]. Transposition of words, clauses, or lines is pointed out by notes in Ps 35.7; Prov 3.21; 4.5. A note on Jer 10.11 says, "This verse is in Aramaic"; see also Ezra 4.7 mg; Dan 2.4 mg.

§ 9 Where R adopts a revised Hebrew text (see § 4 and PART THREE), no note is considered necessary if only the vowels of the Hebrew are changed (see §§ 125, 130f); changes in the consonants also have no note if the reading adopted is attested by three or more Hebrew manuscripts (see § 126); if one or two manuscripts support it, this fact is stated (see § 133); where it is derived from one or more of the ancient Versions (§§ 135ff), these are specifically cited. Readings given in the margin of the Hebrew text are often adopted, usually without a note, by R as well as by J, E, and A (§ 127). Sometimes, but very rarely, R adopts a formula much used by EA, "Another reading is, ..."

As already noted, the formula "Heb uncertain" may refer either to the meaning or to the Hebrew text itself. In 2 Chron 34.6 it indicates simply that the interpretation depends on the word-division and vocalization (§ 131) of the Hebrew (cp E mg, A mg). In several other places it is the text that is uncertain (e.g., Jer 8.13; 33.6; Lam 3.56; 4.6; Ezek 23.42). Sometimes this is more precisely stated (e.g., 1 Chron 26.21; Job 9.19; Prov 26.10).

When the same passage occurs more than once in the OT, with minor variations, R avoids indiscriminate harmonization, but occasionally an obvious mistake in one of the parallel passages is corrected by the other; R then indicates the source of the correction (e.g., 2 Sam 6.7; 2 Chron 3.4; for other examples see § 134).

When no satisfactory correction of a clearly corrupt text is afforded by any of the Hebrew manuscripts or the ancient Versions, R occasionally adopts corrections proposed by competent scholars and approved by a consensus of scholarly opinion. Such corrections are indicated in the footnotes by the abbreviation "Cn." Typical examples, with brief explanations, will be found in § 142.

Various combinations of these different types of notes appear here and there in R; see, e.g., Deut 33.13; 1 Sam 1.5; 2 Sam 6.19; 2 Chron 9.11; Job 9.19; 24.20; Ps 16.2; 145.13; Song 3.1; Is 14.4; Ezek 23.24; Mic 5.1.

Chapter II

THE ELIMINATION OF ARCHAIC LANGUAGE

§10 Differences in spelling between R and J are governed by current American usage, as registered by Webster's International Dictionary. The spelling of J itself, as a matter of fact, has been somewhat modernized. In the original edition of 1611 Psalm 23, for example, begins, "The LORD is my shepheard," and ends, "Surely goodness and mercie shall followe me all the daies of my life; and I will dwell in the house of the LORD for euer." At many points, however, J's spelling is still unnecessarily archaic; e.g., ancles, chapt, cieled, cloke, divers, flotes, lothe, marishes, mixt, morter, musick, plaister, pransing, prised, sope, subtil, traffick, vail. In British usage some words are still spelled as in J, but American usage has changed; e.g., honour, labour, etc., also shew (still sometimes so spelled in Great Britain, though of course pronounced to rhyme with "sew," not with "stew").

§11 R eliminates also obsolete and archaic forms of words, including the old verb endings -est and -eth and the pronouns thou, thy, thine, thee, and ye. There is one important exception, however, to this rule. Most of our churches still use thou and the related forms and the verb ending -est in addressing God; R therefore retains these forms in the language of prayer and praise. In Ps 27.8 R keeps "ye."

R, like A, abandons also J's use of the possessive pronoun "his" for the neuter as well as the masculine gender (e.g., Gen 1.11 etc.; 29.3), and the relative pronoun "which" with masculine and feminine antecedents (e.g., Gen 18.13; Num 27.17). J's use of "which" sometimes produces an unfortunate ambiguity: e.g., [J]The proud have digged pits for me, which are not after thy law—[R]Godless men have dug pitfalls for me, men who do not conform to thy law (Ps 119.85). A similar ambiguity as to gender appears in the archaic use of "that" for "who" or "what" in Ex 3.14, I AM THAT I AM. Here, unfortunately, the Hebrew word is still more ambiguous, being either a relative pronoun or a conjunction; R therefore reads I AM WHO I AM [Or I AM WHAT I AM or I WILL BE WHAT I WILL BE].

J has an archaic use of "be" instead of "have" in the present perfect and past perfect tenses of some English verbs; e.g., [J]is come—[R]has come (Ps 102.13); [J]was set—[R]had set (Gen 28.11). In keeping with the present trend in good English usage, R also abandons almost entirely the subjunctive mood: e.g., [J]until thy brother's anger turn away from thee, and he forget—[R]. . . turns away . . . forgets (Gen 27.45); [J]Except the LORD build . . . keep—[R]Unless the LORD builds . . . watches over (Ps 127.1).

Such simple changes as "I do not know" for "I know not" or "Do not fear" for "Fear not" require no explanation. J, in fact, reads "Do not drink wine" in Lev 10.9; EA, curiously enough, change this to "Drink no wine," which R carries over from A, its basic text. Equally simple and obvious is the change to "twenty-seventh" instead of "seven and twentieth" (Gen 8.14), and the like.

It is not always easy to tell whether a word in J is an older form of a word still in use or a different word. So in Gen 30.37f, pilled white strakes ([R]peeled white streaks), apparently "pill" and "peel" are variant forms of the same word, but "strake" and "streak" come from two different Anglo-Saxon words. Cp astonied, broidered, minish, stablish. J's verb "grave" is rendered by R "engrave" (Ex 28.9, 36; 39.6; Jer 17.1; cp 2 Chron 2.7, 14), "carve" (1 Kings 7.36; 2 Chron 3.7; Is 22.16), or "shape" (Hab 2.18). In Ex 32.16; Job 19.24; Is 49.16 R keeps "graven," and so often in the term "graven image," though this is frequently rendered simply "image" (§ 66). Note also Zech 3.9 [J]graving—[R]inscription.

Archaic forms of the past tense and past participle of many verbs appear in J; e.g., awaked, bare, brake, builded, chode, digged, gat (J also uses got), holden and withholden, holpen, lien (past participle of lie), loaden, shapen, sod (past tense of seethe), spake, strawed, sware.

Archaic plurals of some nouns appear also; e.g., booties (R booty), kine. Curiously, in transliterating certain Hebrew words and names in the plural J adds the English ending -s to the Hebrew ending -im: cherubims, seraphims, Anakims, Emims, Horims, etc. (but Baalim, treated as though it were a proper noun in the singular). Occasionally J seems to the modern reader to confuse the singular and the plural, as in the use of "brick" as a collective plural (Gen 11.3; Ex 1.14; 5.7, 14, 16; but "bricks" Ex 5.8, 18f; Is 9.10). More serious is the confusion caused by J's use of "people" for both singular and plural. Ps 67.3, "let all the people praise thee," has been used to promote active participation in worship by the whole congregation; but what the Hebrew says is "all the peoples" (see § 96 for other examples).

For the plural of "fish" J sometimes uses "fish" (e.g., Gen 1.26, 28; Ps 8.8), sometimes "fishes," which now, according to Webster, usually signifies "diversity in kind or species" but in J has no such implication (e.g., Gen 9.2; 1 Kings 4.33). R says "fish" everywhere.

Many other archaic forms are replaced by their modern equivalents in R. The following forms, for example, though still intelligible, are now obsolete: afore, aforetime, alway (J also uses always), attent, divorcement, exceeding (as adverb, for exceedingly), excellency (now used only in formal titles), forthwith, scarce (for scarcely), tacklings (for a ship's tackle), throughly, twain, unperfect, whiles.

Other old forms are now confusing. Who would guess that "emerod" (Deut 28.27; 1 Sam 5.6 etc.) is an old form of "hemorrhoid," or that "fats" (Joel 2.24; 3.13; cp Hag 2.16) are "vats"? Only the context can give the modern reader any idea of what is meant by the statement that Jezebel "tired her head" (2 Kings 9.30, [R]adorned her head), or by the "round tires like the moon" worn by the ladies of Jerusalem (Is 3.18, [R]crescents). Jer 4.30, "thou rentest thy face with paint," is quite unintelligible. The word rendered "face" means "eyes" (so J mg); "rent" is an obsolete variant of "rend," which is what the Hebrew verb means. R reads, following EA, "you enlarge your eyes with paint" (i.e., make them look larger).

We now say "instead of" but no longer use "stead" by itself

in this sense; hence, e.g., for "Am I in God's stead" R reads "Am I in the place of God" (Gen 30.2; 1 Kings 14.27; in 2 Chron 12.10, however, R reads with EA "in their stead," where J has "Instead of which").

Similar changes in the division or combination of words are the following:

[J]to the mercy seatward—[R]toward the mercy seat (Ex 37.9); [J]Because that —[R]because (Gen 26.5); [J]Forasmuch as—[R]because (Is 29.13); [J]things for to come—[R]things to come (41.22); [J]from off thy neck—[R]from your neck (Gen 27.40, but cp Mic 3.2f); [J]from thence—[R]from there (Gen 11.8); [J]one to another—[R]to one another (v. 3); [J]gave him Bilhah . . . to wife—[R]gave him . . . Bilhah as a wife (30.4); [J]gave her Jacob to wife—[R]gave her to Jacob as a wife (v. 9).

§ 12 No hard line can be drawn between words that are now obsolete and those that are merely archaic or obsolescent, because usage is constantly changing. There are also local or sectional differences, and differences between ordinary prose and more or less poetic or rhetorical discourse.

The following words used in J are almost or entirely obsolete in the United States:

abjects (Ps 35.15, see §§ 127, 176), albeit, all to brake, bestead, bewray, blains, bolled, bray (crush), chapmen, clout, collop, countervail, crossway, delicates (delicacies), disannul, disquietness, draught house (latrine), ear (plow), familiar (as a noun), fine (refine), finer, fining pot, firstripe, goodman (husband), hough (hamstring), husbandman, knop, lade, latchet, leasing, magnifical, meet (right, fitting), mete, meteyard, neesings, noisome, occurrent, ouches, overlived, overpass, overpast, peradventure, privily, purtenance, ravening, ravin, rereward, ringstrake, and strake (see § 3), scrabble, supple (as a verb), tabering, tache, ward (custody), wit (know) and wot. (For a fuller discussion see BWB.)

Other words and expressions in J, while still used occasionally, have an antique flavor and must be considered archaic. R has not entirely eliminated such archaisms; there is consequently at times a certain incongruity in R's English (see especially § 13). One critic has complained that in Ps 15.1 the "highbrow" word "sojourn" is used with the "lowbrow" word "tent." In poetry or rhetorical prose, however, archaic diction may be quite appropriate. R uses poetic language in translating poetry; but in prose archaic diction is only distracting and tends to convey a sense of unreality (§ 3). Only a bare list of typical words can be given here; many will come up for further discussion in connection with the meanings of Hebrew words (see also BWB).

The following words may serve as examples of J's archaic diction:

amerce, appertain, asunder and in sunder, backbite, backslide, beset, betimes, brutish, comely and comeliness (sometimes kept in R), constrain, contemn, damsel, delightsome, discomfit and discomfiture, eschew, froward, furbish, goodly and goodliness, lucre, plenteous, raiment, seemly, straightway, succour, tarry, verily, vesture.

A rather conspicuous exception to the rule of avoiding archaic language is R's frequent use of "Behold" and "Lo." These are good old English words, but their frequent appearance in the Bible is actually a Hebraism rather than an archaism: it reflects the constant, ubiquitous use of a characteristic particle in Hebrew. J uses "Behold" much more often than "Lo." R sometimes changes the former to the latter or vice versa, following a precedent set by EA and even going beyond it (Gen 29.7; Jer 25.29; 30.3; 50.9; Ezek 8.8; Hos 9.6; Amos 4.2; Zech 9.4).

Sometimes R omits "Behold" or "Lo" (e.g., Gen 27.6; 42.27f; Eccles 1.16; Jer 8.19; 36.12; Ezek 13.10; 25.4), or represents the meaning in more modern ways, such as "Look" (1 Sam 20.21f; 2 Kings 4.25) or "See" (Gen 29.6; 2 Kings 5.20; cp Gen 38.23; 1 Sam 9.14; 2 Sam 18.24; Ezek 1.15; 46.19; 47.7). J itself sometimes translates the particle freely; e.g., Here I am (1 Sam 22.12); Here am I (Is 6.8). In Gen 22.1 J has a double translation: Behold, here I am. R adopts this use of "here" in some places (Gen 30.3; 37.19; Num 20.16; Is 52.6; 65.1). Similarly "there" is used (1 Sam 26.7; 2 Chron 23.13; Ps 59.7; Jer 18.3). Still other substitutes for "Behold" or "Lo" are used by R in other places. No attempt is made, however, to eliminate these words entirely; they are retained as an established item of biblical diction.

Chapter III

CHANGES IN THE MEANING, ASSOCIATIONS, OR USE OF WORDS

§13 More unfortunate as a source of misunderstanding than obsolete or archaic words and expressions are those still in use but with changed meanings or associations. There are many more words of this kind than can even be mentioned here. Only a few can be discussed at all, and others listed as examples. Again BWB may be consulted for a more adequate treatment.

Often the shifts in meaning or use produce only mild perplexity or a sense of sometimes ludicrous incongruity, without being seriously misleading. One who has been bored by travelers' tales of their trips to Europe can enjoy J's rendering in Ps 41.6, "when he goeth abroad, he telleth it." The Hebrew, however, means simply, as R puts it, "when he goes out, he tells it abroad" (cp the preceding lines). The judge Ibzan, who sent his thirty daughters abroad, is another example (Judg 12.9). So the reference to a thief "found breaking up" (Ex 22.2), to Jonathan's "artillery" (1 Sam 20.40), the young prophet's instructions to arouse Jehu "and carry him to an inner chamber" (2 Kings 9.2), or the prophecy concerning owls and vultures that "none shall want her mate" (Is 34.16) may cause the reader to smile, though he is aware that the words did not mean in 1611 what they mean to us now.

This is true also of the following words and expressions, used by J with the meanings here given in parentheses:

advertise (tell), advise (consider), amiable (lovely), apparently (clearly), audience (hearing), blow up (used of blowing a trumpet), certify (tell), confectionary (perfumes), eminent (lofty), footmen (infantry), ghost (spirit or soul, in "give up the ghost," i.e., expire), mirth (rejoicing), mischief (harm, calamity), naughty (worthless), notable (conspicuous), overlay (lie upon), overrun (outrun), play with (used of playing a musical instrument), stalled (fattened), stuff (baggage), touching (concerning), wake (stay awake).

An especially conspicuous archaism of this sort in J is the use of "child" for a grown man, especially in the plural in such expressions as "children of Israel," "children of Ephraim," "children of Ammon." R keeps "children of Israel" about 20 times; elsewhere other expressions are used: sons of Israel, descendants of Israel, people of Israel, Israelites. So with reference to the tribes or to foreign peoples, instead of "children" R uses "sons" or "descendants" and also Ephraimites, Ethiopians, Hittites, and the like; cp Joel 3.6, [J]the Grecians [Heb. *the sons of the Grecians*] —[R]the Greeks. For the inhabitants of a city or region R uses "sons" or "men"; J usually says "children," but cp Ezek 27.11, [JR]men of Arvad. For J's children of the east (also children of the east country, men of the east, people of the east, them of the east) R reads everywhere people of the east.

R keeps "children of men" 3 times but elsewhere reads sons of men, men, or mortal men (cp § 53). Note also [J]children of the people—[R]common people (2 Kings 23.6); [J]the people [Heb. *the sons of the people*]—[R]the lay people (2 Chron 35.5, 7, 12); [J]the children of thy people—[R]your people (Ezek 3.11 etc.); [J]the children of her people—[R]her countrymen (Judg 14.17); but cp Lev 20.17, [J]their people—[R]the children of their people.

To speak of men as God's children as J does may be somewhat more appropriate; here too, however, R usually has "sons" with the Hebrew, but cp Is 45.11, [J]my sons—[R]my children (so too of the stars in a constellation, Job 38.32, [J]his sons—[R]its children).

§ 14 Sometimes J's archaisms lead to serious misunderstanding because of the new associations the words have acquired. The danger is greatest when an expression makes sense with a meaning not intended by J; so, e.g., [J]the basest of men—[R]the lowliest of men (Dan 4.17; see also Ezek 29.14f and cp 17.14; Mal 2.9); [J]whither it seemeth good and convenient for thee to go—[R]wherever you think it good and right to go (Jer 40.4; see also v. 5 and cp Prov 30.8). To speak of "meat," meaning "bread" or "food," as J often does, or of "meat offerings," meaning "cereal offerings" (§ 68, No. 4), is decidedly confusing for modern readers.

The designation of Israel as a "peculiar" people is often misunderstood: note, e.g., [J]a peculiar people unto himself—[R]a people for his own possession (Deut 14.2; cp 26.18); [J]a peculiar treasure unto me—[R]my own possession (Ex 19.5; see also Ps 135.4; Eccles 2.8).

J's use of "prevent" is now confusing; e.g., [J]I prevented the dawning of the morning—[R]I rise before dawn (Ps 119.147); [J]Mine eyes prevent the night watches—[R]My eyes are awake before the watches of the night (v. 148); [J]shall my prayer prevent thee—[R]my prayer comes before thee (88.13); [J]thou preventest him—[R]thou dost meet him (21.3; see also 2 Sam 22.6, 19 = Ps 18.5, 18; Job 3.12; 30.27; 41.11; Ps 59.10; 79.8; Is 21.14; Amos 9.10).

The adjective "quick" as used by J is another misleading word for modern readers; e.g., [J]let them go down quick into hell—[R]let them go down to Sheol alive (Ps 55.15); [J]they had swallowed us up quick—[R]they would have swallowed us up alive (124.3).

Very puzzling now is J's translation in 2 Kings 11.15 (cp 2 Chron 23.14), Have her forth without the ranges. R makes it clear: Bring her out between the ranks (cp v. 8).

J uses "stay" in several ways foreign to modern usage; e.g., [J]stayed—[R]waited (Gen 8.10, 12; cp Lam 4.6); [J]be stayed—[R]be averted (2 Sam 24.21 = 1 Chron 21.22); [J]were stayed—[R]shall be stopped (Ezek 31.15); [J]is stayed from (twice)—[R]have withheld . . . has withheld (Hag 1.10; cp 1 Sam 24.7; Job 38.37); [J]Woe to them that . . . stay on horses—[R]Woe to those who . . . rely on horses (Is 31.1; see also 30.12; 50.10; cp 10.20; 27.8; 29.9; Hos 13.13); [J]stay him—[R]help him (Prov 28.17); [J]stay me—[R]sustain me (Song 2.5).

J's use of "strange" also is now misleading; e.g., [J]a strange woman—[R]another woman (i.e., not Gilead's wife, Judg 11.2); [J]strange women—[R]foreign women (of Solomon's wives, 1 Kings 11.1; cp Neh 13.26, [J]outlandish women—[R]foreign women); [J]strange wives—[R]foreign women (Ezra 10.2, 10, etc.); [J]strange woman—[R]adventuress (Prov 23.27; cp 5.20, [J]stranger—[R]adventuress); [J]strange children—[R]alien children (i.e., not the husband's, Hos 5.7), aliens (Ps 144.7, 11); [J]strange gods—[R]foreign gods (Gen

35.2, 4, etc.); [J]strange apparel—[R]foreign attire (Zeph 1.8). So too [J]stranger—[R]alien (Is 1.7, etc.), foreigner (Deut 17.15, etc.), outsider (Ex 30.33, etc.), sojourner (Ex 2.22, etc.).

Similar possibilities of misunderstanding arise from J's use of many other words whose meanings have changed. Arcturus, for example, now the name of a star, used to designate the whole constellation; hence in Job 9.9; 38.32, [J]Arcturus—[R]the Bear. Other words of this sort, with their modern equivalents in R, are the following:

conversation—way; discover—carry on openly, disclose, expose, flaunt, lay bare, lift up, reveal, strip bare, take away, uncover; hardly—greatly, harshly; would hardly—refused to; hold—stronghold; invention—device; let—hinder; munition—fortress, rampart, stronghold; nephew—descendant, grandson, posterity; nourish—educate, rear; occupy—barter; occupier—dealer; open—commit, reveal, solve; ordinary food—allotted portion (in the 17th century "ordinary" meant "orderly," "regular"); policy—cunning; porter—gatekeeper (we still speak of a "porter's lodge," but a porter means for us one who carries baggage); prolong—delay, grow long; ready to die—close to death; ready to perish—about to perish, lost, wandering; ready to be slain—stumbling to the slaughter; road—raid; so that—if only; spoil—despoil, lay waste; store—reserve, treasure; great store of servants—a great household.

Still other words easily misunderstood because of changed meanings or associations may be mentioned (the words given here in parentheses indicate briefly the meaning intended by J; they are not always those used by R):

bunch (hump, of a camel), carefulness (fearfulness), careless (unsuspecting), carriage (baggage), check (censure), convert (turn, revive), convince (refute), cunning (skill), deal (part), denounce (declare), engage (put up as security), evidence (deed, document), flood (stream), fray (frighten), grievance (trouble), heaviness (anxiety, grief), liquor (juice), lust (desire), meat (food, cp § 66, No. 4), passenger (one who passes by or through), persecute (pursue), prefer (promote), rehearse (recount, repeat), revolting (stubborn), science (learning), shroud (shade), suburb (common land, pasture land), suffer (allow), table (tablet), tale (number), tell (count), tempt (test), temptation (trial), title (monument), travail (hardship), undertake (be security), usury (interest), utter (outer), wholesome (gentle). The list might be extended indefinitely, but these examples may suffice to illustrate one reason for a revision of J. (For references see a Concordance; for explanations and other examples see BWB.)

Sometimes what confuses American readers is still accepted as normal in British usage. The most conspicuous example is the use of "corn" for grains and cereals in general. R changes this to "grain." To speak of an "ear of corn" is especially misleading: with barley, rye, or wheat Americans usually say "head"; so R in Job 24.24. Cp [J]cornfloor—[R]threshing floors (Hos 9.1).

Another point of difference between American and British practice is the use of "shall" and "will." Ordinarily for the simple future tense R uses "will" in the second and third persons, reserving "shall" for expressions of determination and commands; in the first person "shall" expresses futurity and "will" determination. R sometimes, however, uses "shall" in the second or third person as a "prophetic future," expressing certainty.

Chapter IV

SIMPLIFIED STYLE, CONDENSATION AND OMISSION

§15 J's literary style, influenced by the uncomplicated structure of the Hebrew language, is much simpler than what was considered good English style in the 17th century; even so it seems cumbersome and involved by present standards. R often simplifies it without altering the meaning; indeed the meaning stands out all the more clearly.

Sometimes J reproduces and R simplifies a Hebraic construction called by grammarians prolepsis: e.g., [J]God saw the light, that it was good—[R]God saw that the light was good (Gen 1.4; cp Ex 2.2; Ps 75.8; see § 99 for another kind of prolepsis). Other expressions, awkward in English, are condensed by R; e.g., [J]every tree, in the which is the fruit of a tree yielding seed—[R]every tree with seed in its fruit (Gen 1.29; cp 6.15; 8.21; 27.8; Ruth 1.5; 1 Chron 6.65; 23.3; 2 Chron 25.21).

Occasionally, where J uses two or more words to translate one Hebrew word, R is more brief; e.g., [J]in the places round about Jerusalem—[R]round about Jerusalem (2 Kings 23.5); [J]the dawning of the day—[R]the dawn (Job 7.4); [J]him that was at peace with me—[R]my friend (Ps 7.4). See also Ps 90.5; 137.3; Mal 3.11. Other examples of simpler English without change of meaning are the following: [J]neither are there any works like unto thy works—[R]nor are there any works like thine (Ps 86.8); [J]while as yet he had not made—[R]before he had made (Prov 8.26); [J]and assembled themselves by troops in the harlots' houses—[R]and trooped to the houses of harlots (Jer 5.7; cp 8.3; 11.17; 38.5; Ezek 31.14; 40.10ff; 44.3; 47.6, 12; Dan 1.7; Zech 9.11).

The Hebrew language often uses expressions which are redundant in English when translated word for word. Thus the excessive frequency of "and" in J reflects the idiomatic use of the Hebrew conjunction. Sometimes this is better represented by other English conjunctions (see § 79); in other places it is better omitted, particularly at the beginning of a sentence. In the first five verses of Genesis J has nine clauses beginning with "and." R omits the conjunction at the beginning of verses 2 and 5. Equally characteristic is the Hebrew idiom rendered in J "And it came to pass." R sometimes reads "It happened" (e.g., Gen 38.1; Neh 1.1), "So it was" (Gen 19.29), or the like, but usually omits the expression with no sacrifice of meaning (e.g., Gen 4.3, 14; Ruth 1.1).

The adverb "now" is often dropped by R where it represents a Hebrew particle (*-nā'*, § 93, No. 3) often attached to a word, usually a verb in the imperative mood, to convey something like the force of a polite request. The translation "now" is sometimes quite misleading, suggesting an expression of time; e.g., [J]Behold, now I know—[R]Behold, I know (2 Kings 5.15). In Gen 18.3, where the particle occurs twice, J translates it in two different ways; R omits it both times. In Num 12.13, where J again has two translations, R drops one of them and keeps the other. (See § 93, No. 3 for other examples and other ways of representing this particle.)

Another Hebrew idiom which is redundant in English is the use of "saying" to introduce a direct quotation. This too is generally omitted by R, whose quotation marks (§ 6) make it unnecessary; e.g., [J]I commanded thee, saying,—[R]I commanded you (Gen 3.17); [J]God talked with him, saying,—[R]God said to him (17.3).

The expression "answered and said" is likewise simplified by R: e.g., [J]And Isaac answered and said unto Esau—[R]Isaac answered Esau (Gen 27.37); [J]Then he answered and spake unto me—[R]Then he said to me (Zech 4.6). This idiom sometimes occurs where nothing has been said; e.g., [J]Then answered David and said—[R]Then David said (1 Sam 26.6; see also 2 Chron 29.31; 34.15; cp 1 Sam 14.12; Ezra 10.2). In Dan 4.30, where Nebuchadnezzar is alone on the roof of his palace, J reads "The king spake, and said," but the Aramaic verb is the one elsewhere translated "answered"; R reads simply, "and the king said." In 1 Sam 18.7 this idiom introduces a song, perhaps implying that it was sung antiphonally. J here reads "answered one another," R "sang to one another."

§ 16 Hebrew grammar or idiom often requires the repetition of words which need not be repeated in English; e.g., [J]the God of heaven, and the God of the earth—[R]the God of heaven and of the earth (Gen 24.3); [J]possession of flocks, and possession of herds—[R]possessions of flocks and herds (26.14). Sometimes the Hebrew repeats a name in a way which is unnatural in English; e.g., [J]And when Rachel saw . . . , Rachel envied—[R]When Rachel saw . . . , she envied (Gen 30.1; cp 31.55; Ex 34.29; Num 21.23; Jer 37.16). So too a common noun or a pronoun may be repeated; e.g., [J]two manner of people . . . ; and the one people shall be stronger than the other people—[R]two peoples . . . ; the one shall be stronger than the other (Gen 25.23; cp Ex 3.2; Dan 11.11). In Gen 36.15–43 and 1 Chron 1.51–4 J uses the word "duke" 30 times; R uses "chief" only 17 times.

Similarly verbs, or expressions represented in English by verbs, are often repeated in Hebrew; e.g., [J]they had brick for stone, and slime had they for morter—[R]they had brick for stone, and bitumen for mortar (Gen 11.3; cp Deut 9.25; 2 Sam 18.8; 1 Kings 2.11; 3.11; Is 14.25; 24.22; Jer 39.13f; 44.1; Ezek 48.11; Hos 2.21).

In descriptions the Hebrew language makes much use of "distributive repetition"; thus J in Ex 25.35, translating word for word, says three times, "under two branches of the same"; R says once, "under each pair of the six branches" (see also, e.g., Ezek 48.31ff). In various other connections also R often eliminates unnecessary repetition; e.g., [J]pools of water, to water therewith—[R]pools from which to water (Eccles 2.6); [J]power over the spirit to retain the spirit—[R]power to retain the spirit (8.8; cp Is 20.1; Jer 16.3; 18.23; Ezek 18.22; 33.13; 47.3–5).

§ 17 Prepositional phrases are used in Hebrew and Aramaic in the same way that we say in English "I bought a hat for myself" or "I bought myself a hat" (cp the Latin "ethical dative" or "dative of interest"). The context often makes such a phrase superfluous, and R omits it; e.g., [J]Lamech took unto him two wives—[R]Lamech took two wives (Gen 4.19); [J]write this song for you—[R]write this song (Deut 31.19).

Words inserted by J in italics (§ 6) are often found unnecessary and omitted by R; e.g., [J]a tower, whose top *may reach* unto heaven—[R]a tower with its top in the heavens (Gen 11.4); [J]to say, *She is* my wife—[R]to say, "My wife" (26.7); [J]The name *of the* LORD—[R]the Name (Lev 24.11, 16). Words not representing anything in the Hebrew are sometimes inserted without italics by J and dropped by R: e.g., [J]make cakes upon the hearth—[R]make cakes (Gen 18.6); [J]made the altar—[R]made it (Ex 38.7).

Pronouns and phrases are sometimes omitted by R where they seem awkward and unnecessary in the context; e.g., [J]pass by me—[R]pass through (Num 20.18); [J]from mine iniquity—[R]from guilt (2 Sam 22.24 = Ps 18.23). In 2 Chron 4.3, to avoid repetition, R omits a whole clause.

Words which are not only unnecessary but confusing or even misleading are occasionally used in J and omitted by R; e.g., [J]Bring it near to me. . . . And he brought it near to him—[R]Bring it to me . . . So he brought it to him (Gen 27.25); [J]the hollow of Jacob's thigh—[R]Jacob's thigh (32.25); [J]the part of the hand—[R]the hand (Dan 5.5, 24). Sometimes J uses several words to bring out the supposed force of a Hebrew word but reads into it more than it actually means: e.g., [J]both yesterday and today—[R]today (Ex 5.14); [J]in the places round about Jerusalem—[R]round about Jerusalem (2 Kings 23.5).

With such omissions as those mentioned thus far no marginal note is needed. Sometimes, however, attention is called to an omission by a note, as in the following instances: [J]thy victuals. So the Levite went in—[R]your living [Heb *living, and the Levite went*] (Judges 17.10); [J]the King's servant, and me thy servant—[R]your servant [Heb *the king's servant, your servant*] (2 Sam 18.29); [J]called the Gibeonites and said unto them—[R]called the Gibeonites [Heb *the Gibeonites and said to them*] (21.2; the omission here avoids an incomplete sentence and a long parenthesis); [J]with fire in the same place—[R]with fire [Heb *fire in the sitting*] (23.7).

Two omissions with unusually long notes involve words (one word in the original) indicating a sudden shift from the Hebrew to the Aramaic language in the text (Ezra 4.7; Dan 2.4).

Chapter V

ADDITIONS

§18 Like J, R occasionally inserts words to clarify the meaning. The subject or object of a verb or the object of a preposition is often expressed in Hebrew only by the form of the verb or by a pronoun (or pronominal suffix), which may be ambiguous. Where a person is referred to, J sometimes uses his name instead of an indefinite pronoun, giving the literal meaning in the margin (e.g., Gen 45.26) or printing the name in italics (e.g., 2 Sam 3.7).

R sometimes retains the inserted name, with a note (e.g., Job 20.23) or without one (e.g., 1 Kings 20.34); often, however, J's insertion seems unnecessary and is discarded (e.g., Gen 45.26). In Job 27.22 R's interpretation of the intended reference differs from J's, which is recognized in the margin: [J]God—[R]It [Or *he* (that is God)]. On the other hand, R frequently inserts a name where J does not, sometimes with a note (e.g., Ex 15.25) but more often without one (e.g., Gen 4.10; Ps 105.24, 37).

Supplying the name frequently avoids possible confusion. In 1 Sam 4.18, for instance, speaking of the messenger who brought to Eli the news of Israel's defeat and the loss of the ark, J reads literally, "And it came to pass, when he made mention of the ark of God, that he fell from the seat backward." But it was not the messenger that fell and broke his neck. R therefore reads, "Eli fell."

In Josh 15.13 R's recognition of a place-name necessitates repetition of a personal name which is a part of it: [J]the city of Arba [or, *Kirjath-arba*] the father of Anak, which city is Hebron—[R]Kiriath-arba, that is Hebron (Arba was the father of Anak). R's "that is" instead of J's "which city is" renders the Hebrew quite literally.

Not only names but common nouns and other words are frequently added by J to complete or clarify the meaning, and R adopts many of these additions (e.g., Ex 27.14). In other places R makes such additions where J does not. Often a noun is substituted for a pronoun to make clear the subject of a verb; thus J's "one" may become in R "a man" (Ezek 33.21; cp 46.9, [J]he shall not return—[R]no one shall return), "the man" (33.22), or "man" (e.g., Deut 5.24); "they" may become "men" (e.g., Is 2.19), "the men" (2 Sam 17.21), "people" (Jer 17.26; Ezek 38.8), "the people" (e.g., Judg 14.11), "her people" (Jer 14.2), or "its people" (Ezek 38.8). Other expressions also are used by R to replace ambiguous pronouns: e.g., [J]they rolled the stone—[R]the shepherds would roll the stone (Gen 29.3); [J]there was written—[R]an edict . . . was written (Esther 3.12).

In the same way the object of a verb is often specified by R where the Hebrew and J leave it indefinite or unexpressed; e.g., [J]let him go free—[R]let the slave go free (Ex 21.26f); [J]measure unto the cities—[R]measure the distance to the cities (Deut 21.2). The object of a preposition also is sometimes similarly indicated; e.g., [J]eaten thereof—[R]eaten of the tithe (Deut 26.14); [J]by their means—[R]through the king's traders (1 Kings 10.29).

§ 19 To complete a sentence or clause, or to clarify the meaning, J often inserts a verb not expressed in Hebrew, particularly in a "nominal sentence" (§ 108), where some form of the verb *be* is implied. In such cases R frequently inserts some verb other than *be* to express the implied meaning; e.g., [J]much increase is by the strength of the ox—[R]abundant crops come by the strength of the ox (Prov 14.4). Other verbs used in this way are endure (Ps 45.6; 102.24; 119.90; in Prov 27.24 J inserts *endure*), last (Prov 27.24), end (Prov 10.28; 11.23), extend (Ps 36.5, covering J's *reacheth* and *is*), reach (48.10), rest (62.7), stand (87.1).

R sometimes inserts a verb where J has none; e.g., [J]In the morning, when it is day—[R]Let us wait till the light of the morning (Judg 16.2); [J]even unto the LORD—[R]they cried to the LORD (2 Sam 22.42; here the verb is suggested by the parallel passage, Ps 18.41).

When intervening words have obscured the connection, it is

helpful to repeat a verb. Thus in Prov 13.2 J repeats "shall eat"; here R, with a somewhat different interpretation, inserts "is for" instead of repeating the verb. Elsewhere R often repeats a verb from the context for coherence; e.g., [J]Save only that which the young men have eaten—[R]I will take nothing but what the young men have eaten (Gen 14.24; cp v. 23); [J]Unto a land—[R]Go up to a land (Ex 33.3; cp v. 7). In Deut 4.15f R simplifies a long sentence by dividing it. This necessitates the insertion of "beware" in v. 16.

Occasionally a Hebrew verb which does double duty, so to speak, must be translated twice in English. In 1 and 2 Kings the beginning of each reign and its length are stated in a formula which varies slightly. Sometimes it appears as in 1 Kings 15.25, "And Nadab . . . began to reign . . . and reigned . . ." Frequently, however, one Hebrew verb stands for both "began to reign" and "reigned." In such instances J sometimes inserts "and reigned," R "and he reigned" (e.g., 2 Kings 13.1, 10); R has this addition also in some places where J does not (e.g., 1 Kings 15.33).

A double translation of one Hebrew verb is given by R in some other places also, where no one English verb is fully adequate; e.g., [J]turn thee behind me—[R]Turn and ride behind me (2 Kings 9.18f); [J]My skin is black upon me—[R]My skin turns black and falls from me (Job 30.30; literally "turns black from upon me").

In other ways too R occasionally expands an expression to make its meaning or connection clearer; e.g., [J]even as the green herb have I given you all things—[R]and as I gave you the green plants, I give you everything (Gen 9.3); [J]in a strong city—[R]when I was beset as in a besieged city (Ps 31.21); [J]they may eat—[R]who are doomed with you to eat (Is 36.12); [J]He is swift as the waters—[R]You say, 'They are swiftly carried away upon the face of the waters' (Job 24.18; the change from "he" to "they" connects the verse with what precedes it).

§ 20 In view of its abandonment of J's italics (§ 6), R has many marginal notes indicating words that have been added. With such additions as have been noted thus far notes have usually been deemed unnecessary, but in other cases the insertions require explanation. The note then gives the literal meaning of the Hebrew (abbreviated "Heb"); e.g., [J]for his righteousness—[R]by his righteousness [Heb *by it*] (Ezek 33.12). So too when R adds words but J does not; e.g., [J]he shall—[R]the one who hurt her shall [Heb *he shall*] (Ex 21.22). Occasionally another formula is used; e.g., [J]O LORD God of Israel—[R]The LORD, the God of Israel, be witness [Heb lacks *be witness*] (1 Sam 20.12).

Occasionally more elaborate notes are needed. In Num 26.4, for example, R has a long addition (cp J), with the note, "Supplying *take a census of the people* Compare verse 2." A whole clause is moved by R from Jer 38.28 to the beginning of 39.3, with the note, "This clause has been transposed from the end of chapter 38."

At one place where something is missing in the Hebrew text it is impossible now to supply what has been lost. In 1 Sam 13.1 J reads "Saul reigned one year [Heb. *the son of one year in his reigning*]." The Hebrew expression is actually an idiomatic way of stating a person's age, but Saul was not one year old when he became king; the number indicating his age is missing. Unable to supply it, R reads, "Saul was . . . years old when he began to reign [The number is lacking in Heb]." In the latter half of the same verse J reads, "and when he had reigned two years over Israel." But Saul's son Jonathan was at this time a grown man; R therefore assumes another gap in the text and reads, "and he reigned . . . and two years [*Two* is not the entire meaning. Something has dropped out]."

§ 21 In some cases words added by R involve points of interpretation on which R differs, or seems to differ, from J. While these belong logically in Part Two, a few examples may be cited here to illustrate this kind of addition.

Sometimes R presents a specific interpretation where J is at best ambiguous. In Gen 1.30 the clause "wherein there is life" seems in J to apply only to "everything that creepeth upon the earth," though this may not have been intended by J and was certainly not meant by the Hebrew author. To preserve the connection with beasts and fowls as well as creeping things R reads "everything that has the breath of life." In 46.30 Jacob says to Joseph, according to J, "Now let me die, since I have seen thy face, because thou art yet alive." The conjunction rendered "because" (§ 80, No. 3) means also "that," and this is surely its meaning here. R therefore reads, "I have seen your face and know that you are still alive."

At the end of Hos 5.15 R inserts "saying" to show that what follows (6.1–3) is not part of what God says, but the expected response of penitent Israel. The addition of a phrase in Jon 3.3 makes an ambiguous expression definite: [J]Nineveh was an exceeding great city of three days' journey—[R]Nineveh was an exceedingly great city, three days' journey in breadth. Both the use of a different verb and the addition of other words reflect a different interpretation in Ps 42.4: [J]went with them—[R]led them in procession.

Occasionally an addition apparently implying a different interpretation is actually made merely for the sake of clearer or more idiomatic English; e.g., [J]and how saidst thou—[R]how then could you say (Gen 26.9); [J]the heavens also dropped—[R]the heavens poured down rain (Ps 68.8). Other additions in R, like those in J, are intended simply to express the meaning more fully; e.g., [J]cried unto the LORD—[R]cried to the LORD for help (Judg 4.3; "for help" is part of the meaning of the Hebrew verb).

Sometimes the identification or grammatical form of a Hebrew word is in question; e.g., [J]in pride [Or, *to deal proudly*]—[R]he dealt proudly (Dan 5.20). In Nahum 2.11 what J takes for a noun meaning "old lion" is recognized by R as a verb and rendered "brought his prey."

Somewhat difficult points of interpretation are involved in some of R's additions. In 2 Sam 12.31, referring to David's treatment of the people of Rabbath Ammon, J says that he "put them under saws, and under harrows of iron, and under axes of iron, and made them pass through the brickkiln." David was undoubtedly capable of cruelty, but it is not necessary to attribute quite such a frightful atrocity to him. The Hebrew means literally "set them in saws" or "with saws," etc. R takes the verb "set" to mean "set to labor," translates literally the phrase "with saws," etc., and so reads, "set them to labor with saws," etc.

Still more complicated instances of additions involving interpretation may be seen in Is 64.5; Jer 40.10; Ezek 48.1; Dan 9.27.

Chapter VI

CHANGES IN THE ORDER OF WORDS

§ 22 No translation can follow exactly the order of words in the original language. English word-order is exceptionally flexible, yet what is normal in another language is often strange and awkward in English.

Since the English language has no case-endings of nouns, the subject and object of a verb can often be distinguished only by the order of the words. In other ways also the lack of inflections in English makes the word-order important to prevent ambiguous or erroneous connections of ideas. It is therefore frequently necessary in translating the Bible to change the order of words. J often departs from the Hebrew word-order. Sometimes, in fact, it does so unnecessarily, and R returns to the original order, e.g., [J]on the twentieth day of the second month, in the second year—[R]in the second year, in the second month, on the twentieth day of the month (Num 10.11); [J]how will he then vex [Heb. *do hurt*] himself, if we tell him that the child is dead?—[R]how then can we say to him the child is dead? He may do himself some harm (2 Sam 12.18).

In some cases a return to the Hebrew order is occasioned by R's recognition of poetic form. For example, in 2 Kings 19.21 J turns a bit of Hebrew poetry into plain English prose by shifting to the normal English word-order: [J]The virgin the daughter of Zion hath despised thee, and laughed thee to scorn; the daughter of Jerusalem hath shaken her head at thee—

> [R]She despises you, she scorns you—
> the virgin daughter of Zion;
> she wags her head behind you—
> the daughter of Jerusalem.

So too Job 30.1: [J]But now they that are younger than I have me in derision—

> [R]But now they make sport of me,
> men who are younger than I.

§ 23 In many places, however, where J retains the Hebrew or Aramaic order of words, R changes to a more idiomatic English order: e.g., [J]Of Haran are we—[R]We are from Haran (Gen 29.4); [J]The secret which the king hath demanded cannot the wise men . . . shew unto the king—[R]No wise men . . . can show to the king the mystery which the king has asked (Dan 2.27).

In Hebrew a possessive pronoun often precedes its antecedent, but this is awkward in English: e.g., [J]His own iniquities shall take the wicked himself—[R]The iniquities of the wicked ensnare him (Prov 5.22).

Many common expressions have an established order in English which is adopted by R instead of J's literal rendering of the Hebrew: e.g., [J]between me and thee—[R]between you and me (Gen 13.8; 31.44, 48–50); [J]Isaac went unto Abimelech king of the Philistines unto Gerar—[R]Isaac went to Gerar, to Abimelech . . . (26.1); [J]Esau my brother—[R]my brother Esau (27.11); [J]little children and women—[R]women and children (Esther 3.13, but cp 8.11); [J]With arrows and with bows—[R]with bow and arrows (Is 7.24); [J]with nails and with hammers—[R]with hammer and nails (Jer 10.4); [J]upon my knees and upon the palms of my hands—[R]on my hands and knees (Dan 10.10).

Some changes of word-order are made in R simply for the sake of a smoother reading: e.g., [J]pulled her in unto him into the ark—[R]brought her into the ark with him (Gen 8.9); [J]all the wells which his father's servants had digged . . . , the Philistines had stopped them, and filled them with earth—[R]the Philistines had stopped and filled with earth all the wells which his father's servants had dug . . . (26.15).

Many of R's changes in the order of words are intended to bring out the right connections between parts of a sentence. A good example is Gen 1.11, [J]the herb yielding seed, and the fruit tree yielding fruit after his kind, whose seed is in itself—[R]plants yielding seed, and fruit trees bearing fruit in which is their seed, each according to its kind. By moving the phrase "according to its kind" down to follow "in which is their seed," R shows that it modifies "plants" as well as "fruit trees." The clause "in which is their seed" also directly follows "fruit," with which it belongs.

In some cases the change of order is a matter of emphasis as well as coherence: e.g., [J]How thou didst drive out the heathen . . . , and plantedst them; how thou didst afflict the people, and cast them out—[R]Thou . . . didst drive out the nations, but them thou didst plant; thou didst afflict the peoples, but them thou didst set free (Ps 44.2).

Chapter VII

FREE vs. LITERAL TRANSLATION

§24 The most literal translation is not always the most accurate. J is by no means a literal translation; the scholars who made it knew both their Hebrew and their English too well for that. R, in fact, is often more literal than J. Where the latter translates freely and gives a literal translation in the margin, R sometimes adopts the marginal rendering (as it also often adopts marginal renderings of EA): e.g., [J]How old art thou? [Heb. *How many are the days of the years of thy life?*]—[R]How many are the days of the years of your life (Gen 47.8); [J]the whole age of Jacob [Heb. *the days of the years of his life*]—[R]the days of Jacob, the years of his life (v. 28); [J]mourned [Heb. *wept*]—[R]wept (50.3).

In other instances R agrees in general with J mg but does not follow it exactly: e.g., [J]And the evening and the morning were [Heb. *And the evening was, and the morning was*] the first day—[R]And there was evening and there was morning, one day (Gen 1.5; cp vv. 8, 13, 19, 23, 31); [J]for as much money as it is worth [Heb. *full money*]—[R]for the full price (23.9).

§25 A word in one language does not always correspond exactly to any one word in another language; there is often a certain overlapping of meaning among several related words. J therefore rightly makes no attempt at uniformity or consistency in its renderings of Hebrew words; in fact it seeks rather variety. Even where a Hebrew word appears twice in the same context with no change of meaning, J often avoids repeating the same English word: e.g., children of Heth (Gen 23.5, 7, 10), sons of Heth (vv. 3, 16); sons of Belial (1 Kings 21.10), children of Belial (v. 13); valley (Gen 14.17), dale (same v.); famine (Gen 41.30f, 56f), dearth (v. 54); earth (Ex 10.15), land (same v.); gore

(Ex 21.28, 31), push (vv. 32, 36), push with his horn (v. 29); gates (Job 38.17), doors (same v.). Examples of such gratuitous variety of rendering of the same Hebrew could be multiplied indefinitely.

EA reacted against J's excessive variations by endeavoring, so far as possible, to use the same English word everywhere for a given Hebrew word. Such extreme, mechanical consistency is avoided by R. When the meaning of a Hebrew word is not the same in two places, only the use of different English words can do justice to it. Even differences of rendering in the same context for stylistic variety are used occasionally in R, though far less often than in J: e.g., [J]And they that went in, went in . . .—[R]And they that entered . . . went in (Gen 7.16); [J]waxed great . . . became very great—[R]became rich . . . became very wealthy (26.13).

Note also kill, slay (Gen 4.8, 14f, 23, 25; 34.25f); attack, kill, slay (Josh 7.3, 5); grave, tomb (Gen 35.20); throw, cast (37.20, 22, 24); shore, haven (49.13); generous, willing (Ex 35.5, 22); end, termination (Num 34.4f, 8f, 12); choicest gifts, rich yield, abundance, best gifts (Deut 33.13–15); food, bread (1 Kings 21.4f, 7); encompass, are round about (Ps 22.12, 16); hills, mountains (104.10, 13); obey, listen (Jer 7.23f, 26–8); likeness, form (Ezek 1.5); wicked deeds, evil works, wickedness (Hos 7.1–3).

§ 26 As a Hebrew word may be rendered by any of several English words, so the same English word may be used for more than one Hebrew word. A glance at Strong's or Young's Concordance will show that any English word used at all frequently in J represents several different Hebrew words. This is true also of R, but to a lesser extent. Here again, J sometimes goes farther than necessary, ignoring real distinctions of meaning between different Hebrew words.

For instance, "creeping thing" or "thing that creepeth" usually stands in J for a Hebrew noun translated in the same way in R (e.g., Gen 1.24f; 7.23); in Gen 7.21, however, "every creeping thing that creepeth" represents a quite different noun and verb, namely, those used in 1.20, where J has "bring forth abundantly," R "bring forth swarms" (cp 8.19; 9.2f; Ex 8.3).

In Gen 26.25, where JR both read "pitched his tent," the Hebrew verb means literally "stretched"; in v. 17 J's "pitched his tent" stands for a verb which R translates literally "encamped." J uses "pitch" with reference to tents 80 times for the verb in v. 17, 8 times for the one in v. 25, 3 times for a third verb, twice for a fourth, and once for still another. In vv. 20–22 J has "strive" once and "strove" 3 times, but the verb in the last clause of v. 20 is not the same as the one in the other places; R uses "quarrel" and "contend." J uses "defiled" in 34.2 for a verb rendered differently everywhere else; in v. 5 "defiled" stands for another verb. R reads "humbled" in v. 2, "defiled" in v. 5. In 37.29 and 34 "clothes" stands for two different Hebrew nouns, which R distinguishes by using "clothes" and "garments."

§ 27 In other ways, too, R often comes closer to the Hebrew than J does. Among innumerable instances of more literal translation in R, the following may be noted:

[J]a wild man—[R]a wild ass of a man (Gen 16.12); [J]grew—[R]were fruitful (47.27); [J]which another challengeth to be his—[R]of which one says, 'This is it' (Ex 22.9); [J]after he had made it a molten calf—[R]and made a molten calf (32.4); [J]they came to Hebron at break of day—[R]the day broke upon them at Hebron (2 Sam 2.32); [J]a thousand chariots and seven hundred horsemen—[R]a thousand and seven hundred horsemen (8.4); [J]chief rulers [Or, *princes*]—[R]priests (v. 18); [J]Until the day break—[R]Until the day breathes (Song 2.17); [J]the dark mountains—[R]the twilight mountains (Jer 13.16); [J]after three years [Heb. *three* years of *days*]—[R]every three days (Amos 4.4); [J]this man shall be the peace—[R]this shall be peace (Mic 5.5).

Not always, however, is R more literal than J. Under some circumstances R translates more freely. A few examples must suffice here by way of illustration; others will appear later. We have seen that R, to escape ambiguity, sometimes alters the word-order, or makes specific what in J is indicated only by an indefinite pronoun. Other changes made for the same purpose sometimes involve a less literal translation than J's, though by no means always;

e.g., [J]And she again bare his brother Abel—[R]And again, she bore his brother Abel (Gen 4.2; cp v. 22); [J]I will not again curse the ground any more for man's sake—[R]I will never again curse the ground because of man (8.21); [J]to be his wife—[R]as a wife (16.3—Sarah was not resigning in favor of Hagar); [J]Joseph's ten brethren—[R]ten of Joseph's brothers (42.3

—Benjamin too was his brother); [J]neither shalt thou take a wife to her sister to vex her—[R]and you shall not take a woman as a rival wife to her sister (Lev 18.18); [J]avenge the LORD of Midian—[R]execute the LORD's vengeance on Midian (Num 31.3); [J]and went on crying—[R]and went away, crying aloud as she went (2 Sam 13.19); [J]shall not be satisfied with bread —[R]have not enough to eat (Job 27.14); [J]their maidens were not given to marriage—[R]their maidens had no marriage song (Ps 78.63); [J]sick of love —[R]sick with love (Song 2.5; 5.8); [J]and another third kingdom—[R]and yet a third kingdom (Dan 2.39).

§ 28 In spite of J's freedom in dealing with the Hebrew, its language is not always normal, idiomatic English. What is now alien to our idiom may of course have been more familiar in the 17th Century. The expressions "take to wife" and "give to wife," for examples, may be considered idiomatic but archaic English; in any case R avoids them (e.g., Gen 12.19; 34.8, 12; 38.14). Words are sometimes changed by R merely to obtain a more natural phrasing: e.g., [J]preeminence above—[R]advantage over (Eccles 3.19); [J]kneeled upon his knees—[R]got down upon his knees (Dan 6.10).

J sometimes follows Hebrew on Aramaic idiom too closely in the use of prepositions: e.g., [J]answered before the king—[R]answered the king (Dan 2.10); [J]tell the interpretation thereof before the king—[R]tell the king its interpretation (v. 36). In Gen 41.44 J's "without thee" means "without your consent" (so R; cp Mt 10.29).

Following the Hebrew, J uses possessive pronouns in ways foreign to our idiom: e.g., [J]his sin that he hath sinned—[R]the sin which he has committed (Lev 5.13); [J]thy days approach that thou must die—[R]the days approach when you must die (Deut 31.14); [J]thy flesh and thy body—[R]your flesh and body (Prov 5.11).

The attempt to reproduce certain forms of the Hebrew verb sometimes produces awkward English in J, even defeating its own end. There is a "reflexive" form, for example (Stem VII, § 106), which J translates literally in Is 57.4: [J]do ye sport yourselves—[R]are you making sport. More conspicuous is the construction "cause to come," etc., representing the "causative" form of the Hebrew verb (Stem V, § 106). This is not wholly alien to English usage; in fact, R introduces it sometimes where J does not have it (e.g., Lam 1.14; 2.8; Ezek 36.11, 21; 37.6). Its excessive frequency in J, however, is an example of "translation English," for which R often substitutes smoother and more natural expressions; e.g., [J]I will cause the sword to fall out of his hand—[R]I will make the sword fall from his hand (Ezek 30.22).

§ 29 Words used idiomatically in Hebrew are often rendered more freely in J than in R; in other connections, however, the same words may be translated literally by J and more freely by R. The word for "day," for example, has many idiomatic uses in Hebrew. An expression which means literally "all the day" occurs frequently, with various shades of meaning and with the following renderings in J and R:

J	R	
continually	continually	(Ps 42.3)
continually	All the day	(Ps 52.1)
all day	continually	(Is 28.24)
all the day long	continually	(Ps 44.8)
daily	continually	(Ps 42.10)
daily	all the day	(Ps 74.22; 86.3; Jer 20.7)
daily	all day long	(Ps 56.1f; 88.17; Jer 20.8)
every day	all day long	(Ps 56.5)

Such apparently arbitrary shifts in rendering reflect the judgment of the various translators as to the exact meaning of the expression in each context. In some cases rhythm also has been a consideration.

Other expressions involving the same word are similarly rendered in various connections:

[J]all their days—[R]continually (2 Kings 13.3); [J]perpetually—[R]for all time (2 Chron 7.16; lit. all the days); [J]daily—[R]all the day (Ps 13.2); [J]daily—[R]day after day (61.8); [J]daily—[R]Every day (88.9); [J]in the daytime—[R]by day (Is 4.6; cp v. 5 [JR]by day); [J]daily—[R]day after day (Jer 7.25); [J]daily the seven days—[R]on each of the seven days (Ezek 45.23; later in the same verse [JR]daily).

J offers in marginal notes four different literal translations of an idiomatic expression which occurs fifteen times in the OT:

a matter of a day in his day (Ex 5.13), the portion of a day in his day (16.4), the thing of a day in his day (1 Kings 8.59), the matter of the day in his day (Ezra 3.4; Jer 52.34). In the text J translates this expression in twelve more or less different ways:

your daily tasks (Ex 5.13, 19), a certain rate every day (16.4), every thing upon his day (Lev 23.37), at all times, as the matter shall require (1 Kings 8.59), a daily rate for every day (2 Kings 25.30=Jer 52.34), as every day's work required (1 Chron 16.37), after a certain rate every day (2 Chron 8.13), as the duty of every day required (v. 14; Ezra 3.4), his daily portion (2 Chron 31.16), due for every day (Neh 11.23), every day his portion (12.47), a daily provision (Dan 1.5).

R keeps J's rendering, with a slight change, in Ex 5.13; elsewhere it reads as follows:

your daily number (Ex 5.19), a day's portion every day (Ex 16.4), each on its proper day (Lev 23.37), as each day requires (1 Kings 8.59), every day a portion (2 Kings 25.30), as each day required (1 Chron 16.37; Ezra 3.4), as the duty of each day required (2 Chron 8.13f; 31.16), as every day required (Neh 11.23), the daily portions (12.47), according to his daily need (Jer 52.34), a daily portion (Dan 1.5).

Various renderings are similarly used for an idiom whose literal meaning J mg gives as follows: gone into days (Gen 24.1), come into days (Josh 23.1), entered into days (1 Kings 1.1). It is translated in the text by J and R respectively as follows:

[J]well stricken in age—[R]advanced in age (Gen 18.11); [J]well stricken in age—[R]well advanced in years (24.1); [J]stricken in years—[R]advanced in years (Josh 13.1 twice; 1 Kings 1.1); [J]stricken in age—[R]well advanced in years (Josh 23.1f).

§ 30 Variations in the treatment of still other expressions involving the word "day" illustrate the same problems and principles of translation. Only occasionally do J and R differ in their understanding of the Hebrew. In the following instances J's renderings are, at least relatively, more literal than those of R:

[J]this day—[R]now (1 Sam 18.21); [J]to day—[R]just now (9.12); [J]to day—[R]first (1 Kings 1.51; 22.5; 2 Chron 18.4); [J]as it is this day—[R]this day (1 Kings

3.6); [J]at his day—[R]on the day he earns it (Deut 24.15); [J]until those days—[R]yet (1 Kings 3.2); [J]from that day—[R]henceforth (Ezek 48.35); [J]before the day was—[R]henceforth (Is 43.13); [J]all thy days—[R]so long as you live (1 Sam 25.28); [J]all the days of his life—[R]as long as he lived (2 Kings 25.30=Jer 52.34, but cp the preceding v.; in Deut 12.19 J reads as long as thou livest [Heb. *all thy days*]); [J]to thy days—[R]to your life (Is 38.5); [J]the days of my vanity—[R]my vain life (Eccles 7.15); [J]him that is full of days—[R]the very aged (Jer 6.11); [J]many days—[R]for a long time (32.14); [J]in the days of old—[R]long ago (Lam 2.17); [J]the days of Baalim—[R]the feast days of the Baals (Hos 2.13).

In other places J and R have different but equally free translations:

e.g., [J]Did I then begin to enquire—[R]Is today the first time that I have inquired (1 Sam 22.15); [J]at the day appointed [Or, *the new moon*]—[R]at full moon (Prov 7.20); [J]presently [Heb. *in that day*]—[R]at once (12.16); [J]many days and years—[R]In a little more than a year (Is 32.10); [J]in the clear day—[R]in broad daylight (Amos 8.9).

"In the day that" or "in the day of" often means simply "when." Note, e.g., [J]When—[R]in the day when (Ps 56.9). R reads "in the day that you eat of it" in Gen 2.17, but changes to "when" in 3.5; 5.1f; cp [J]in the day of vengeance—[R]when he takes revenge (Prov 6.34).

In Prov 3.16, where J translates literally "Length of days," R reads "Long life." The same Hebrew expression with the preposition "to" is rendered by both J and R "for ever" in Ps 23.6 [R mg Or *as long as I live*]. Corresponding to this is the expression "prolong thy (or your) days," so translated by both J and R in Deut 4.40 and 6.2 but changed by R to "live long" in 4.26; 5.33; 11.9; 22.7 (cp Eccles 8.12, where the Hebrew omits "days"); Prov 10.27 (with a different Hebrew verb).

The Hebrew word for "day" is sometimes translated "time";

e.g., [J]about this time—[R]one day (Gen 39.11); [J]about this time [Heb. *to day*]—[R]immediately (1 Sam 9.13); [J]in time of snow—[R]on a day when snow had fallen (2 Sam 23.20; in 1 Chron 11.22 J reads "in a snowy day"); [J]the same time—[R]on that day (2 Chron 15.11; cp Ezek 38.10); [J]in time of trouble—[R]in the day of trouble (Ps 41.1); [J]in the times of old—[R]in the days of old (44.1).

R uses "time" in some places where J has "day":

e.g., ^{J}according to the days—^{R}as at the time (Lev 12.2); ^{J}in the day—^{R}at the time (Num 3.1; Hos 2.15); ^{J}until the days be fulfilled—^{R}until the time is completed (Num 6.5; cp v. 13); ^{J}the days . . . were forty years—^{R}the time . . . was forty years (1 Kings 2.11); ^{J}after certain days—^{R}after some time (Neh 13.6); ^{J}in the days of evil—^{R}in times of trouble (Ps 49.5); ^{J}at the end of the days—^{R}At the end of the time (Dan 1.18).

In much the same way "while" is used for "day" by both J and R, but not always in the same places. R follows J in reading "a while" in 1 Sam 9.27 and 1 Kings 17.7 and "all the while" in 1 Sam 25.16 and 27.11, but in 1 Sam 22.4; 25.7 changes "all the while" to "all the time," and in 1 Sam 7.2 changes "while the ark abode" to "From the day that the ark was lodged." In Gen 24.55 where the Hebrew says literally "days or ten," J reads "a few days, at the least ten," R "a while, at least ten days."

In Aramaic the word for "hour" is used idiomatically: e.g., ^{J}the same hour—^{R}immediately (Dan 3.6, 15; 4.33; 5.5); ^{J}for one hour—^{R}for a moment (4.19). J's literal rendering of these expressions is misleading.

§ 31 Other idiomatic forms of speech may be mentioned. (1) A characteristic Hebrew idiom is "lift up the horn." In some places (e.g., Ps 75.4f; 89.17, 24; 92.10) R retains J's literal translation of this expression; in others a less literal rendering is adopted;

e.g., ^{J}my horn is exalted—^{R}my strength is exalted (1 Sam 2.1); ^{J}exalt the horn of his anointed—^{R}exalt the power of his anointed (v. 10); ^{J}to lift up the horn—^{R}to exalt him (i.e., the king, 1 Chron 25.5); ^{J}he hath set up the horn of thine adversaries—^{R}and exalted the might of your foes (Lam 2.17). "Horn" is used in this way also with other verbs; e.g., ^{J}defiled my horn in the dust—^{R}laid my strength in the dust (Job 16.15); ^{J}cut off . . . all the horn of Israel—^{R}cut down . . . all the might of Israel (Lam 2.3).

(2) The adverb "how" is idiomatically rendered by R in some connections;

e.g., ^{J}how shall I do—^{R}what else can I do (Jer 9.7); ^{J}how is she become a desolation—^{R}What a desolation she has become (Zeph 2.15).

(3) The verb "know" has many idiomatic uses in Hebrew and Aramaic. It is not always translated literally by J: e.g., [J]I am sure—[R]I know (Ex 3.19). In many instances, however, where J reads "know," R uses a different English verb;

e.g., choose (Gen 18.19), consider (Deut 11.2; Ps 90.11), find out (Prov 10.9), gain (Prov 4.1), have (Dan 2.21), perceive (Is 43.19), recognize (Lam 4.8), regard (Ps 95.10, cp 144.3), take heed of (31.7), take note (Jer 5.1), take notice (Ps 142.4), understand (73.16; Prov 30.18; Is 42.25; Jer 17.9).

Other uses and renderings of this verb that should be noted are the following: [J]know to refuse—[R]knows how to refuse (Is 7.15f; cp 8.4, [J]shall have knowledge to cry—[R]knows how to cry); thou shalt not know—[R]you cannot (47.11); [J]are not known—[R]were unseen (Ps 77.19); [J]is known—[R]has shown himself (48.3).

(4) How misleading a literal translation may be is shown by the expression used in 1 Kings 20.22, 26: [J]at the return of the year—[R]in the spring. A reader of J might well suppose that the beginning of January was meant. J is literal but obscure in Gen 18.10: [J]according to the time of life—[R]in the spring. Cp [J]About this season according to the time of life—[R]At this season, when the time comes round (2 Kings 4.16); [J]at that season that Elisha had said unto her, according to the time of life—[R]about that time the following spring, as Elisha had said to her (v. 17). Another idiom whose force is entirely lost in J's literal translation appears in Eccles 3.12, [J]do good—[R]enjoy themselves.

§ 32 Frequently a word of broad, general meaning is replaced in R by one more specific, expressing more exactly what it means in the particular context. Instances of this have already been encountered incidentally, and others will appear later; suffice it here to mention some of these words and R's more specific renderings:

[J]another tongue—[R]an alien tongue (Is 28.11); [J]bind—[R]Harness (of horses, Mic 1.13); [J]broken—[R]wrecked (of a ship, 1 Kings 22.48; Ezek 27.26, 34); [J]bring thee up in my net—[R]haul you up in my dragnet (32.3); [J]cometh in—[R]breaks in (of a thief, Hos 7.1); [J]entered—[R]invade (Lam 1.10); [J]caused . . . to enter—[R]drove into (of arrows, 3.13); [J]Enflaming yourselves—Ryou who burn with lust (Is 57.5); Ja great oppressor—Ra cruel oppressor (Prov 28.16); Jhole of the pit—Rquarry (Is 51.1); Jholes—Rsockets (of eyes, Zech 14.12); Jones—Rwomen (Jer 2.33); Jpiece—Rloaf (of bread, 37.21); Jpile—Rpyre (Is 30.33); Jreturn—Rbe sheathed (of a sword, Ezek 21.5); Jshod them—Rgave them sandals (2 Chron 28.15); Jsing—Rhoot . . . croak (translated twice by R to fit two different subjects, Zeph 2.14); Jturned—Rswung open (of a gate, Ezek 26.2); Jwalk—Rprowl (Lam 5.18); Jwaters—Rpool (Jer 41.12); Jwater—Rtears (Lam 1.16; 3.48); Jword—Rthreat (2.17).

The following words also are sometimes replaced in R by various more specific terms:

Jbring in—Rharvest; Jbuild—Rrebuild, build up, besiege, fortify, help to build; Jcall—Rannounce, appoint, invite, proclaim, speak of as, summon, give names, name; Jcome down—Rbe felled, step down; Jcome up—Rgrow up; Jcover—Rclothe, hide, wrap, set under, forgive, pardon; Jcut—Rgash; Jcut down—Rfell, hew down; Jfat—Rfull of sap, proud, rich, stout, strong, wanton; Jmake fat—Renrich, refresh, gorge, make rich, richly supply, make strong; Jfatness—Rabundance; Jfear—Rdread, object of dread, dread wrath, those who fear, what they fear, panic, terror, trembling, turmoil; Jfill—Rgorge; Jbe filled—Renjoy, have more than enough, take their fill, to the full, ever thirsty, wet; Jfly—Rhover, swoop; Jgift—Rbribe; Jgo—Rflee, float, flow, glide away; Jgreat—Rhard, thick; Jherdmen—Rshepherds; Jissue—Rflow; Jissues—Rescape, springs; Jplant—Rpitch, transplant; Jrestingplace—Rfold; Jrun—Rcharge, dart, flow, make haste, race; Jtake—Rcarry, seize, cut off; Jwrite—Rdecree, enroll, inscribe, prescribe, record.

§ 33 R sometimes substitutes for J's rendering of a Hebrew word one that is less literal but more appropriate in the context:

e.g., Jput . . . my bridle in thy lips—Rput . . . my bit in your mouth (2 Kings 19.28; Is 37.29); Jlet loose the bridle—Rcast off restraint (Job 30.11); Jthe generations of Jacob—Rthe history of the family of Jacob (Gen 37.2; what follows is narrative, not a genealogy); Jget a snare—Rentangle yourself in a snare (Prov 22.25); Jbe healed—Rbecome fresh (of water, Ezek 47.8); Jheavy—Rdull (of the ear, Is 59.1); Jhide—Rclose (of the ear, Lam 3.56); Juncircumcised—Rclosed [Heb *uncircumcised*] (of the ear, Jer 6.10); Jthe furrows of her plantation—Rthe bed where it was planted (Ezek 17.7); Jplantings of a vineyard—Ra place for planting vineyards (Mic 1.6); [J]poured out—[R]scattered (of stones, Lam 4.1); [J]make I my bed to swim—[R]I flood my bed with tears (Ps 6.6); [J]the people whither—[R]the peoples among whom (Ezek 29.13); [J]wife—[R]widow (1 Sam 30.5; 2 Sam 3.3, cp 2.2).

In other cases R's translation is both more appropriate than J's and equally literal:

e.g., [J]claws—[R]hoofs (of sheep, Zech 11.16); [J]cut off—[R]breaks (of a dog's neck, Is 66.3). Sometimes, indeed, the words used by R are virtually synonyms of those in J but better suited to the context: e.g., [J]disperse—[R]spread (of knowledge, Prov 15.7); [J]exalted—[R]lifted up (of valleys, Is 40.4); [J]shall fall—[R]have sunk (of shipwrecked men and goods, Ezek 27.34); [J]intermission—[R]respite (Lam 3.49); [J]jealousy—[R]jealous wrath (Ps 79.5); [J]join themselves together—[R]make an alliance (Dan 11.6); [J]lean not unto—[R]do not rely on (Prov 3.5); [J]nursing fathers—[R]foster fathers (Is 49.23; R keeps "nursing mothers"); [J]nursed—[R]carried (60.4); [J]plentiful—[R]fruitful (of a field, 16.10); [J]pluckt off—[R]freshly plucked (Gen 8.11); [J]prosper—[R]thrive (of a vine, Ezek 17.9f); [J]sea—[R]lake (Job 14.11); [J]trickleth down—[R]will flow (Lam 3.49); [J]wash herself—[R]bathe (Ex 2.5); [J]weak—[R]lovesick (Ezek 16.30).

§ 34 Somewhat similar to these more appropriate but less literalistic readings are a few euphemisms to which R resorts out of deference to modern canons of taste. The word "beget," for example, is not avoided where the context calls for it (e.g., Deut 4.25; 1 Chron 14.3). Its constant recurrence in J in genealogies, however, does not enhance the impressiveness of these passages; R therefore uses such renderings as "became the father of" (Gen 5.3 etc.), "was the father of" (4.18 etc., cp Eccles 5.14), or simply "had" (Gen 6.10 etc.); cp [J]begat children of—[R]had children by (1 Chron 2.18); [J]after he begat—[R]after the birth of (Gen 11.11 etc.); [J]which thou begettest—[R]born to you (48.6).

Other expressions are somewhat toned down by R: e.g., [J]he that shall come forth out of thine own bowels—[R]your own son (Gen 15.4; cp Ex 1.5; Judg 8.30). The idiomatic Hebrew use of "know" as in Gen 4.1, "Adam knew Eve his wife," is usually rendered literally in R, but cp 38.26. R only partly interprets another characteristic Hebrew idiom in Deut 22.30 (cp 27.20).

The word "seed" in the sense of offspring is kept by R six

times in the OT (see § 146); elsewhere it is translated according to the context as child or children, son or sons, descendants, descent, family, house, kind, line, people, posterity, race, or stock; cp [J]the seed of Israel—[R]the Israelites (Neh 9.2); [J]the seed of the righteous—[R]those who are righteous (Prov 11.21); [J]of the seed of the Medes—[R]by birth a Mede (Dan 9.1); [J]with the seed of men—[R]in marriage (2.43). Where the sense requires it, R translates the same noun "semen" (Gen 38.9; Lev 15.16–18, 32; 22.4).

In Deut 23.13 a euphemistic Hebrew expression is paraphrased by J but translated literally by R; later in the same verse J translates another expression literally and R interprets it. The Hebrew euphemism "cover his feet" is represented in R by an equivalent English euphemism, "relieve himself" (Judg 3.24; 1 Sam 24.3). The idiom used in 1 Sam 25.22, 34 and elsewhere is as meaningless as it is shocking to modern readers; it is therefore given a less literal but clearer rendering in R than in J.

Following its basic text, A (§ 2), R often prefers "body" to "belly." It says "harlot" instead of "whore" and in the OT changes "fornication" to "harlotry," "unfaithfulness," or the like. In Ezek 16.25 it changes "and hast opened thy feet" to "offering yourself."

J uses freely the verb "stink," but sometimes uses other renderings when the Hebrew verb is used figuratively: e.g., [J]ye have made our savour to be abhorred—[R]you have made us offensive (Ex 5.21; cp 1 Sam 27.12); [J]was had in abomination—[R]had become odious (1 Sam 13.4; cp 1 Chron 19.6). In other places, however, even though the meaning is figurative, J translates literally: e.g., [J]to make me to stink—[R]by making me odious (Gen 34.30; cp 2 Sam 10.6). R sometimes changes the word even when the meaning is literal: e.g., [J]stink—[R]become foul (Ex 7.18; 16.24; cp 7.21; 16.20); in 8.14, however, R keeps "the land stank."

§ 35 Idiomatic translation involves more than the occasional substitution of one word for another. By changing the grammatical structure of an expression R sometimes achieves more idiomatic English while remaining as close as J to the meaning of the Hebrew;

e.g., [J]the gathering together of the waters—[R]the waters that were gathered together (Gen 1.10); [J]no rest for the sole of her foot—[R]no place to set her foot (8.9); [J]before my death—[R]before I die (27.7; cp v. 10); [J]burn him on the wood with fire—[R]burn it on a fire of wood (Lev 4.12); [J]be unto him a people of inheritance—[R]be a people of his own possession (Deut 4.20); [J]the priests the Levites—[R]the Levitical priests (17.9, 18 and often); [J]and that they may learn, and fear—[R]and learn to fear (31.12); [J]and the goings out of that coast were at the sea—[R]and comes to its end at the sea (Josh 15.4; cp vv. 7, 11; 16.3, 7 etc.).

Some of the changes that have been mentioned may be classified under the head of paraphrase. Other renderings belong even more clearly to that category. To convey the meaning and force of the original in natural and intelligible English it is sometimes necessary to recast an expression more or less completely, giving its essential meaning in a quite different form. J and all the revisions resort to paraphrase in this sense on occasion.

Examples of paraphrase in J where R translates more literally have been noted in § 27; others are the following:

[J]according as the cattle . . . and the children be able to endure—[R]according to the pace of the cattle . . . and according to the pace of the children (Gen 33.14); [J]he spake unto them by an interpreter—[R]there was an interpreter between them (42.23); [J]in process of time—[R]in the course of those many days (Ex 2.23).

Sometimes both J and R paraphrase, but in different ways:

e.g., [J]I have accepted thee concerning this thing—[R]I grant you this favor (Gen 19.21); [J]and fallen in decay—[R]and cannot maintain himself (Lev 25.35); [J]there shall none of you be freed from being bondmen—[R]some of you shall always be slaves (Josh 9.23); [J]Amnon thought it hard for him—[R]it seemed impossible to Amnon (2 Sam 13.2); [J]if he will shew himself—[R]if he proves to be (1 Kings 1.52); [J]them that were in the king's presence—[R]the king's council (2 Kings 25.19; cp Jer 52.25).

In many places R introduces a paraphrase which interprets the Hebrew more clearly and even more accurately than J's more literal rendering;

e.g., [J]The end of all flesh is come before me—[R]I have determined to make an end of all flesh (Gen 6.13); [J]for all the goods of his master were in his hand—[R]taking all sorts of choice gifts from his master (24.10); [J]I pray thee, if I have found favour in thine eyes—[R]If you will allow me to say so (30.27); [J]Peace be to you—[R]Rest assured (43.23); [J]the way of them that dwelt in tents—[R]the caravan route (Judg 8.11); [J]sent abroad—[R]gave in marriage outside his clan (12.9); [J]He maketh a path to shine after him—[R]Behind him he leaves a shining wake (Job 41.32).

Part Two

Differences of Interpretation

Chapter VIII

NEW UNDERSTANDING OF THE MEANINGS OF WORDS

§36 The most important differences between R and J are not different ways of expressing the same meaning. Far more basic are the new interpretations arising from a better understanding of the original words.

It has been said that the Bible is a book about three subjects: war, agriculture, and religion. The fact is that it is concerned with the whole of human life and man's whole environment. It deals with the past and the future as well as the present, and not only with what the senses and reason can discern but also with the world of the imagination, the world of feeling, and above all the world of faith. Its major concern, of course, is spiritual; but the great spiritual themes of the Bible are presented in terms of the common interests and activities of everyday life.

Naturally, therefore, the vocabulary of the Bible is a large one. Strong's Concordance lists 8674 Hebrew and Aramaic words used in the OT. A great many of these, moreover, have not one but several more or less related meanings. If we are to get the message of the Bible, and get it right, we must first of all understand the words in which it is expressed.

In no area of biblical scholarship has greater progress been made since 1611, and even since 1901, than in lexicography, the study of words and their meanings. So rapid, indeed, is the advance of knowledge in this field that a new Hebrew and Aramaic dictionary begins to be antiquated by the time it is printed.

Many of the words in the OT, to be sure, refer to comparatively unimportant things, the earthen vessels in which the spiritual treasure has come to us. Salvation does not depend upon knowing whether *tidhār* means a pine tree or a plane tree, or whether a *šaḥap* is a "cuckow" (*sic*) or a sea gull. The OT Section of the Standard Bible Committee sometimes felt that it had to spend more time on mint, anise, and cummin than on the weightier matters of the law, more on the minutiae of the high priest's vestments or the architectural details of the temple than on the words for justice, mercy, and faith.

There is some comfort, to be sure, in that very fact. On the whole it is the things that pertain to salvation that are so plain that he may run who reads them, and the things that are obscure and uncertain are things that it is not necessary to understand. No man will be led astray from the path to life by reading any honest, moderately accurate translation of the Bible. At the same time, if the true meaning of the Bible is important at all, no translation can be too accurate. No sharp line can be drawn between what is and what is not important. "He who is faithful in a very little is faithful also in much" (Luke 16.10).

§ 37 Among the most important sources of new understanding is archeology. By disclosing the ancient Near Eastern way of life, the results of excavation have illuminated many expressions used in the OT. In 2 Chron 34.11, for example, J speaks obscurely of "timber for couplings." The word rendered "couplings" appears elsewhere only in 1 Chron 22.3, where it clearly means something made of iron ([J]joinings, [R]clamps). The remains of ancient buildings excavated in the Near East show that wooden beams were used as binders in brick or stone walls (cp Ezra 5.8; 6.4); R therefore reads in 2 Chron 34.11 "timber for binders."

1 Sam 13.21, an obscure verse at best, is partly clarified by a discovery which reveals the meaning of the Hebrew word *pīm*, found only here in the OT. J (see mg) takes it as a plural form meaning "mouths." Recently, however, small stone weights with this word engraved on them have been excavated in Palestine. The preceding noun, rendered "file" in J, appears now by comparison with other Semitic languages to mean something like "demand." Measures of weight were of course used as measures of value before coins were invented. R therefore translates these two words "the charge was a pim."

A word employed somewhat more often in the OT (*ḥammān*) is translated "image" or "idol" in J, "sun-image" in J mg and EA (Lev 26.30; 2 Chron 14.5; 34.4, 7; Is 17.8; 27.9; Ezek 6.4, 6). A small altar for incense found at Palmyra has this word engraved on it. The language of Palmyra was Aramaic, not Hebrew, and this altar comes from a period later than OT times. The meaning "incense altar," however, fits the use of the word in the OT, and R accordingly so translates it.

Customs presupposed in the OT are illuminated by ancient texts found by archeologists. In connection with Jeremiah's redemption of his uncle's property reference is made in Jer 32.11, 14 to the deed of purchase, "that which was sealed . . . and that which was open," as J reads. Babylonian documents of this sort were recorded on clay tablets, which were often enclosed in an outer coating of clay inscribed with the same text. R therefore reads here, "the sealed deed . . . and the open copy."

In Gen 50.23 J speaks of Joseph's grandchildren as "brought up [Heb. *borne*] upon Joseph's knees." R translates literally, "born upon Joseph's knees." Receiving a baby at its birth on one's knees was a rite of adoption in the ancient Near East, attested by texts found in excavations.[1]

§ 38

The ancient texts uncovered in excavations include many thousands in languages akin to Hebrew: Akkadian (Babylonian-Assyrian), Aramaic, Phoenician, Moabite, and Ugaritic (the language of ancient Ugarit, at the place in northern Syria now called Ras Shamra). These languages, most of which were unknown in the time of King James, have vastly enlarged our understanding of biblical Hebrew.

(1) From Akkadian texts we learn the meaning of the noun *'pēr:* [J]ashes—[R]a bandage (1 Kings 20.38, 41). It occurs only here in the OT; J confuses it with *'ēper* (dust, ashes).

(2) In 2 Kings 18.17 there are what J takes to be three proper names: Tartan, Rabsaris, and Rabshakeh. The third one occurs repeatedly throughout the chapter and in its parallel, Is 36; the second appears also in Jer 39.3, 13 with a fourth, Rabmag; Assyrian texts show that these were Assyrian military titles. R

[1] For further examples and discussion see Introd. RSVOT, Chapter VII.

makes this clear by inserting the definite article: "the Tartan, the Rabshakeh," etc.

(3) Another Assyrian term (*ṭipšar*) occurs in Jer 51.27 and Nahum 3.17. J translates it "captain." R reads "marshal" in Jeremiah, "scribes [Or *marshals*]" in Nahum. The word means primarily "scribe," and it is apparently used in that sense in Nahum; in Jeremiah, however, the context shows that it refers to a military officer.

(4) A noun which occurs only in Dan 9.25 in the OT (*ḥārūṣ*) is translated "wall" by J. It too is an Assyrian word, used also in Aramaic inscriptions, meaning "moat" or "trench." R renders it "moat."

(5) A word used only in Hab 2.6 (*'abṭīṭ*) is treated by J as a combination of two words meaning "thick clay." It is related, however, to a verb (*'BṬ*) which means "pledge," with cognate forms in Assyrian and Aramaic. R reads "pledges" in Hab 2.6.

(6) A verb which ordinarily means "forget" (*ŠKḤ*) is so translated by J in Ps 137.5, but this necessitates the insertion of an object, "her cunning." Ugaritic texts show that there was a verb identical with this in sound and spelling which meant "wither." This fits the context in Ps 137.5 and requires no object. R therefore reads, "let my right hand wither!"

The evidence of cognate languages is not always so helpful. (7) The inscription of King Mesha on the famous Moabite stone contains the word *ariel* (*'rī'ēl*), which appears in 2 Sam 23.20 (=1 Chron 11.22). Unfortunately the context does not reveal the meaning of the word, either in the OT or in the inscription. J takes it as two words and reads "lionlike men [Heb. *lions of God*]." R simply transliterates it, "ariels," with a note, "The meaning of the word *ariel* is unknown."

§ 39 In addition to such ancient inscriptions we have abundant literary texts in later Semitic languages and dialects which help us to understand Hebrew words. A verb (*MWQ*) found only in Ps 73.8 in the OT is translated by J "They are corrupt." It appears in Jewish Aramaic, Palestinian Christian Aramaic, and Syriac in the sense "scoff" and is so interpreted here by some of the ancient Versions (§§ 135ff). R therefore so renders it.

J speaks in Ezek 46.14 of "oil, to temper with the fine flour." The Hebrew verb is not either of the two translated "temper" elsewhere (*BLL, MLḤ*), but one which occurs only here (*RŚŚ*). It has cognates in Aramaic, Syriac, and Arabic meaning "moisten"; consequently R reads, "to moisten the flour."

In Nahum 2.7 J says, "her maids shall lead her as with the voice of doves." The point of the simile is not clear, and "her" is not in the Hebrew. The verb is actually not the common one meaning "lead" (*NHG*) but another, identical in sound and spelling, which means "moan" or "lament," as shown by its use in Syriac and Arabic. For the sake of the meter R translates this rather freely:

> her maidens lamenting,
> moaning like doves.

A noun used only twice in the OT (*māzōr*) is translated "wound" by J in Hos 5.13, but in Jer 30.13 it is taken as a verbal form meaning "bound up." Once more Syriac and Arabic come to the rescue, showing that the root is not one meaning "close" or "press together" (*ZWR*) but a quite different one (*MZR*) which means "putrefy," to which the idea of an incurable wound has been attached. R reads "wound" in both Jeremiah and Hosea.

Arabic, having an extensive literature and many colloquial dialects, and being closer than any other extant language to "proto-Semitic," the common ancestor of all the Semitic languages, is especially useful for recovering the meanings of Hebrew words, especially those which occur only once or twice in the OT. A good example is the puzzling statement in Gen 6.3, when J reads, "My spirit shall not always strive with man." This has no connection with the context. The Septuagint (see § 135) says "shall not remain in man," and a cognate verb in Egyptian Arabic shows this to be a quite possible meaning for the Hebrew. The connection with the context is then clear: God's spirit, the breath of life, "shall not abide in man for ever" (so R; i.e., man cannot live for ever), "but his days shall be a hundred and twenty years."

A noun in Job 39.4 (*bar*), translated by J "corn" (cp § 14) is actually another word, well known in Arabic, which sounds and looks the same but means "open country." R reads "in the open."

Very few Hebrew words begin with *w*. Where that letter appears at the beginning of a word it almost always represents a conjunction ("and," "but," etc.; see § 79). Not unnaturally, therefore, J takes *wāzār* in Prov 21.8 to mean "and strange." A cognate word in Arabic, however, suggests that we have here a rare Hebrew adjective meaning "guilty," which goes with "man" instead of "froward." R reads therefore "the guilty."

Other changes dictated by a new understanding of Hebrew words in the light of their Arabic cognates are the following:

^{J}flow together—^{R}be radiant (Is 60.5; so Jer 31.12, but cp 51.44); ^{J}thou trustedst—^{R}you fall down (Jer 12.5); ^{J}reeds—^{R}bulwarks (51.32); ^{J}made of cedar—^{R}made secure (Ezek 27.24); ^{J}shall be grieved—^{R}shall be afraid and withdraw (Dan 11.30); ^{J}get you down—^{R}tread (Joel 3.13); ^{J}the forest of the vintage—^{R}the thick forest (Zech 11.2).

§ 40 Better knowledge of the life of OT times enables us to correct a number of anachronisms in J, or expressions that present to us now an anachronistic picture, whatever they may have meant in the seventeenth century. The following terms used in J, with the words used to replace them in R, are good examples:

^{J}barn—^{R}threshing floor; ^{J}barrel—^{R}jar; ^{J}bottle—^{R}skin, waterskin, wineskin, jar (R keeps "bottle" in Ps 56.8); ^{J}brass—^{R}bronze, copper; ^{J}candle—^{R}lamp; ^{J}candlestick—^{R}lampstand; ^{J}coat—^{R}robe, tunic (R uses "coat" 12 times); ^{J}cottage—^{R}booth, hut (for two different Hebrew nouns; cp, with a third noun, Zeph 2.6, ^{J}cottages—^{R}meadows); ^{J}duke—^{R}chief, prince; ^{J}furnace—^{R}fire pot, kiln (R uses "furnace" 24 times); ^{J}hinge—^{R}socket (ancient Near Eastern doors swung in sockets, not on what we call hinges); ^{J}parlour—^{R}hall; ^{J}pitcher—^{R}jar; ^{J}printed—^{R}inscribed; ^{J}range for pots—^{R}stove; ^{J}shoe—^{R}sandal (R keeps "shoe" 7 times).

Chapter IX

PROPER NAMES

§ 41 J's spelling of Hebrew proper names was considerably revised by EA. As a rule R simply follows A, its "basic text" (§ 2), in this matter. In a few places, however, a name is adjusted to the form it has elsewhere:

^{J}Gashmu [Or, *Geshem*]—^{R}Geshem [Heb *Gashmu*] (Neh 6.6; cp v. 1); ^{J}Gibeath—^{R}Gibeah [Heb *Gibeath*] (Josh 18.28); ^{J}Megiddon—^{R}Megiddo (Zech 12.11).

Instead of transcribing the Hebrew name of a city or country, J sometimes gives its modern or classical equivalent, and R restores the Hebrew name;

e.g., ^{J}Armenia—^{R}Ararat (J reads Ararat in Gen 8.4); ^{J}Ethiopia—^{R}Cush (but cp next paragraph); ^{J}Idumea—^{R}Edom; ^{J}Lybia [Heb. *Phut*]—^{R}Put; ^{J}Lydia—^{R}Lud; ^{J}Palestina, Palestine—^{R}Philistia; ^{J}The Red Sea [Or, *Zuph*]—^{R}Suph (Deut 1.1, probably not here the sea but a city); ^{J}Syria—^{R}Aram.

In some other places, however, where J keeps the Hebrew name, R substitutes a later form;

e.g., ^{J}Achmetha [Or, *Ecbatana*]—^{R}Ecbatana; ^{J}Ashur—^{R}Assyria (R sometimes keeps Asshur, and J often reads Assyria); ^{J}Bethshemesh—^{R}Heliopolis (not the Palestinian Bethshemesh); ^{J}Cush—^{R}Ethiopia (cp last paragraph); ^{J}Chittim—^{R}Cyprus (R reads Kittim in Num 24.24; Dan 11.30); ^{J}Hiddekel—^{R}the Tigris; ^{J}Japho—^{R}Joppa (J sometimes reads Joppa); ^{J}Mizraim—^{R}Egypt (so usually J); ^{J}No—^{R}Thebes; ^{J}populous No [Heb. *No Amon*]—^{R}Thebes [Heb *No-Amon*]; ^{J}Noph—^{R}Memphis; ^{J}Sihor —^{R}the Nile; ^{J}Sin [Or, *Pelusium*]—^{R}Pelusium.

In several places what is now seen to be a compound place-name is taken by J as two separate names:

e.g., [J]Atroth, Shophan—[R]Atroth-shophan (Num 32.35); [J]Hazor, Hadattah, and Kerioth, and Hezron—[R]Hazor-hadattah, Kerioth-hezron (Josh 15.25); see also Josh 19.7, 33; Neh 7.59. Cp, however, [J]to the sea of Joppa—[R]to the sea, to Joppa (Ezra 3.7).

The fact that Habor is the name of a river, as attested by Assyrian texts, makes possible another correction: [J]in Habor by the river of Gozan—[R]on the Habor, the river of Gozan (2 Kings 17.6; 18.11; in 1 Chron 5.26 Habor is apparently a city). In Hebrew Babylon, the city, and Babylonia, the country, are both called Babel. This has twice misled J in Ezra: [J]to Babylon—[R]to Babylonia (2.1); [J]in all the province of Babylon—[R]in the whole province of Babylonia (7.16).

The OT often uses the name of a country, as we do, for its people or rulers. J therefore frequently translates the name of the country by the name of the people, sometimes even where this meaning is not intended; e.g., [J]to the Egyptians, and to the Assyrians—[R]to Egypt, and to Assyria (Lam 5.6); see also Ps 83.7; Jer 25.25; 46.9; Dan 5.13; but cp [J]Egypt—[R]the Egyptians (Ex 9.6).

As a native of Beirut is now called in Arabic a Beiruti, or an inhabitant of Iraq an Iraqi, so the Hebrew language attaches the ending *-ī* to a place-name to indicate a person's home or place of origin. J usually represents this by the ending -ite; R more often, though not always, uses "of" with the place-name; e.g., [J]the Anethothite—[R]of Anathoth (2 Sam 23.27; cp 1 Chron 27.12); cp [J]the stonesquarers [Or, *Giblites*]—[R]the men of Gebal (1 Kings 5.18). Sometimes J mistakes this form for a person's name; e.g., [J]Cushi—[R]the Cushite; [J]Geshuri—[R]the Geshurites; [J]Shiloni—[R]the Shilonite.

The same ending is used also to designate tribal or family connections. In Num 3.21 the family name itself (cp v. 18) ends in *-ī* and is thus indistinguishable from the adjective: [J]the Shimites —[R]the Shimeites. In Zech 12.13 J mistakes the adjective for the name, although it has the definite article: [J]of Shimei—[R]of the Shimeites.

§ 42 Like such English names as Carpenter or Smith, most Hebrew names are common nouns or verbs, or combinations of such words. J sometimes sees a name, or part of a name, where R sees a common noun. In some instances J mg gives R's reading as a possible alternative. Note the following examples: [J]Allon—[R]the oak; [J]Ashdoth-Pisgah—[R]the slopes of Pisgah; [J]Assir—[R]the captive; [J]Asuppim [Heb. *Gatherings*]—[R]the storehouse; [J]Bithron—[R]forenoon; [J]Gibeah—[R]the hill; [J]the son of Hammelech [Or, *of the king*]—[R]the king's son. Sometimes J reads a common noun but gives a proper name in the margin as an alternative. R may or may not agree; e.g., [J]the company of two armies [Or, *of Mahanaim*]—[R]a dance before two armies [Or *dance of Mahanaim*]; [J]from the south [Or, *Teman*]—[R]southward.

There are also many places where a name (usually a place-name) is recognized by R but not by J. The new interpretation is sometimes indicated by the use of capitals:

e.g., [J]beyond the river—[R]the province Beyond the River (cp § 85, No. 1); [J]the city of salt—[R]the City of Salt; [J]the fuller's field—[R]the Fuller's Field; [J]the king's high way—[R]the King's Highway; [J]the rocks of the wild goats—[R]the Wildgoats' Rocks; [J]the dragon well—[R]the Jackal's Well (cp §§ 46, 73).

In other instances R transliterates the name. Outstanding examples of this are three geographical terms frequently used to designate specific areas in Palestine. (1) *‘rābāh* (the low valley running south from the Dead Sea to the eastern arm of the Red Sea): [J]champaign, desert, plain, wilderness—[R]Arabah. (2) *špelāh* (the line of low hills between the coastal plain and the central plateau): [J]plain, low plains, low country, vale, valley—[R]Shephelah (also sometimes lowland). (3) *negeb* (south in general, but also in particular the southernmost region of Palestine): [J]south, south country, southward—[R]Negeb (40 times; also the South, the extreme South). R's recognition of the specific territorial reference of these terms clarifies the historical picture in many places.

Other geographical terms also are sometimes treated in the same way. The noun (4) *y'ōr,* meaning "river" or "stream," often refers so clearly to the Nile River that R translates it "the Nile."

Similarly the common word for "sea," (5) *yām,* is applied to the Nile River in Is 18.2 and 19.5, and R renders it "the Nile." The usual word for "river," (6) *nāhār,* is sometimes used practically as a proper name for the Euphrates; R then reads "the River" or "the Euphrates." Two nouns meaning "forest" are taken by R as place-names in one or more places: (7) *ḥōreš,* [J]in the wood—[R]at Horesh (1 Sam 23.15f, 18f); (8) *ya'ar,* [J]the wood—[R]Jaar (Ps 132.6).

Many other common nouns, rendered as such by J, are used as names or parts of names, geographical or personal. Place-names beginning with "Beth-" ([J]house of) are especially common. Cp Ps 95.8, [J]as in the provocation [Heb. *contention*], and as in the day of temptation—[R]as at Meribah, as on the day at Massah (cp § 58, No. 5). Note also the astronomical name, (9) *kīmāh:* [J]the seven stars—[R]the Pleiades (Amos 5.8, cp Job 9.9, [JR]the Pleiades).

An important instance of J's translating, indeed mistranslating, a proper name as a common noun is (10) *š'ōl,* the name of the underworld or place of the dead: [J]the grave (Gen 37.35 etc., 30 times), hell (Deut 32.22 etc., 31 times), the pit (Num 16.30, 33; Job 17.16); [R]Sheol (cp § 46, No. 1).

In a few instances J confuses a proper name with a noun with which it has no real connection, though resembling it in sound or appearance. A poetic form of the Hebrew name of Egypt, (11) *māṣōr,* in the four verses where it occurs, is taken by J as a common noun which looks and sounds exactly like it: [J]besieged places—[R]Egypt (2 Kings 19.24; Is 37.25); [J]the brooks of defence—[R]the branches of Egypt's Nile (Is 19.6; cp § 42, No. 4); [J]the fortified cities . . . the fortress—[R]Egypt . . . Egypt (Mic 7.12). Cp Ezek 27.11, [J]with thine army—[R]and Helech [Or *and your army*]; here what J understands as a noun with a possessive suffix is more probably a form of the name Cilicia, or perhaps Chalcis.

The fact that Hebrew names usually consist of one or more common words makes it difficult sometimes to choose between transliterating and translating them. The name Adam, for instance, means simply "man"; it is the word used in that sense, e.g., in Gen 1.26ff. In 5.2 it is applied to both Adam and Eve. R changes Adam to Man here and nine times in chapters 2f, but keeps Adam eight times in chapters 3–5. The symbolic names in Hos 1f are transliterated by J with translations in the margin; R translates them, except that in 2.22 Jezreel is kept, with a note. In Is 62.4 J translates the first two names, Forsaken and Desolate, and R follows with notes. J then, however, shifts to transliteration with translations in the margin; R puts the readings of J's notes in the text and *vice versa.* In Jer 23.6 and 33.16 J and R both translate the name. Several place-names are transliterated in J and translated in R; e.g., ᴶMaktesh—ᴿthe Mortar (Zeph 1.11); ᴶthe stone Zoheleth—ᴿthe Serpent's stone (1 Kings 1.9).

Some of the differences in names between J and R reflect different readings of the Hebrew text (see Part Three).

Chapter X

DIVINE BEINGS

§43 The number of Hebrew and Aramaic words in the interpretation of which R differs from J is much too large to permit even a bare list of them here. Some idea of the range and nature of the differences, however, may be given by presenting a selection of such words, grouped under general headings. This manner of presentation is convenient because there is often much overlapping of meaning among several words.

In a great many cases R's choice of a different rendering does not reflect a different understanding of the Hebrew word but the Committee's judgment as to the best way of representing its meaning in the particular context. Sometimes considerations of rhythm or metrical form have determined the choice. In other cases a slightly different shade of meaning may be conveyed by the use of a word which is synonymous with the one in J. Only changes expressing a real difference of interpretation, and only a sampling of these, can be noted here.

Some changes involve the Hebrew words for God. (1) *'lōhīm*. Since this word is plural in form even when applied to the one true God, only the context can tell whether it is so intended or refers to pagan gods. Usually the reference is quite clear, but not always. In Hos 14.3, for instance, "the work of our hands" may refer to several pagan idols; J assumes this and reads, "neither will we say any more to the work of our hands. . . . Ye are our gods." R, however, sees here a reference to an image representing God himself, and so reads, "we will say no more, 'Our God,' to the work of our hands." On the other hand J makes the Philistines say in 1 Sam 4.7, "God is come into the camp"; in R they say, "The gods have come . . ." (cp v. 8).

In Ex 7.1 J takes this noun to mean "a god"; R reads "God."

Sometimes, however, R says "the gods" where J has "God" (e.g., Ezek 28.2; Dan 11.37; cp Deut 4.34, God—any god). J sometimes even says "a God," "any God," "that God," or "no God"; R in such places reads "god" (Ezek 28.2, 9; cp Jonah 1.6; also in Aramaic Dan 3.15, 28f; 6.7).

The same Hebrew noun is supposed by J, following a rabbinic tradition, to refer to human judges in Ex 21.6; 22.8f: [J]unto the judges—[R]to God (cp 22.28, [J]the gods [Or, *judges*]—[R]God; 1 Sam 2.25, [J]the judge—[R]God). Ancient texts have made clear the real meaning in these places. Among the Hurrians of northern Mesopotamia, with whom the Hebrews had many cultural affinities, when a man was accused of crime and subjected to trial by ordeal, he was said to be "brought before the gods," i.e., before the idols in the temple. The Hebrews had no idols in the tabernacle or temple, but they carried over the idea of bringing a man accused of crime into the presence of God in the sanctuary to be judged.

In Ps 50.1 *'lōhīm* is used together with (2) *'ēl,* a related word for God which J here translates as an adjective, "mighty," R "The mighty One." Both this noun and No. 1 appear in several idiomatic expressions. In one of these *'ēl* is used in the sense of "power" (probably its original meaning): e.g., [J]in the power of my hand—[R]in my power (Gen 31.29; cp Deut 28.32; Prov 3.27).

Another idiom means literally "cedars of God," "mountain of God," or the like; here too the noun is usually represented in J by an adjective: goodly, great, or mighty. R sometimes follows this precedent even where J translates literally; e.g., [J]the hill of God—[R]mighty mountain (Ps 68.15); [J]The chariots of God—[R]mighty chariotry (v. 17; but cp 36.6); cp Eccles 8.2, [J]the oath of God—[R]your sacred oath.

In other places, where the meaning is more literal, R reads "the mighty," though the Hebrew does not have the definite article; e.g., [J]the congregation of the mighty—[R]the divine council (lit. congregation of God, Ps 82.1). So too when the noun is used in the plural J sometimes renders it "the mighty," and in one case R follows, adding a footnote: [J]the mighty—[R]the mighty [Or *gods*] (Job 41.25). Here divine beings are clearly meant; so also when the noun in the plural follows "sons" (cp § 53): [J]O ye mighty—[R]O heavenly beings [Heb *sons of gods*] (Ps 29.1); [J]the sons of the mighty—[R]the heavenly beings [Or *sons of gods*] (89.6).

A noun meaning "rock," (3) *ṣūr,* is sometimes used in the OT in the sense of "God" or "god." J translates it literally in Deut 32.4, 15, 30f, 37; but cp [J]the mighty One [Heb. *Rock*] of Israel—[R]the Rock of Israel (Is 30.29); [J]there is no God [Heb. *rock*]—[R]there is no Rock (44.8).

Translating idioms freely, J sometimes introduces the word "God" without italics where the Hebrew does not have it: e.g., [J]God forbid—[R]Far be it, Far from it; [J]Would (to) God—[R]Would (that); [J]God save the king [Heb. *Let the king live*]—[R]Long live the king. In Neh 6.9, R follows J in inserting "O God" for clarity.

Several names or epithets of God appear in the OT, such as Almighty, Everlasting, and Most High; but there is practically no difference between J's and R's ways of treating them. In Ps 56.2, [J]O thou most High—[R]proudly, the word used, (4) *mārōm* (lit. height), is not the one usually rendered "Most High." Note also (5) *'ābīr:* [J]the mighty God—[R]the Mighty One (Gen 49.24; Ps 132.2, 5; cp *'abbīr,* § 47, No. 3; § 73, No. 3). (6) *neṣaḥ:* [J]Strength—[R]Glory (1 Sam 15.29).

§ 44 The ancient name of the Hebrew God presents a difficult problem for the translator. In early times only the consonants of the Hebrew language were written (see §§ 9, 125); the name of God was therefore represented only by its four consonants, *YHWH* (the "Tetragrammaton"). By the time that vowels came to be indicated the divine name was considered too holy and dangerous to be pronounced aloud; the vowels of a noun meaning "Lord" (*'dōnāy*) were therefore attached to the consonants of the name in the manuscripts to remind readers to say "Lord" instead of uttering the sacred name.

Not until many centuries later was it supposed that these consonants and vowels were ever pronounced together, making the name Yehowah, or in Latin (which uses J for the sound of Y and V for the sound of W) Jehovah. This unhistorical form of the divine name is used by J in four places (Ex 6.3; Ps 83.18; Is 12.2; 26.4), and as part of three place-names (Gen 22.14; Ex 17.15; Judg 6.24). Elsewhere, following Jewish tradition, J reads "LORD," spelled with capitals to show that it stands for the sacred name. R (see footnote on Ex 3.15) adopts this practice even where J has "Jehovah," not only because "Jehovah" is not really Hebrew at all, but also because R is intended for use in worship, and for Christians as for Jews the one God needs no proper name to distinguish him from other deities.

In Gen 6.5 J reads "GOD," though the Hebrew has the name; R reads "the LORD." Twice J has "LORD" with capitals where the Hebrew says "Lord" (*'dōnāy*): in Ps 90.17 R correctly reads "Lord" but in Mal 1.12 keeps "LORD." Cp [J]my Lord—[R]the LORD (Num 14.17); [J]the Lord—[R]the LORD (Ps 130.6; in both places many Hebrew manuscripts have the name); [J]my Lord—[R]my lords (Gen 19.18, addressing the two angels); [J]My lord—[R]O Lord (Is 21.8, apparently addressed to God but not clear).

A variant form of the divine name has only two consonants, *YH*. In Ps 89.8 and 94.7 both J and R use "LORD" for this also; in Ps 68.4 J reads "Jah," R "LORD."

Sometimes the sacred name is combined with "God" (*'lōhīm*, § 43). In Gen 2f both J and R read "the LORD God"; elsewhere varying combinations produce minor variations in translation; e.g., [J]the LORD God of heaven—[R]the LORD, the God of heaven (Gen 24.7; cp vv. 27, 48; see also Ex 3.15, 18; 5.1; Is 37.21); cp [J]The LORD, the LORD God, merciful—[R]the LORD, the LORD, a God merciful (Ex 34.6).

Sometimes the name and "Lord" are used together; in the Hebrew the name is then given the vowels of the word for "God" (*'lōhīm*) to avoid saying "Lord" twice. In such places J usually has "GOD" for the name; R keeps this in Ps 109.21 but in 140.7 reads "O LORD, my Lord" (cp Ps 8.1). Cp [J]the Lord GOD of hosts—[R]the Lord, the LORD of hosts (Is 10.23f; in 22.5 R follows J).

Twice the divine name is used idiomatically in the OT: in Song 8.6 both J and R read "a most vehement flame" (lit. "a flame of Yah"); in 1 Sam 20.8 J translates literally "a covenant of the LORD," R says "a sacred covenant," with a note, "Heb *a covenant of the* LORD."

R inserts "the LORD" in two places to make the meaning clear: [J]that feareth—[R]who fears the LORD (Prov 28.14); [J]and shall consume—[R]the LORD will destroy (Is 10.18).

§ 45 Several names of pagan deities appear in the OT. (1) The name Baal requires no comment except that where J has the Hebrew plural form, "Baalim," omitting the definite article, R reads "the Baals" (Judg 2.11 and often). The name Baal-peor occurs six times in J; R takes it as a place-name in Deut 4.3 (first time) and Hos 9.10; in Deut 4.3 (second time) and Ps 106.28 it reads "the Baal of Peor" and in Num 25.3, 5 "Baal of Peor."

(2) A god Chiun is named by J in Amos 5.26. R recognizes here the God Kaiwan, mentioned in Akkadian and other ancient sources. The Hebrew name has the same consonants (J uses *ch* for *k*); the vowels, which are those of a noun meaning "abomination" (*šiqqūṣ*), are probably inserted to indicate that the reader should use this word instead of pronouncing the shameful pagan name.

(3) With Baal or the Baals J sometimes mentions "groves." The Hebrew word is *asherah* (*'šērāh*); it is often applied to a cult-object (see § 65, No. 3), but in 1 Kings 15.13; 18.19; 2 Kings 21.7; 23.4; and 2 Chron 15.16 it is the name of the goddess Asherah, called Athirat in the Ugaritic texts (§ 38). The plural form Asheroth in Judg 3.7 indicates a class of such goddesses, corresponding to the Baals.

(4) The god Molech is named several times (Lev 18.21 etc.); in Amos 5.26 J spells the name Moloch, but the correct reading there is "your king," as in J mg and R. Cp [J]the king—[R]the king [Or *Molech*] (Is 30.33); [J]the king—[R]Molech [Or *the king*] (57.9). The question in these places is what vowels should be read with the consonants *MLK* (see §§ 19, 130). A variation of this name is that of the Ammonite god, Milcom (1 Kings 11.5, 33; 2 Kings 23.13). This differs only in its vowels from the Hebrew noun and suffix meaning "their king" (*malkām*). In three verses where the Hebrew says "their king" it should be "pointed" (§125) "Milcom": [J]their king's crown—[R]the crown of their king [Or *Milcom*] (2 Sam 12.30); [J]their king [Or, *Melcom*]—[R]Milcom (Jer 49.1, 3); [J]Malcham—[R]Milcom (Zeph 1.5).

Other names of pagan deities appear only rarely. They are not always recognized by J:

e.g., (5) [J]for that troop . . . unto that number—[R]for Fortune . . . for Destiny (Is 65.11); (6) [J]are . . . swept away—[R]has Apis fled (Jer 46.15, a matter of vowels and word-division, § 131); (7) [J]the multitude [Or, *nourisher.* Heb. *Amon*]—[R]Amon (v. 25); (8) [J]the sin of Samaria—[R]Ashimah of Samaria (Amos 8.14; cp 2 Kings 17.30, Ashima); (9) [J]the tabernacle [Or, *Sikkuth*]—[R]Sakkuth (Amos 5.26).

§ 46 As modern poets make allusions to Greek and Roman mythology, so the Hebrew poets sometimes alluded to the myths of their ancestors or their neighbors. Ancient sources enable us now to recognize such allusions. Thus the personification of (1) "hell" (*š'ōl,* § 42, No. 10), (2) "destruction" (*'baddōn*), and (3) "death" (*māwet*), doubtless only a figure of speech for the Hebrews, had a mythological background: [J]Hell . . . and destruction—[R]Sheol . . . and Abaddon (Job 26.6; cp Prov 15.11; 27.20); [J]Destruction and death—[R]Abaddon and Death (Job 28.22; cp 31.12; Ps 88.11; Is 28.18).

The names of two mythological monsters are used in Job 40f as poetic designations of natural creatures: (4) [J]behemoth [Or, *the elephant,* as some think]—[R]Behemoth [Or *the hippopotamus*] (40.15); (5) [J]leviathan [i.e., *a whale,* or, *a whirlpool*]—[R]Leviathan [Or *the crocodile*] (41.1; see also Is 27.1). Both the name Leviathan and the terms applied to this monster in Is 27.1 (see also Job 26.13, where the name is not used) have now appeared in Ugaritic mythological texts (see § 38).

(6) Another term drawn from pagan mythology (*hēylēl*) is applied to the king of Babylon in Is 14.12: [J]O Lucifer [Or, *O day star*], son of the morning—[R]O Day Star, son of Dawn. The word rendered "morning" and "Dawn" (*šaḥar*) is the name of a god in the Ugaritic texts.

(7) The Hebrew noun translated "the deep" (*thōm*) in Gen 1.2 is related to the Babylonian name of the primeval dragon of chaos, Tiamat. In Is 51.10 this word appears in connection with a reference to (8) a mythological monster, Rahab (v. 9). The name Rahab is used also as a figurative designation of Egypt; in Ps 87.4; 89.10, it is recognized as such by J, but cp Job 9.13, [J]the proud helpers—[R]the helpers of Rahab. The Babylonian creation epic speaks of "the helpers of Tiamat." See also 26.12f; Is 30.7.

(9) The word translated "dragon" by JR in Is 51.9 (*tannīn*) is used in 27.1 in connection with Leviathan; it appears also in many other places. Often it refers actually to wild animals (see § 73, No. 14); R keeps "dragon," however, in Ps 74.13 and Ezek 29.3, as well as Is 27.1 and 51.9.

The Ugaritic texts speak of (10) a god whose name is a common Semitic word for "sea" (*yām*); in other words, the sea, like the earth and sky, was deified. For the Hebrew poets this god would be a mythological creature. (11) In Job 9.8, "and treadeth upon (R trampled) the waves of the sea," the word translated "wave" (*bāmāh*) usually means "high place" in Hebrew (see § 65, No. 2); in Ugaritic, however, it means "back." R therefore adds a note, "Or *trampled the back of the sea dragon.*"

§ 47 Hebrew words designating angels, demons, etc. cause some difficulty. (1) The common word for "angel" (*mal'āk*), like the corresponding Greek noun, means primarily "messenger."

Note, e.g., Ja messenger—Ran angel (Job 33.23); Jthe angel—Rthe messenger [Or *angel*] (Eccles 5.6). The fact that (2) the Hebrew word for "spirit" (*rūaḥ*) means also "wind" (§ 50, No. 4) creates additional confusion in Ps 104.4, JWho maketh his angels spirits—Rwho makest the winds thy messengers (see also §§ 94, 123).

Other words are occasionally translated "angel." (3) One so rendered by both J and R in Ps 78.25 (*'abbīr,* § 73, No. 3) is closely related to the one translated "mighty" or "Mighty One" when applied to God (*'ābīr,* § 43, No. 5). In Ps 8.5, where J reads "a little lower than the angels," the Hebrew, as translated literally by R, says "a little lower than God" (*'lohīm*). See also §§ 43 and 53 for "sons of God," meaning divine beings.

The words (4) "cherub" and (5) "seraph" are simply taken over from the Hebrew for lack of equivalent English words. In the plural (§ 11) J adds an *s* to the Hebrew plural ending *-im;* R keeps the Hebrew ending only.

J uses "devil" for two Hebrew nouns; R translates one of them (6) *šēd,* "demon" (Deut 32.17; Ps 106.37), the other, (7) *sā'īr,* "satyr" (Lev 17.7; 2 Chron 11.15). The (8) "doleful creatures" (*'ōḥīm,* R "howling creatures") of Is 13.21 are possibly demonic beings but more probably beasts of prey; the (9) "screech owl" (J) of 34.14, however, is a female demon (*līlīt,* R night hag), attested by both Assyrian and later Jewish sources.

(10) In Lev 16.8, 10, 26 J preserves an old but erroneous interpretation: [J]scapegoat [Heb. *Azazel*]—[R]Azazel. The Hebrew word is the name of a wilderness demon, and the sacrificial goat is sent into the wilderness not "to be a scapegoat" or "for a scapegoat" but "to Azazel."

(11) In New Testament times Belial was a name for Satan (2 Cor 6.15). In the OT it is still an abstract noun with its original meaning, "worthlessness" (lit. without profit). J often recognizes this meaning (see § 61, No. 10), but sometimes renders the word as a proper name, especially when it is used idiomatically with "son" (see § 25; § 52, No. 2):

[J]children of Belial—[R]base fellows (Deut 13.13; Judg 20.13), worthless fellows (1 Sam 10.27), worthless scoundrels (2 Chron 13.7); [J]sons of Belial—[R]base fellows (Judg 19.22; 1 Kings 21.10), worthless men (1 Sam 2.12), godless men (2 Sam 23.6); [J]such a son of Belial—[R]so ill-natured (1 Sam 25.17); [J]daughter of Belial—[R]base woman (1.16).

Similarly the word is used with "man" instead of "son":

[J]man of Belial—[R]ill-natured fellow (1 Sam 25.25), worthless fellow (2 Sam 16.7); [J]men of Belial—[R]base fellows (1 Kings 21.13); [J]all the wicked men and men of Belial—[R]all the wicked and base fellows (1 Sam 30.22, lit. every man of evil and of worthlessness).

(12) The name Satan itself was originally a common noun, meaning "adversary." It is still often so used in the OT. In legal terminology it designates the plaintiff or prosecutor (see § 54, No. 1). In a few places, however, R keeps "Satan," with or without a note: [J]Satan [Heb. *the Adversary*]—[R]Satan [Heb *the adversary*] (Job 1.6; JR without note vv. 7, 9, 12; 2.1–4, 6f; also 1 Chron 21.1); [J]Satan [i.e., *an adversary*]—[R]Satan (Zech 3.1).

Chapter XI

MAN: PHYSIOLOGICAL AND PSYCHOLOGICAL TERMS

§ 48 With a few exceptions, J and R do not differ much as to the literal meaning of Hebrew terms for the body and its parts or constituent elements (bone, flesh, blood, etc.). There are many differences, however, in English terminology. Several of the Hebrew words in question, like some of our own, are often used with derived or figurative meanings and in idiomatic expressions. Sometimes both J and R translate freely, and in such cases they do not always agree in their interpretations of the idioms;

e.g., ^{J}in the time of thine anger—^{R}when you appear (lit. at the time of your face, Ps 21.9); ^{J}The anger [Or, *face*] of the LORD—^{R}The LORD himself (Lam 4.16); ^{J}by labour [Heb. *with the hand*]—^{R}little by little (Prov 13.11); ^{J}cannot get [Heb. *his hand reach not*]—^{R}cannot afford (Lev 14.21; cp vv. 22, 30, 32; Ezek 46.7).

More often, however, J translates such expressions literally and R interprets them.

The following examples may be noted: ^{J}blood—^{R}lifeblood, life, bloodshed, bloodguilt, death, homicide, murder; ^{J}thy flesh—^{R}you; ^{J}his own flesh—^{R}himself; ^{J}my flesh—^{R}my kinsmen; ^{J}fat—^{R}rich; ^{J}make fat—^{R}enrich; ^{J}fatness—^{R}abundance; ^{J}They are inclosed in their own fat—^{R}they close their hearts to pity (Ps 17.10); ^{J}face—^{R}favor, presence, edge, front, surface; ^{J}turn away the face of—^{R}repulse; ^{J}in the eyes of—^{R}in the sight of; ^{J}covering of the eyes—^{R}vindication; ^{J}hath an evil eye—^{R}is stingy, a miserly man; ^{J}in the ears of—^{R}in the hearing of (J sometimes uses "audience" in this sense for "ears," § 13); ^{J}the smell of thy nose—^{R}the scent of thy breath; ^{J}mouth—^{R}speech, talk, word; ^{J}cry with my mouth—^{R}cry aloud; ^{J}from my mouth—^{R}at my dictation; ^{J}harden the neck—^{R}be stubborn; ^{J}lift up the hand—^{R}swear; ^{J}strike hands—^{R}give pledges, give security; ^{J}though hand join in hand—^{R}Be assured (lit.

hand to hand, Prov 11.21; 16.5); [J]according to the state of the king [Heb. *according to the hand of the king*]—[R]according to the bounty of the king (Esther 1.7; cp 2.18); cp [J]at hand—[R]near; [J]out of hand—[R]at once (where J uses these two phrases the Hebrew does not have "hand"); [J]from the belly—[R]from birth (cp Hos 9.11, [J]from birth—[R]no pregnancy, see § 84); [J]from my mother's belly—[R]since my mother bore me; [J]all that openeth the womb—[R]all their first-born; [J]the offspring of thy bowels—[R]your descendants; [J]forgotten of the foot—[R]forgotten by travelers; [J]at his feet—[R]close behind; [J]at thy feet—[R]in thy steps; [J]to his foot—[R]at every step.

Sometimes R merely substitutes for J's words more modern or more customary terms without any difference of meaning;

e.g., [J]countenance, visage—[R]face; [J]paps—[R]breasts; [J]teats—[R]breasts, bosom; [J]reins—[R]kidneys (Or *heart*); [J]maw—[R]stomach; [J]navel—[R]flesh [Heb *navel*]; [J]stones—[R]testicles.

§ 49 No difference as to the literal meaning of the Hebrew is implied when R, in order to make the meaning of an expression clearer for modern readers, substitutes one part of the body for another, or the whole body for one of its parts;

e.g., [J]bones—[R]body, limbs; [J]skin—[R]body; [J]crown of the head—[R]brow, head, scalp; [J]mouth to mouth—[R]face to face; [J]in thine hands—[R]on your back (lit. between your hands, Zech 13.6); [J]liver—[R]entrails; [J]fifth rib—[R]belly, body; [J]belly—[R]body, womb; [J]womb—[R]body; [J]bowels—[R]body, stomach, womb; [J]at thy side—[R]in the arms; [J]upon her sides—[R]on her hip; [J]back parts—[R]side; [J]buttocks—[R]hips; [J]reins—[R]loins, waist; cp [J]the girdle of their loins—[R]a waistcloth; [J]stones—[R]thighs; [J]thigh—[R]legs; [J]feet—[R]legs.

Such substitutions are often made when an organ is used to indicate feeling, thought, or will, because the notions of the ancient Hebrews concerning these matters differed considerably from ours. Like other ancient peoples, the Hebrews did not think of the brain as the organ of thought. What we call the mind they located in the heart;

hence, e.g., [J]heart—[R]mind (J too sometimes reads "mind" for Hebrew "heart"), sense, understanding; cp [J]understanding [Heb. *heart*]—[R]sense (Prov 17.18; without note Hos 7.11); [J]wisdom [Heb. *heart*]—[R]understanding (Job 36.5). Hebrew has many idiomatic uses of "heart," sometimes expressing attitude, purpose, or will; e.g., [J]heart—[R]conscience, courage, soul, spirit, will; [J]with a perfect heart—[R]with full intent; [J]purposed in his heart—[R]resolved; [J]said in his heart—[R]said to himself; [J]spoke kindly unto [Heb. *to the heart of*]—[R]spoke tenderly to (Gen 34.3); [J]Speak ye comfortably [Heb. *to the heart*]—[R]speak tenderly (Is 40.2; cp 2 Sam 19.7; 2 Chron 30.22). R uses "heart" for a different word (*qereb,* lit. midst) in Ps 5.9; 94.19; Is 16.11. In Deut 10.15 and Jer 8.21 R uses "heart" to translate other expressions idiomatically.

In contrast with such differences of rendering rather than interpretation, R differs from J on the meaning of some physiological terms, or words taken as such in J:

(1) *gab:* [J]body—[R]defense (Job 13.12 twice). (2) *qaneh:* [J]the bone [Or, *the chanelbone*]—[R]its socket (Job 31.22). (3) *ḥammūq:* [J]joints—[R]rounded (Song 7.1). (4) *qtar* (Aramaic): [J]the joints [Or, *girdles.* Is 5.27. Chald. *bindings,* or *knots*] of his loins—[R]his limbs (Dan 5.6 with *ḥraṣ*). (5) *'ōrēq:* [J]my sinews—[R]the pain that gnaws me (Job 30.17, lit. my gnawers). (6) *ṣammāh:* [J]locks—[R]veil (Song 4.1, 3; 6.7). (7) *raqqāh:* [J]temples—[R]cheeks (4.3; 6.7). (8) *zīw* (Aram.): [J]countenance [Chald. *brightness*]—[R]color (Dan 5.6, 9f; 7.28). (9) *ṣawwārōn:* [J]neck—[R]necklace (Song 4.9). (10) *'tīn:* [J]breasts [Or, *milk pails*]—[R]body [The meaning of the Hebrew word is uncertain] (Job 21.24). (11) *ṭuḥāh:* [J]inward parts—[R]clouds [same note] (Job 38.36). (12) *śekwī:* [J]heart—[R]mists [same note] (same v.). (13) *šarīr:* [J]navel—[R]muscles (Job 40.16). (14) *ṣēla':* [J]side—[R]stumbling (Job 18.12). (15) *nāšeh:* [J]which shrank—[R]of the hip (Gen 32.32 twice). (16) *'āqēb:* [J]heel—[R]persecutor (Ps 49.5).

There are a few differences also in the interpretation of terms designating physical afflictions, diseases, etc., aside from such obvious changes in English terminology as "blemish" for "spot" or "plague" for "pestilence":

(17) *'ōpel:* [J]emerod (i.e., hemorrhoid, see § 11)—[R]ulcer (Deut 28.27), tumor (1 Sam 5.6, 9.12; 6.4f). (18) *ṭḥōr:* [J]emerod—[R]tumor (1 Sam 6.11, 17). (19) *ṣārebet:* [J]burning—[R]scar (Lev 13.28). (20) *sappaḥat:* [J]scab—[R]eruption (13.2, 6ff; 14.56). (21) *yabbelet:* [J]wen—[R]discharge (22.22).

§ 50 No Hebrew word has the same meaning or range of meanings as our word "soul," yet no Hebrew word has more varied and at the time important meanings than (1) *nepeš,* the noun usually translated "soul" (about 470 times in J). Its original meaning was apparently "throat," then "breath," etc.

It has many different renderings in both J and R. Not much more than a bare list of them can be given here, but this may serve to show the broad connotations and associations of the word in the OT. Here again, while J and R use many of the same English words, they frequently interpret the Hebrew word differently in particular places.

The following renderings of *nepeš* may be noted:

[JR]soul, life, person, myself etc., man, heart, mind, desire, appetite; [J]ghost,[1] lust (see § 14), pleasure, will; [R]craving, greed, hunger, fancy, courage, spirit, strength, slave. Cp [J]He that laboureth—[R]A worker's appetite (Prov 16.26; J paraphases the supposed meaning, "A laboring person"); [J]my mind—[R]I; [J]thy mind—[R]you; [J]slay him [Heb. *smite him in life*]—[R]wound him mortally (Deut 19.6, cp v. 11); [J]beast for beast [Heb. *life for life*]—[R]life for life (Lev 24.18); [J]the soul that—[R]he who; [J]the soul of the people—[R]the people; [J]make his soul enjoy good [Or, *delight his senses*]—[R]find enjoyment (Eccles 2.24); [J]tablets [Heb. *houses of soul*]—[R]perfume boxes (Is 3.20); [J]ponds for fish [Heb. *of living beings*]—[R]will be grieved (19.10, lit. grieved of soul; J mistakes for a noun meaning "pool" an adjective spelled and pronounced like it but of different derivation).

Combined with an adjective (*ḥay*) meaning "alive" or "living," *nepeš* is rendered as follows:

[J]a living soul—[R]a living being (Gen 2.7); [JR]living creature (Gen 1.21, 24); [J]creature that hath life—[R]living creature (v. 20); [J]life [Heb. *a living soul*]—[R]the breath of life (v. 30); [J]thing that liveth—[R]living creature (Ezek 47.9).

Both with and without the adjective "dead," *nepeš* also sometimes (very strangely to us) means "dead body"; so JR Num 6.6, 11; 9.6f, 10; 19.11, 13; Hag 2.13.

J uses "soul" also for two other Hebrew nouns, (2) *ndībāh* (Job 30.15, [J]my soul [Heb. *my principal one*]—[R]my honor), and (3) *nšāmāh* (Is 57.16, [J]the souls—[R]the breath of life). The latter is the noun translated "breath" in Gen 2.7; 7.22; and often. It is

[1] Job 11.20, [J]the giving up of the ghost [Or, *a puff of breath*]—[R]to breathe their last; Jer 15.9, [J]she hath given up the ghost—[R]she has swooned away; elsewhere "give up the ghost" stands for a verb meaning "perish."

also translated "spirit" by JR in Job 26.4; Prov 20.27. Cp [J]blast—[R]breath (Job 4.9); [J]inspiration—[R]breath (32.8).

Used in parallelism with this noun in the two places just cited is (4) *rūaḥ,* the word most commonly rendered "spirit": [J]the breath of his nostrils—[R]the blast of his anger (Job 4.9); [JR]spirit (32.8). Like corresponding nouns in Greek, Latin, and other languages, *rūaḥ* means primarily "wind." Both J and R often so render it;

e.g., [JR]wind (Gen 8.1 and often); [J]wind—[R]air (Jer 14.6), blast (Is 27.8), breath (Job 7.7); [J]a destroying wind—[R]the spirit of a destroyer (Jer 51.1); [J]tempest—[R]wind (Ps 11.6); cp [J]whirlwind—[R]stormy wind (Ezek 1.4, with *s'ārāh*); [J]blast—[R]spirit (2 Kings 19.7; Is 37.7; cp Is 25.4, [JR]blast).

From this the transition to "breath" is easy;

note, e.g., [JR]breath (Ps 146.4; Ezek 37.8, 10); [J]breath—[R]breath [Or *spirit*] (Job 12.10; Ezek 37.5f): [J]wind [Or, *breath*]—[R]breath (Ezek 37.9, 1st time); [J]wind—[R]breath [Or *wind* or *spirit*] (same v., 2d and 3d times); [J]breath [Or, *spirit*]—[R]spirit (Job 17.1).

Like *nepeš, rūaḥ* may be used as the equivalent of a personal pronoun; e.g., [J]my breath—[R]I (Job 19.17). In Is 26.9, indeed, both nouns are used practically as the subjects, or in apposition with the subjects, of verbs in the first personal singular: [J]With my soul have I desired thee . . . yea, with my spirit within me will I seek—[R]my soul yearns for thee . . . my spirit within me earnestly seeks.

Thus the idea of "spirit" is reached;

so, e.g., [JR]spirit (Eccles 8.8); [J]spirit—[R]wind (Job 26.13; Eccles 1.14, 17; 2.11, 17, 26; 4.4, 6, 16; 6.9); [J]spirit [Or, . . . *wind*]—[R]wind (Mic 2.11); [J]spirits—[R]winds (Ps 104.4, see § 44, No. 2); [J]the four spirits [Or, *winds*] —[R]the four winds (Zech 6.5; cp Ezek 37.9, [JR]the four winds); [J]the Spirit of the LORD—[R]the wind of the LORD (Is 59.19, cp § 7).

The ambiguity of this Hebrew noun creates a difficulty for the interpreter already in Gen 1.2, where R agrees with J in reading "Spirit," but recognizes the view of many commentaries in a note, "Or *wind*."

Chapter XII

ETHNIC AND SOCIAL RELATIONSHIPS

§ 51 From the first chapter of Genesis on, the OT recognizes the unity of mankind. The relatively modern but now antiquated concept of race is quite alien to the Bible. In J the word "race" occurs twice in the OT and twice in the NT; in all four places it refers to an athletic contest. R introduces it in Ezra 9.2, where J translates literally "seed" (see § 34).

The historical divisions of mankind into peoples and nations are indicated by several Hebrew words, of which the following are the most important:

(1) *gōy:* [JR]nation, people; [J]Gentiles, heathen (R keeps "heathen" only in Ps 79.1). (2) *'am:* [JR]people; cp [J]people—[R]peoples (often; J uses "people" for both singular and plural), nations, men, multitude, army, soldiers, troops, kindred. (3) *l'ōm:* [J]people—[R]peoples, nations; [J]folk—[R]nations.

(4) *maṭṭeh:* [JR]tribe; cp [J]rod—[R]tribe (Mic 6.9); [J]rod, staff, [R]stem, shaft. (5) *šēbeṭ:* [JR]tribe; cp [J]rod [Or, *tribe*]—[R]tribe (Ps 74.2; without note Jer 10.16; 51.19; cp Ps 125.3, [J]rod—[R]scepter; Judg 5.14, [J]pen—[R]staff). (6) *pluggah:* [J]division—[R]clan, grouping. (7) *'elep:* [J]family, thousand—[R]clan. (8) *mišpāḥāh:* [J]family—[R]clan, tribe, people; [J]household, kind, kindred—[R]family. (9) *bayit* (lit. house): [J]in families [Heb. *in a house*]—[R]a home (Ps 68.6). Cp *bēt 'āb:* [JR]father's house, family; [J]father's household, principal house, families of the fathers.

§ 52 There is no uncertainty as to the primary meaning of the basic words for "father," "mother," "son," "daughter," etc.; but some of them are occasionally used with extended or figurative meanings which may be misunderstood if the words are rendered literally.

Thus (1) *'āb:* [J]father—[R]ancestor (Judg 18.29); [J]the tribes of their fathers—[R]their ancestral tribes (Num 1.16, 47).

(2) *bēn* (son): [J]sons—[R]grandchildren (Gen 31.55), young men (Song 2.3); [J]nephews [Heb. *sons' sons*]—[R]grandsons (Judg 12.14; cp § 14 for J's use of "nephew"). This noun is often used idiomatically; e.g., [J]the son of wickedness—[R]the wicked (Ps 89.22); [J]came up in a night [Heb. *was the son of the night*]—[R]came into being in a night (Jon 4.10; cp same v., [JR]perished in a night, lit. a son of night perished). For other examples see § 14 on J's use of "children"; also § 43, No. 2, and § 53 on "son of man" and "son of God."

(3) *bat* (daughter): [J]daughter [Or, *granddaughter:* See ver. 18]—[R]granddaughter (2 Kings 8.26); [J]daughter—[R]maiden (Song 2.2; 6.9; 7.1), woman (Gen 27.46 three times, etc.); [J]king's daughter—[R]princess (Jer 43.6); [J]daughter dwelling in, daughter that dost inhabit—[R]inhabitant of (Jer 48.18f); [J]daughters of Canaan—[R]Canaanites (Gen 36.2); [J]daughter of Tyre—[R]people [Heb *daughter*] of Tyre (Ps 45.12); cp daughter of Jerusalem, daughter of Zion (for Jerusalem or its people, JR often); [J]the daughter of my people—[R]my people (Jer 8.11; 9.7; JR often read daughter of my people). The villages clustered about a large town are called in Hebrew its daughters; hence, e.g., [J]her daughters—[R]its villages (i.e., of Rabbah, Jer 49.2; cp Num 21.25 and often, [JR]villages; Josh 15.45–61 and often, [J]towns—[R]villages).

(4) *'āḥ* (brother): [J]brother—[R]kinsman, fellow; [J]every man against his brother—[R]to one another (Mal 2.10). In the plural R uses "brothers" for the literal meaning, "brethren" for extended or figurative meanings: [J]brethren—[R]brothers (Gen 9.22 etc., 122 times), brethren (Lev 10.4 etc., 53 times); cp [J]brethren—[R]kinsmen, kinsfolk, people; [J]their brethren the priests—[R]their fellow priests (Ezra 6.20); [J]the brotherly covenant [Heb. *the covenant of brethren*]—[R]the covenant of brotherhood (Amos 1.9). See also § 63, No. 5 (*gō'ēl*).

§ 53 Especially important among the idiomatic uses of "son" is the expression "son of man," because of its later use as a Messianic title. In the OT it means simply a member of the human race, but it was well adapted for Messianic use, meaning "the Man." Once it had come to be used in this way, several OT passages were naturally interpreted as Messianic though not originally so intended.

The following examples illustrate the use and translation of this idiom:

[J]son of man—[R]man (Jer 49.33; cp Job 16.21, [JR]a man); [J]sons of men—[R]men (Ps 4.2; Eccles 9.3; Jer 32.19), man (Eccles 2.8; cp Prov 8.31; Eccles 9.12 [JR]sons of men). R keeps "son of man" where the expression is used in parallelism with another word for "man," e.g., Ps 8.4; Jer 51.43; cp [J]sons of man—[R]sons of men (Prov 8.4). See also "children of men," § 13.

The use of "son of man" as a form of address for the prophet in Ezekiel (2.1 etc.) requires no change of translation.

A variation of the idiom occurs in Ps 62.9, using two different words for "man" (*'ādām* and *'îš*): [J]men of low degree . . . men of high degree—[R]men of low estate . . . men of high estate (lit. sons of mankind . . . sons of a man).

As a "son of man" is a human being, so a "son of God" is a divine being. For the Hebrews this could only mean an angel or the like (see § 43), as in Gen 6.2, 4; Job 1.6; 2.1; 38.7. Among polytheists, however, or when used with reference to one of their deities, it meant simply a god. In Psalms 29 and 89 this polytheistic background is still evident, though obscured by J's rendering "the mighty" (cp § 43), which agrees with a few Hebrew manuscripts: [J]ye mighty [Heb. *ye sons of the mighty*]—[R]O heavenly beings [Heb *sons of the gods*] (Ps 29.1); [J]the sons of the mighty—[R]the heavenly beings [Or *sons of gods*] (89.6).

In Ps 82.6 the "gods" (cp v. 1) are called "sons of the Most High" (J "children of the most High," cp § 13). Here, as in Ps 58.1, the reference is probably to the pagan rulers whose claims to be divine are thus ironically recalled.

Sometimes the redeemed people of God are called his sons: [J]my sons—[R]my children (Is 45.11); [J]the children—[R]my sons (Jer 3.19), his sons (Hos 11.10; cp 1.10, [JR]sons of the living God; 11.1, [JR]my son; Jer 31.20, [JR]my dear son).

In a special sense the Hebrew king was called God's son. Promising David a son to succeed him, God says in 2 Sam 7.14, "I will be his father, and he shall be my son." Here again the expression acquired new meaning later when it was applied to the promised Messiah, and this meaning was then read back into the OT where it was not intended. So especially Ps 2.7, [J]Thou art my Son—[R]You are my son. Here J assumes that Christ, the Messiah, is addressed; R understands the psalm as a coronation ode for the king, who is "begotten," i.e., adopted, as God's son when he is anointed (for v. 12 see § 142).

In Dan 3.25 J again sees a reference to Christ, though the Aramaic expression does not have the "determinate" form which would justify the translation "the Son of God," and the words are spoken by the pagan king, Nebuchadnezzar. R sees here the ancient idiom and therefore reads "a son of the gods," i.e., a god.

Chapter XIII

LEGAL TERMINOLOGY

§ 54 The major themes of Sin, Judgment, and Salvation are commonly presented in the OT in the language of ancient Hebrew court procedure. The terms thus used are therefore of more than cultural interest; in fact the OT uses them figuratively, with a religious application, far more often than in their literal sense. The words used for the charge or accusation, the plaintiff or prosecutor, the controversy or case, and the like, have a religious significance which is better understood when their original meaning is recognized.

(1) We have seen (§ 47, No. 12) that the name Satan is a word meaning "adversary," used in legal terminology for the plaintiff or prosecutor. This noun, *s̀āṭān,* is often translated "adversary" (so JR Num 22.22; 1 Sam 29.4; 2 Sam 19.22; 1 Kings 5.4; 11.14, 23, 25); cp Ps 109.6, [J]Satan [Or, *an adversary*]—[R]an accuser. The plaintiff in a Hebrew trial evidently stood at the right side of the defendant; hence, in the verse just cited, [J]stand at his right hand—[R]bring him to trial [Heb *stand at his right hand*] (in v. 31 the expression is effectively used in a different sense). Note also Zech 3.1, where the high priest is arraigned before the angel of the Lord, with "Satan standing at his right hand to accuse him." In these same passages and others we find also (2) the verb *S̀ṬN:*

[J]are my adversaries—[R]accuse me (Ps 109.4); [J]mine adversaries—[R]my accusers (participle, vv. 20, 29); [J]them . . . that are adversaries to my soul—[R]my accusers (Ps 71.13, cp § 50); [J]to resist him [Heb. *to be his adversary*]—[R]to accuse him (Zech 3.1).

Several words are used for the legal process as a controversy:

(3) *rīb:* [J]cause—[R]case, suit; [J]controversy—[R]cause, dispute, indictment; [J]strife—[R]contention, quarrel; cp Job 31.35, mine (R my) adversary (lit. the man of my dispute). (4) *RYB:* [J]contended with—[R]brought a complaint against; [J]contend thou—[R]plead your case; [J]called to contend—[R]was calling for a judgment; [J]debate—[R]contend; [J]plead—[R]complain, contend; [J]strive—[R]contend, bring into court. R sees a participle of this verb where J sees an adjective in Is 19.20, [J]a great one—[R]will defend. Sometimes this verb is used with the noun (No. 3) as cognate object (§ 103): [J]Debate thy cause—[R]Argue your case; [J]pleaded the cause of—[R]avenged; [J]plead my cause—[R]defend my cause; [J]thou hast pleaded the cause of my soul—[R]thou hast taken up my cause. (5) *YKH̱* (§ 56, No. 4): [J]plead—[R]contend, make an argument; [J]plead for—[R]maintain the right of. (6) *biqqōret:* [J]she [Or, *they*] shall be scourged [Heb. *there shall be a scourging*]—[R]an inquiry shall be held (Lev. 19.20).

§ 55 Several very important words are formed from a root which means determining what is right, maintaining or restoring the rights of those who are wronged, and punishing wrongdoers.

(1) *ŠPṬ* (JR usually judge): [J]defend—[R]give justice to; [J]judge—[R]defend, defend the cause of, do justice to, bring judgment on, decide, give judgment, hold judgment, pass judgment on, pronounce judgment, administer justice, govern, rule, try, vindicate; [J]be the judge—[R]execute judgment. Stem II (see § 105): [J]be judged—[R]be brought to trial; [J]plead—[R]argue, bring to judgment, execute judgment, go to law; [J]reason—[R]plead. (2) *šōpēṭ* (I participle of No. 1, used as noun, JR usually judge): [J]their judges—[R]those who shall condemn them; [J]judge—[R]ruler. (3) *mšōpēṭ* (III participle of No. 1): [J]to my judge—[R]to my accuser [Or *for my right*] (Job 9.15). (4) *šĕpeṭ* (always plural, [JR]judgments 9 times): [J]judgments—[R]acts of judgment, judgment, condemnation.

(5) *mišpāṭ* (JR often judgment): [J]judgment—[R]decision, justice, just, what is just, just measure, ordinance (representing a specific type of law, 86 times; JR ordinance 8 times), right, what is right, rule, sentence, way; [J]thy judgments—[R]my case (Jer 12.1; neither "thy" nor "my" is in the Hebrew); [J]come unto judgment—[R]come to court; [J]for want of judgment—[R]through injustice; [J]disannul my judgment—[R]put me in the wrong; [J]execute judgment—[R]judge; [J]stand in judgment—[R]act as judges; [J]they whose judgment was not to—[R]those who did not deserve to; [J]do justly—[R]do justice; [J]right—[R]rights, justice, just; [J]without right—[R]with injustice; [J]sentence—[R]vindication; [J]in measure—[R]in just measure.

Another root also provides words of similar meaning.

(6) *DYN:* [J]contend—[R]dispute; [J]plead the cause of—[R]maintain the rights of, uphold the cause of; [J]judge—[R]execute judgment, rule, vindicate. (See § 39 on Gen 6.3) (7) *dīn:* [J]cause—[R]rights; [J]judgment—[R]case, justice, rights, sentence; [J]strife—[R]quarreling. Also Aramaic: [J]judgment—[R]court, just. Cp (8) *middīn* (probably plural of *mad*): [J]in judgment—[R]on rich carpets [The meaning of the Hebrew word is uncertain] (Judg 5.10). (9) *dayyān:* [J]judge—[R]protector (Ps 68.5; cp 1 Sam 24.15, [JR]judge).

Note also (10) *PLL:* [J]judge—[R]mediate for, make judgment favorable for. (11) *plīlāh:* [J]judgment—[R]justice. (12) *plīlīyyāh:* [J]judgment—[R]giving judgment.

(13) *dābār* (lit. word): [J]the case of—[R]provision for; [J]sentence—[R]decision, verdict; [J]the sentence which—[R]what. (14) *qesem:* [J]A divine sentence [Heb. *Divination*]—[R]Inspired decisions (Prov 16.10).

(15) *RŠʿ* (cp § 61, No. 6), Stem V: [J]condemn—[R]confute, declare guilty, declare to be in the wrong.

§ 56 Punishment is not always regarded in the OT as disciplinary, educational, or redemptive. The idea of vengeance is all too often present. It is true, however, that the same terms often combine the ideas of discipline and instruction, punishment and teaching. An extreme example is Judg 8.16, where it is said that Gideon "taught the men of Succoth" with thorns and briers. There are several words whose meaning includes discipline and instruction.

(1) *YSR:* [JR]chasten; [J]chastise, correct, instruct; [R]discipline, direct, warn. (2) *yissōr:* [J]instruct—[R]a faultfinder (Job 40.2; J does not recognize the noun, which occurs only here). (3) *mūsār:* [JR]chastisement, discipline, instruction; [J]chastening, correction; [R]punishment, warning. (4) *YKḤ* (§ 54, No. 5): [J]correct—[R]chastise, reprove; [J]for correction—[R]for chastisement (lit. to chastise). (5) *tōkēḥāh, tōkaḥat:* [J]correction—[R]reproof; [J]punishment—[R]chastisement.

A very common and characteristic verb, difficult to translate because its meaning varies in different connections, is

(6) *PQD* (J usually and R often, visit, which like the Hebrew verb may denote either blessing or punishment): [JR]punish; [J]avenge; [R]attend to, give attention to, care for, have regard for, help, make inquiry, inspect, be mindful of, miss, muster, seek, set over, enjoin upon. (7)

pquddāh: [J]visitation—[R]care, punishment. (8) *'NŠ:* [J]punish—[R]fine, impose a fine on; [J]be punished—[R]suffer; [J]the condemned [Or, *such as have been fined,* or *mulcted*]—[R]those who have been fined (Amos 2.8). (9) *'āwōn* (§ 59, No. 7): [J]punishment [Or, *iniquity*]—[R]chastisement [Or, *iniquity*] (Lam 4.6); [J]the punishment of their iniquity—[R]their punishment (Ezek 14.10); [J]punishment—[R]iniquity (same v. twice).

§ 57 The terms used for a favorable outcome of the legal process—acquittal, innocence, righteousness, etc.—are important for the language of salvation in the New Testament as well as the Old. The Greek words of the New Testament can be rightly understood only when it is remembered that they are the words used in the Greek OT to translate these Hebrew terms. It does not follow that salvation is thought of literally as a legal or forensic transaction, but the legal background and associations of the language used indicate at least an important aspect of the subject.

(1) *ZKH:* [J]and be clear—[R]and blameless (Ps 51.4); [J]cleanse—[R]keep clean, keep pure. (2) *zākū* (Aramaic): [J]innocency was found in me—[R]I was found blameless (Dan 6.22). (3) *NQH* ([JR]be innocent 3 times): [J]be innocent [Or, *unpunished*]—[R]go unpunished; [J]be clear—[R]be free; [J]acquit—[R]clear. See also § 64, No. 2. (4) *nāqī* ([JR]innocent 29 times): [J]the poor innocents—[R]guiltless poor (Jer 2.34; cp 19.4, [JR]innocents). (5) *niqqāyōn:* [J]innocency—[R]innocence (Gen 20.5; Ps 26.6; 73.13); [J]attain to innocency—[R]are pure (Hos 8.5; see BWB, p. 189). Cp (6) *ḥap:* [J]innocent—[R]pure (Job 33.9). (7) *hinnām:* [J]innocent—[R]without cause (1 Kings 2.31). (8) *PLṬ* (§ 62, No. 10): [J]be delivered—[R]be acquitted (Job 23.7).

The background of the New Testament doctrine of "justification" is to be found in the next four words.

(9) *ṢDQ:* [J]be righteous—[R]be innocent, be in the right, be justified; [J]be justified—[R]be righteous, be proved right, triumph, be vindicated; [J]be cleansed [Heb. *justified*]—[R]be restored to its rightful state (of the sanctuary, Dan 8.14); [J]If I justify myself—[R]though I am innocent (Job 9.20). Stem III (see § 106): [J]hast justified thy sisters—[R]have made your sisters appear righteous (Ezek 16.51f). V (§ 106): [J]justify you—[R]say that you are right (Job 27.5): [J]justify many—[R]make many to be accounted righteous (Is 53.11); [J]hath justified herself more—[R]has shown herself less guilty (Jer 3.11); [J]do justice to—[R]maintain the right of (Ps 82.3).

(10) *ṣedeq:* [JR]justice, right, the right, righteousness; [J]righteous cause; [R]what is just, justly, just cause, what is right, righteous, righteously, rightful, honest evidence, true, truth, deliverance, salvation, victory, victorious, vindication. Cp Deut 16.20, [J]that which is altogether just [Heb. *Justice, justice*]—[R]Justice, and only justice.

(11) *ṣdāqāh:* [JR]right, righteousness, righteous act; [J]justice, righteous help, moderately; [R]acquittal, command, equity, honesty, prosperity, uprightness, saving help, deliverance, salvation, righteous deed, saving act, saving deed, triumph, vindication.

(12) *ṣaddiq:* [JR]just, righteous; [R]a good man, innocent, right, in the right, Righteous One, triumphant, upright.

Chapter XIV

SIN AND SALVATION

§ 58 Temptation to sin appears in the OT in two aspects, incitement and testing. The words used are the same ones used elsewhere for incitement to action of any kind and for testing in general.

The idea of incitement to sin is expressed by the verb used for David's being tempted to take a census,

(1) *ŠWT:* [J]moved—[R]incited (2 Sam 24.1; cp 1 Chron 21.1, [J]provoked —[R]incited); elsewhere [JR]entice, stir up; [J]persuade, remove, set on, take away; [R]allure, deceive, draw away, mislead, urge.

The idea of testing, much more common in this connection, is represented by several words, two or three of which sometimes appear together, as in Ps 26.2. Apart from their use for testing things or materials, they refer sometimes to God's testing of man, sometimes to God's being put to the test by man. They are so close in meaning that the choice of a rendering may be governed by suitability to the immediate context or by rhythm.

(2) *BḤN:* [JR]prove, try; [J]examine, tempt; [R]assay, test, put to the proof, put to the test. (3) *bōḥan:* [J]trial—[R]testing; [J]tried—[R]tested. (4) *NŠH:* [JR]prove, try; [J]adventure, assay; [R]attempt, be used to, make trial, test, make a test, venture. (5) *maššāh:* [JR]trial; [J]temptation. See § 42 on Ps 95.8. A different Hebrew noun, spelled and pronounced the same but from a different root, is used in Job 9.23, [J]trial—[R]calamity [The meaning of the Hebrew word is uncertain]. (6) *ṢRP:* [JR]try; [R]refine, test; [J]is tried [Or, *refined*]—[R]proves true (2 Sam 22.31; Ps 18.30). Cp § 64, No. 10.

§ 59 The vocabulary of the OT is extraordinarily rich in words for guilt, iniquity, sin, and the like. The primary meanings of these words clarify the Hebrew conception of sin as crookedness, rebellion, treachery, missing the mark, etc. Where J uses a few general synonyms for several Hebrew words, R tries to bring out more clearly, where possible, the specific meaning of each term, though of course with no attempt to use a different English word for each Hebrew word, or to use the same English word everywhere for a particular Hebrew word.

(1) *'ŠM:* [J]offend, trespass; [R]be guilty, become guilty, incur guilt, do the wrong. Cp [J]acknowledge their offence—[R]acknowledge their guilt (Hos 5.15); [J]hold themselves not guilty—[R]go unpunished (Zech 11.5). (2) *'āšām:* [J]guiltiness, guilty, sin, trespass; [R]guilt, guilty ways. See also § 68, No. 7. (3) *'ašmāh:* [J]sin, trespass; [R]guilt, wrong. Cp [J]whereas we have offended against the LORD—[R]to bring upon us guilt against the LORD (lit. for the guilt of the LORD upon us, 2 Chron 28.13). See also § 68, No. 8.

(4) *'āwen:* [JR]iniquity; [J]unjust, unrighteous, wicked; [R]crime, evil, mischief, misfortune, trouble, wickedness, godless, iniquitous. Also in the expression, *pō'lē 'āwen:* [JR]them that (R those who) work iniquity, men that (R who) work iniquity; [J]workers of iniquity; [R]workers of evil, those who work evil, evildoers.

(5) *'WH:* [J]commit iniquity—[R]do wrong; [J]deal perversely with—[R]subvert. (6) *'aw'eh,* plural with *rūaḥ* (§ 50, No. 4); [J]a perverse spirit [Heb. *a spirit of perverseness*]—[R]a spirit of confusion (Is 19.14). (7) *'āwōn* (§ 56, No. 9): [JR]iniquity, punishment, sin; [R]corruption, guilt.

(8) *'WL:* [J]deal unjustly—[R]deal perversely; [J]unrighteous—[R]unjust (participle). (9) *'awwāl:* [J]wicked—[R]unrighteous. (10) *'āwel:* [JR]unrighteousness; [J]iniquity; [R]injustice, wrong. (11) *'awlāh:* [JR]wickedness; [J]iniquity, perverseness; [R]crime, falsehood, injustice, perversion of justice, unrighteousness, wrong. Cp [J]unto iniquity—[R]to do wrong; [J]workers of iniquity —[R]wrongdoers; [J]children of iniquity—[R]wayward people; [J]children of wickedness—[R]violent men.

(12) *'āmāl:* [J]iniquity [Or, *grievance*]—[R]wrong; [J]perverseness—[R]trouble. (13) *lzūt:* [J]perverse—[R]devious. (14) *lūz:* [JR]devious, perverse; [J]froward. (15) *'iqqēš:* [JR]perverse; [J]froward; [R]crooked. (16) *'iqqšūt:* [J]froward—[R]crooked, devious. (17) *hpakpak:* [J]froward—[R]perverse, perverted. (19) *PTL:* [J]froward [Heb. *wreathed*]—[R]twisted; [J]froward—[R]wily; [J]shew thyself froward [Or, *wrestle*]—[R]show thyself perverse (Ps 18.26). (20) *muṭṭeh:* [J]perverseness [Or, *wresting of judgment*]—[R]injustice. (21) *ŠLP:* [J]pervert

—[R]subvert, bring to ruin. (22) *šelep:* [J]perverseness—[R]crookedness. (23) *gēzel:* [J]perverting—[R]taken away. (24) *ŠWB* (lit. turn): [J]pervert—[R]lead astray.

§ 60 Other terms are rendered offence, sin, transgression, or trespass.

(1) *mikšōl:* [J]offence—[R]stumbling; [J]offence of heart—[R]pangs of conscience (cp § 49). (2) *BGD:* [J]offend against—[R]be untrue to; [J]transgress —[R]be treacherous; [J]transgressed [Or, *dealt treacherously*]—[R]dealt treacherously. Participle: [J]transgressor—[R]faithless, treacherous; [J]wicked transgressors—[R]those who treacherously plot evil (with *'āwen,* § 59, No. 4).

(3) *ḤṬ'* ([JR]usually sin): [J]offend—[R]sin; [J]What have I offended—[R]What wrong have I done; [J]sinneth against his own soul—[R]forfeits his life (Prov 20.2, cp Hab 2.10; see § 50); [J]sin [Or, *err*]—[R]miss (Job 5.24; cp Judg 20.16, [JR]miss, of slinging a stone); [J]sinneth against me—[R]misses me (Prov 8.36); [J]sinneth—[R]misses his way (19.2). Stem V: [J]cause the land to sin—[R]bring guilt upon the land (Deut 24.4). See also § 64, No. 3. (4) *ḥēṭ':* [JR]sin, offence, [R]crime, sinfully. (5) *ḥaṭṭā'āh, ḥaṭṭā't* ([JR]usually sin or sin offering, cp § 68, No. 6; see also § 64, No. 4): [J]sin—[R]sinful thing.

(6) *M'L:* [JR]transgress, trespass; [R]be false, be unfaithful, break faith, deal treacherously, do wrong, sin. (7) *ma'al:* [J]transgression, trespass; [R]breach of faith, faithlessness, treachery, treason. As cognate object (§ 103) with No. 6: [J]have committed a trespass [Heb. *trespassed a trespass*]—[R]have acted faithlessly (Ezek 15.8); [J]commit a trespass—[R]act unfaithfully, break faith; [J]their trespass that they have trespassed—[R]the treachery which they have committed; [J]the trespasses whereby they have trespassed—[R]the treachery which they have practiced.

(8) *'BR* (lit. pass over; cp. § 62, No. 13): [J]have transgressed my covenant—[R]have broken my covenant (Hos 8.1); [J]ye make the LORD's people to transgress [Or, *to cry out*]—[R]the people of the LORD spreading abroad (1 Sam 2.24).

(9) *PŠ':* [JR]transgress; [J]trespass; [R]rebel, do wrong; [J]whereby they have transgressed—[R]their rebellion. (10) *peša':* [JR]transgression; [J]sin, trespass; [R]offense, sinful way, treason, breach of trust; [J]for the transgression of a land—[R]when a land transgresses (Prov 28.2). As cognate object (§ 103) with No. 9: [J]their transgressions wherein they have transgressed—[R]their transgressions which they have committed (1 Kings 8.50).

§61 Still other words are translated evil, wickedness, wrong, etc. They often combine the conceptions of evil as wrong and as calamity.

(1) *R‘‘:* [JR]do evil; [J]bring evil, evil entreat; [R]bring calamity, do harm, do ill, do wickedly, do wrong, work evil, treat harshly; [J]if it seem evil unto you—[R]if you be unwilling; [J]and thine eye be evil—[R]and your eye be hostile; [J]his eye shall be evil—[R]will grudge food; [J]her eye shall be evil —[R]will grudge. Participle as noun: [JR]evildoer, the wicked; [J]evil men, [R]evil. (2) *R‘H:* [J]He evil entreateth—[R]they feed on (Job 24.21; R understands here the common word for "feed," "be shepherd," which is also *R‘H).*

(3) *ra‘:* [JR]evil, evil man; [J]naughty (cp § 13), wicked, wicked person, wickedly, wickedness; [R]bad, deadly, destroying, what was evil, evil doer, with malice, ruin, unpleasant, vile. Cp [J]evil beast—[R]wild beast; [J]evil-favouredness—[R]defect (lit. evil thing). (4) *rā‘āh:* [JR]wickedness; [R]doom, evil doing, evil works, wicked deeds. (5) *rō‘:* [JR]evil; [J]naughtiness, wickedness; [R]bad.

(6) *RŠ‘:* [J]be wicked—[R]be condemned, be guilty; [J]do wickedly against —[R]violate. (7) *rāšā:* [JR]wicked; [J]condemned, ungodly; [R]bad, guilty. (8) *reša‘:* [JR]iniquity; [J]wickedness; [R]evil.

(9) *hawwah, hōwāh:* [J]iniquity, mischief, naughtiness, naughty, perverse thing, wickedness; [R]calamity, destruction, disaster, lust, ruin, mischievous, wicked. (10) *bliyya‘al:* (cp §47, No. 11) [JR]wicked; [J](usually with note, Heb. *Belial*) evil, naughty, ungodly; [R]base, deadly, worthless, perdition, villainy.

Many other terms of similar meaning must be passed over here. One instance of quite different interpretation of the Hebrew, however, should be mentioned,

(11) *NK’:* [J]they were viler than the earth—[R]they have been whipped out of the land (Job 30.8; cp § 84).

Chapter XV

SALVATION

§62 The Hebrew vocabulary of salvation is as rich and varied as the vocabulary of sin, consisting not of technical theological terms, but of the same words used for deliverance from any kind of hardship or danger. Here again, since the language of the Bible is not scientific but literary, there is much overlapping of meanings among the various terms. English words too, of course, often have varied meanings: "deliver," for example, may mean "rescue, save," or "hand over, give up."

Several words are derived from a root meaning "save," from which the name Jesus is derived.

(1) *YŠ‘:* [JR]deliver, help, save, get victory; [J]defend, preserve, bring salvation, have salvation; [R]give victory, defend the cause of, give deliverance to, give help, bring victory, victorious. (2) *mōšī‘:* [JR]saviour ([R]savior), deliverer. Cp [J]thou that savest—[R]savior (Ps 17.7). (3) *yēša‘:* [JR]safety, salvation; [R]deliverance, help. (4) *yšū‘āh:* [JR]help, salvation; [J]health, saving health; [R]deliverance, saving power, victory. (5) *mōšā‘āh* (only Ps 68.20): [JR]salvation. (6) *tšū‘āh:* [JR]deliverance, help, salvation, victory; [J]safety; [R]deeds of salvation.

Several other words also have much the same meanings.

(7) *ḤLṢ:* [JR]deliver; [R]rescue, plunder. (8) *MLṬ:* [J]deliver, preserve; [R]rescue, save. (9) *NṢL:* [JR]deliver, save; [R]rescue. (10) *PLṬ* (§ 57, No. 8): [J]deliver—[R]rescue, save. (12) *plēṭāh:* [J]deliverance [Or, *they that escape*] —[R]those that escape (Obad 1.17); [J]deliverance—[R]those who escape (Joel 2.32); [J]deliverance—[R]remnant (Ezra 9.13); [J]escaping—[R]any to escape (v. 14). (12) *PṢH:* [J]delivery, rid; [R]rescue. (13) *‘BR* (§ 60, No. 8): [J]were delivered [Heb. *passed away*]—[R]were freed (Ps 81.6). (14) *ŠYZYB* (Aramaic): [JR]deliver; [R]save.

§63 The Hebrew words for atonement, ransom, and redemption refer primarily to such human matters as blood-revenge, bribery, inheritance, and the ransoming of captives. Recognition of these basic meanings makes clearer their religious applications.

(1) *KPR:* with human subjects, ^{JR}appease, make atonement; with God as subject, ^{JR}forgive, pardon. Also ^{J}be merciful, be pacified, purge, purge away, put off, reconcile, make reconciliation; ^{R}atone for, expiate, make expiation. (2) *kōper:* ^{JR}bribe, ransom; ^{J}satisfaction, sum of money; ^{R}compensation. (3) *kippurīm:* ^{JR}atonement, atonement money.

(4) *G'L:* ^{JR}redeem; ^{J}deliver, ransom, do the kinsman's part, do the part of a kinsman, perform the part of a kinsman; ^{R}do the part of the next of kin. Cp ^{J}the year of my redeemed—^{R}my year of redemption [Or *the year of my redeemed*] (Is 63.4); ^{J}redeem thou my right to thyself—^{R}Take my right of redemption yourself (Ruth 4.6). (5) *gō'ēl* (participle of No. 4 used as a noun): ^{JR}avenger, kinsman, near kinsman, redeemer, Redeemer; ^{J}revenger; ^{R}next of kin. Cp ^{J}one of our next kinsmen [Or, *one that hath the right to redeem*]—^{R}one of our nearest kin (Ruth 2.20); ^{J}redeemer—^{R}Redeemer [Or *Vindicator*] (Job 19.25). (6) *g'ullāh:* ^{JR}redemption; cp ^{J}right—^{R}right of redemption (Ruth 4.6).

(7) *PDH:* ^{JR}deliver, redeem; ^{R}buy back, ransom, rescue. Cp ^{J}those that are to be redeemed—^{R}the redemption (Num 3.46), their redemption price (18.16); ^{J}them that were redeemed—^{R}those redeemed (3.49), redemption (v. 51, see § 128). (8) *pidyōn:* ^{JR}ransom, redemption. (9) *QNH:* ^{J}redeemed—^{R}bought back (Neh 5.8).

(10) *ŠKK:* ^{J}was appeased—^{R}had abated (Esther 2.1, of the king's wrath). (11) *ŠQṬ:* ^{J}appease—^{R}quiet (Prov 15.18). (12) *KPH:* ^{J}pacifieth—^{R}averts (Prov 21.14). (13) *NWḤ:* ^{J}pacify—^{R}make amends for (Eccles 10.4).

§64 Such terms as "blot out" and "cleanse" are often used in the sense of "forgive" in the OT. Several verbs are used for cleansing from sin in Ps 51; here J and R do not differ in translating them, but the same verbs and others like them are rendered differently in some other places.

(1) *MḤH:* ^{JR}blot out; ^{R}sweep away, wash off. (2) *NQH* (§ 57, No. 3): ^{JR}cleanse; ^{R}clear. (3) *ḤṬ'* (§ 60, No. 3): ^{JR}purge, purify; ^{R}cleanse. Cp ^{J}purify themselves—^{R} are beside themselves (Job 41.25). (4) *ḥaṭṭā't* (§ 60, No. 5): ^{J}purifying—^{R}expiation (Num 8.7). (5) *KBŠ:* ^{JR}wash. (6) *BRR:*

[J]be ye clean—[R]purify yourselves (Is 52.11); [J]purge—[R]cleanse (Dan 11.35). (7) *DWḤ:* [JR]wash; cp [J]purged—[R]cleansed (Is 4.4); [J]hath cast me out—[R]has rinsed me out (Jer 51.34). (8) *ṬHR:* [JR]be clean, pronounce clean, cleanse, purge, purify. (9) *ZQQ:* [J]purge—[R]refine (Mal 3.3). (10) *ṢRP* (§ 58, No. 6); [J]purge away—[R]smelt away (Is 1.25).

(11) *NS'* (lit. lift): [JR]forgive. (12) *ŚLḤ:* [JR]forgive, pardon; [J]spare. (13) *śallāh:* [J]ready to forgive—[R]forgiving. (14) *ślīḥāh:* [JR]forgiveness; cp [J]ready to pardon—[R]ready to forgive (Neh 9.17, lit. of pardons). (15) *RṢH:* [J]accept—[R]approve, have delight in; [J]approve—[R]be pleased with; [J]accept of the punishment of—[R]make amends for; [J]acceptable to—[R]the favorite of (passive participle). (16) *rāṣōn:* [JR]acceptable, accepted; cp [J]an acceptable time—[R]a time of favor (Is 49.8); [J]to be accepted for you—[R]that you may find acceptance (Lev 23.11). (17) *DŠN* (lit. make fat): [J]accept [Heb. *turn to ashes,* or *make fat*]—[R]regard with favor. (18) *ḥēpeṣ:* [J]acceptable words [Heb. *words of delight*]—[R]pleasing words (Eccles 12.10).

Chapter XVI

PUBLIC WORSHIP

§ 65 Several words used in the OT apply only or chiefly to Canaanite or pagan religion. A distinctive term for the priests of Israel's idolatrous neighbors is (1) *kāmār:* [JR]idolatrous priest; [J]Chemarims. The common term for a Canaanite place of worship is (2) *bāmāh* (cp § 46, No. 11): [JR]high place; [R]height, shrine.

Two characteristic objects at the Canaanite shrines are often mentioned. Misled by a tradition as old as the Septuagint (§ 135), J erroneously calls the first of these, (3) *'šērāh,* a grove. Except where it is the name of the goddess Asherah (§ 45, No. 3), the word designates a wooden cult-object, either an image of the goddess or a tree or post representing her. R simply transliterates, Asherah in the singular and Asherim in the plural.

The other characteristic object can be more exactly identified, because such an object, being made of stone, does not decay like wood but can still be found now and then in an archeological excavation. It is a crudely carved stone pillar, the (4) *maṣṣēbāh:* [JR]pillar; [J]image, standing image ([Jmg]often *statue*); cp [J]images [Heb. *statues,* or, *standing images*]—[R]obelisks (Jer 43.13, referring to Egypt); [J]garrisons—[R]pillars (Ezek 26.11).

There are several Hebrew words for idols of various kinds.

(5) *'līl* (lit. nothing): [JR]idol; [R]worthless idol; cp [J]the idol shepherd —[R]my worthless shepherd (Zech 11.17; cp v. 15, with a different Hebrew word, *'wilī,* [J]foolish shepherd—[R]worthless shepherd). (6) *'ēlīm:* [J]with idols—[R]among the oaks (Is 57.5). J takes this as the plural of *'ēl,* god (§ 43, No. 2); R as the plural of *'ayil,* oak (§ 72, No. 13). (7) *mipleṣet:* [J]idol—[R]abominable image, image. (8) *'āṣāb:* [JR]idol, image. (9) *'ōṣeb:* [JR]idol (Is 48.5); see also § 142 on Hos 10.6. Cp (10) *'eṣeb:* [J]idol—[R]pot (Jer 22.28). This noun, confused by J with Nos. 8 and 9, is from a dif-

ferent root, meaning "form," "fashion," "shape" (cp Job 10.8). (11) *gillūl:* [JR]idol, image; cp [J]the sins of your idols—[R]your sinful idolatry (Ezek 23.49). (12) *ṣelem:* [JR]image; cp [J]their image—[R]their phantoms (Ps 73.20, of dreams); [J]in a vain shew—[R]as a shadow (39.6).

(13) *pesel:* [JR]graven image; [J]carved image; [R]idol, image. (14) *psīl:* [JR]graven image; [J]carved image; [R]image. (15) *nesek* (cp. § 68, No. 19): [JR]molten image; [R]image. (16) *maššēkāh:* [JR]molten image; [R]metal image. (17) *maskīt:* [J]image of stone [Or, *figured stone.* Heb. *a stone of pictures*] —[R]figured stones (Lev 26.1); [J]pictures—[R]figured stones (Num 33.52); [J]image [Heb. *statue*]—[R]pillar (2 Kings 3.2; 10.27).

Hebrew rather than Canaanite, but listed here because of its idolatrous nature, is (18) *trāpīm* (always plural, at least in form): [JR]image [Heb. *teraphim*], teraphim, idolatry; [J]images [Heb. *teraphim*], images [Or, *teraphim*], idols [Heb. *teraphim*]; [R]household gods.

§ 66 Other terms are used for Hebrew sacred persons, places, and objects.

(1) *kōhēn:* [JR]priest. Cp [J]chief rulers [Or, *princes*]—[R]priests (2 Sam 8.18). This is a conspicuous instance of mistranslation in J due to a dogmatic presupposition which distorted the history of Hebrew religion: the makers of J simply could not believe that David's sons, not being of the tribe of Levi, could be priests, even though the Hebrew plainly said that they were. Note also 2 Sam 20.26, [J]a chief ruler [Or, *a prince*]—[R]priest; 1 Kings 4.2, [J]priest [Or, *chief officer*]—[R]priest. With *gādōl* (lit. great): [JR]high priest; cp [J]he that is the high priest—[R]The priest who is chief (Lev. 21.10).

(2) *lēwī, lēwiyyī:* [JR]Levite. With No. 1: [J]the priests the Levites—[R]the Levitical priests; [J]the Levites, the priests—[R]the Levitical priests; cp, without No. 1, [J]the Levites—[R]the Levitical priests (Jer 33.22). Note also 2 Chron 5.12, [J]the Levites which were the singers—[R]the Levitical singers. (3) *mnaṣṣēḥ* (III participle of *NṢḤ*): [J]were overseers—[R]directed (2 Chron 34.13; see § 69, No. 11). (4) *šō'ēr:* [J]doorkeeper, porter (see § 14); [R]gatekeeper; cp [J]porter toward the east—[R]keeper of the east gate (2 Chron 31.14); [J]porters [Heb. *for the gate*]—[R]appointed to the gate (1 Chron 16.42). (In Ps. 84.10, [JR]be a doorkeeper, the Hebrew word is different.) (5) *ntīnīm* (always plural); [J]Nethinims—[R]temple servants [Heb *nethinim*].

Various terms are used for the Hebrew place of worship. Three general words for "sanctuary" or the like may be mentioned.

(6) *qōdeš* (lit. holiness): [JR]sanctuary; [R]holy, the holy, holy place, what is sacred; cp [J]the border of his sanctuary—[R]his holy land (Ps 78.54, cp § 71, No. 6). (7) *miqdāš:* [JR]holy place, sanctuary; [J]chapel (Amos 7.13); [R]holy things, sacred area, temple. (8) *mōʿēd* (§ 67, No. 3): [J]his places of the assembly—[R]the place of his appointed feasts (Lam 2.6); [J]congregations—[R]holy place (Ps 74.4); [J]synagogues—[R]meeting places (v. 8).

The portable shrine of the period of wandering in the desert is designated usually by one of two nouns.

(9) *ʾōhel* (lit. tent), with No. 8: [JR]tent of meeting; [J]tabernacle of the congregation. Cp [J]tabernacle—[R]tent (of the tent pitched by David at Jerusalem for the ark, 2 Sam 6.17; of the temple, Ps 15.1; 27.5f). (10) *miškān* (lit. dwelling place): [JR]habitation, tabernacle; [R]abode, dwelling, dwelling place. R keeps "tabernacle" wherever the reference is to the Mosaic tabernacle (for the "tabernacles" of the annual festival see § 67, No. 6).

For the temple also two nouns are used.

(11) *bayit* (lit. house): [J]house—[R]temple (Jer 38.14; 43.13; often in Ezek 40–48); [J]the king's court [Heb. *house of the kingdom*]—[R]a temple of the kingdom (Amos 7.13). (12) *hēkal:* [JR]temple; cp [J]temple—[R]temple [Or *palace*] (Amos 8.3); [J]temples—[R]temples [Or *palaces*] (Joel 3.5); [J]temples—[R]palaces (Hos 8.14). This noun is used also for the outer hall or "holy place" of the temple: [J]temple—[R]nave (often in 1 Kings 6f; 2 Chron 3f; Ezek 41). The inner shrine or "most holy place" is often called the (13) *dbīr:* [J]oracle—[R]sanctuary (Ps 28.2), inner sanctuary (often in 1 Kings 6–8; 2 Chron 4f).

The many terms designating other elements in the architecture of the temple cannot be considered here, though there are some differences in their interpretation in J and R. Such items of the equipment of the sanctuary as the ark, altar, and table have for the most part the same designations in R as in J, but with some differences in detail. There are variations also in the names given by J and R to the vessels and utensils used in the tabernacle and temple, but these too, being of minor importance, must be omitted here for lack of space.

§ 67 For the sacred times and gatherings of Hebrew worship R usually retains such well-established terms as sabbath, passover, unleavened bread, and ingathering; but there are some exceptions.

(1) *šabbāt:* [JR]sabbath, the sabbath day; [R]Sabbath (Ps 92, title). Cp [J]seven sabbaths shall be complete—[R]seven full weeks shall they be (Lev 23.15); [J]seven sabbaths of years—[R]seven weeks [Or *sabbaths*] of years (25.8). (2) *mišbāt:* [J]her sabbaths—[R]her downfall (lit. ceasing, Lam 1.7).

(3) *mō'ēd* (§ 66, No. 8): [JR]appointed feast, assembly, meeting; [J]congregation, feast, set feast, solemn feast, solemn assembly, solemnity; [R]feast day, festival, annual feast, set time. (The word is used also in more general ways and with other renderings: [JR]appointed, appointed time, time appointed, season; [J]set time, appointed season, appointed sign; [R]appointment, hour, time, appointed signal.) (4) *ḤGG:* [J]keep holyday—[R]keep festival. (5) *ḥāg, ḥag:* [JR]feast; [J]feast day, solemn feast, solemn feast day, solemnity, sacrifice; [R]festival, festal procession, offering. (6) *sukkāh;* with No. 3: [J]feast of tabernacles—[R]feast of booths [Or *tabernacles*] (Lev 23.34; without note Deut 16.13, 16; 31.10; Ezra 3.4; Zech 14.16, 18f). (Used more generally: [JR]booth, pavilion; [J]cottage, tabernacle, tent; [R]abode, shelter.) (7) *'ṣārāh, 'ṣeret:* [JR]solemn assembly; [J]assembly, solemn meeting; [R]company.

Two Hebrew nouns are important, through their Greek renderings in the Septuagint (§ 135), for the background of the New Testament word "church."

(8) *'ēdāh:* [JR]congregation (so R regularly when the reference is to the formal gathering of Israel as the people of God), assembly, company, swarm (Judg 14.8, of bees); [J]people; [R]band, council. With No. 9: [J]the congregation and assembly—[R]the assembled congregation (Prov 5.14). (9) *qahal:* [JR]assembly (so R regularly of the formal assembly of Israel, to distinguish this word from No. 9), company, congregation; [J]multitude; [R]horde, host; cp [J]the assembly of the people—[R]the assembled people (Jer 26.17); [J]company—[R]crew (of a ship, Ezek 27.34). Note also (10) *maqhēl:* [J]congregations—[R]great congregation. (11) *miqrā':* [JR]convocation; [R]assembly.

§ 68 The basic Hebrew term for the central act of Hebrew worship, the killing and offering of a sacrificial animal, is (1) *ZBḤ:* [JR]sacrifice; [J]offer; [R]slay; cp [J]offer—[R]offer . . . a sacrifice of . . . [Or *make . . . your sacrifice* . . .] (Ps 50.14). The cognate noun is (2) *zebaḥ:* [JR]sacrifice; cp [J]sacrifice [Or, *slaughter*] —[R]sacrificial feast (Ezek 39.17, 19); [J]sacrifices [Or, *good cheer*]— [R]feasting (Prov 17.1; sacrifice and feasting went together for the Hebrews). Several other verbs and the nouns corresponding to some of them are used for offering and sacrifice, but their interpretation ordinarily poses no problem. An exception is the use of (3) *'LH* in 1 Kings 12.33; 2 Kings 16.12, [J]offered—[R]went up. The form here is ambiguous; J takes it as Stem V (lit. cause to go up), R as Stem I (see §§ 105f).

Several nouns designate particular kinds of offerings.

(4) *minḥāh:* [JR]oblation, offering; [J]meat offering (for J's archaic use of "meat" see § 14), present, evening sacrifice; [R]burnt offering, cereal offering, sacrifice, tribute. (5) *šlāmīm* (always plural in Hebrew, often with No. 2): [JR]peace offerings, sacrifice of peace offerings; [R]sacrifices for peace offerings, sacrifices. See § 141 on Ps 69.22. (6) *ḥṭā'āh, ḥaṭṭā'āh, ḥaṭṭā't* (§ 59, No. 5): [JR]sin offering; cp [J]for the sin—[R]for a sin offering (Lev 4.14). Cp No. 35. (7) *'āšām* (§ 59, No. 2): [JR]an offering for sin (Is 53.10); [J]trespass offering; [R]guilt offering. (8) *'ašmāh* (§ 59, No. 3): [J]trespass offering [Or, . . . *being found guilty*. Heb. . . . *trespass*]— [R]guilt offering (Lev 6.5). (9) *mas'ēt:* [J]oblation—[R]gifts (Ezek 20.40).

(10) *trūmāh:* [JR]offering: [J]oblation, heave offering; [R]contribution, freewill offering, to be offered, that is offered, portion, portion set apart, priest's portion; cp [J]oblation of the holy portion—[R]holy portion (Ezek 48.18), holy district (45.7 twice); [J]oblation . . . that is offered—[R]special portion from the holy portion (48.12). See § 142 on 2 Sam 1.21. With No. 30: [J]the heave shoulder—[R]the thigh that is offered (Lev 7.34). (11) *tnūpāh:* [JR]wave offering; [J]offering [Heb. *wave offering*]— [R]wave offering (Num 8.11, 13, 15, 21).

(12) *kālīl:* [JR]whole burnt offering; [J]whole burnt sacrifice; [J]every whit—[R]as a whole burnt offering (Deut 13.16). (13) *tāmīd:* [JR]continual burnt offering: [J]daily sacrifice. (14) *'ōlāh:* [JR]burnt offering, burnt sacrifice. (15) *ndābāh:* [JR]freewill offering; [J]free offering, voluntary offering; cp [J]a freewill offering . . . which thou hast promised—[R]what you have promised (Deut 23.23); [J]freely—[R]With a freewill offering (Ps 54.6). With Nos. 14 and 5: [J]a voluntary burnt offering or peace

offerings voluntarily—^{R}a freewill offering, either a burnt offering or peace offerings as a freewill offering (Ezek 46.12).

(16) *leḥem pānīm* (lit. bread of face): ^{J}shewbread—^{R}bread of the Presence. (17) *leḥem maʿreket* (lit. bread of row, i.e., set out in rows): ^{J}shewbread—^{R}showbread. (18) *NSK:* ^{J}offer—^{R}pour, pour out. (19) *nēsek* (cp § 65, No. 15): ^{J}drink, offering—^{R}libation. (20) *mimsāk:* ^{J}drink offering—^{R}mixed wine (Is 65.11). (21) *QṬR:* ^{JR}burn incense, offer incense; cp ^{J}burn incense upon it—^{R}burn it (Ex 30.7f); ^{J}offer [Heb. *offer by burning*]—^{R}offer (Amos 4.5). (22) *qṭōret:* ^{JR}incense; cp ^{J}incense—^{R}smoke of the sacrifice (Ps 66.15); ^{J}perfume—^{R}incense (Ex 30.35). (23) *lbōnāh:* ^{J}incense—^{R}frankincense. (24) *nīḥōḥ:* ^{J}sweet odours—^{R}incense (Dan 2.46). *rēḥ nīḥōḥ:* ^{J}sweet savour [Heb. *savour of rest*]; ^{R}pleasing odor, pleasing odors, soothing odors. (25) *rōqaḥ:* ^{J}confection—^{R}blended; ^{J}ointment—^{R}mixing. (26) *šemen:* ^{JR}fat, oil, ointment; ^{R}anointing oil. (27) *RBK:* ^{J}fry—^{R}mix with oil.

Other terms in the interpretation of which J and R differ designate animals used for sacrifice, or parts of such animals.

(28) *ben šānāh* (lit. son of a year, cp § 52, No. 2): ^{J}of the first year—^{R}a year old. (29) *pesaḥ* (^{JR}passover, referring to the festival): ^{J}passover—^{R}the passover lamb; ^{J}sacrifice the passover—^{R}offer the passover sacrifice. (30) *šōq:* ^{J}shoulder—^{R}thigh, leg. (31) *yōteret:* ^{J}caul—^{R}appendage. (32) *sgōr,* with *lēb* (heart): ^{J}the caul of their heart—^{R}their breast (Hos 13.8). (33) *'alyāh:* ^{J}rump—^{R}fat tail.

Several miscellaneous cultic terms may be noted also.

(34) *ZRQ:* ^{JR}sprinkle; ^{R}throw (Ex 9.10 of ashes; 24.6 and often of blood). (35) *ḤṬ'* (§ 60, No. 3), Stem III: ^{J}cleanse—^{R}offer a sin offering for (Ex 29.36, of the altar). Cp No. 6. (36) *mōqdāh:* ^{J}burning—^{R}hearth. (37) *ZKR,* Stem V: ^{J}to bring to remembrance—^{R}for the memorial offering (titles of Ps 38; 70). (38) *'azkārāh:* ^{J}memorial—^{R}memorial portion. (39) *hlīkāh:* ^{J}goings—^{R}solemn processions, processions (Ps 68.24). (40) *ʿSR:* ^{JR}give the tenth, take the tenth, tithe; cp ^{J}tithing—^{R}paying (Deut 26.12). (41) *maʿsēr:* ^{JR}tenth, tithe; ^{J}tenth part. (42) *neder:* ^{JR}vow; ^{R}votive offering.

§ 69 In the Psalms, and especially in their titles, several obscure terms are used. Some but not all of them are now better understood than they were three centuries ago. (1) *selāh* (used 70 times in Ps, also Hab 3.3, 9, 13; meaning unknown): R, like J, simply transliterates, "Selah," but italicizes it and separates it from the line after which it occurs, since it is clearly not a part of the text but some kind of liturgical rubric or "stage direction." So also (2) *higgāyōn,* which accompanies *šelāh* at the end of Ps 9.16: [J]Higgaion [That is, *Meditation*]—[R]Higgaion; cp 92.3, [J]with a solemn sound [Or, *upon the solemn sound* . . . Heb. *Higgaion*]—[R]to the melody of.

The titles of the psalms also do not belong to the text itself, but they are included in translations because they are in the Hebrew manuscripts and are undoubtedly very ancient. Some of the terms used in them can only be transliterated, since there are no equivalent English words. For their meaning much depends upon the particular senses in which the accompanying prepositions are used (see §§ 82ff).

Some of these terms designate forms or types of composition.

(3) *maskīl* (lit. wise or making wise): [J]Maschil [Or, A Psalm *giving instruction*]—[R]A Maskil; cp 47.7, [J]with understanding [Or, every one *that hath understanding*]—[R]with a psalm [Heb *Maskil*]. (4) *miktām:* [J]Michtam—[R]A Miktam. (5) *šiggāyōn:* [J]Shiggaion—[R]A Shiggaion (cp No. 23).

(6) *mizmōr:* [JR]psalm. (7) šīr: [JR]song. (8) *šīr ma'lōt:* [J]a song of degrees—[R]a Song of Ascents (Ps 120–134, referring probably to the "going up" of pilgrims to Jerusalem). (9) *tpillāh:* [JR]prayer. (10) *llammēd:* [J]to teach—[R]for instruction. (11) *lamnaṣṣēḥ* (cp § 66, No. 3): [J]To the chief Musician—[R]To the choirmaster (often; in Ps 4 J mg adds, Or, *overseer*); cp Hab 3.19, [J]To the chief singer—[R]To the choirmaster. (12) *liydūtūn:* [JR]to Jeduthun (Ps 39); cp [J]to Jeduthun—[R]according to Jeduthun (Ps 62, 77).

Some expressions in psalm titles are apparently the names of tunes to which the psalms were sung, possibly the first words of familiar secular songs sung to the same tunes.

(13) *'ayyelet haššaḥar:* [J]Aijeleth Shahar [Or, *the hind of the morning*]—[R]The Hind of the Dawn (Ps 22). (14) *yōnat 'ēlem rḥōqīm:* [J]Jonathelemrechokim—[R]The Dove on Far-off Terebinths (Ps 56, cp § 72, No. 13). (15) *šōšannīm:* [J]Shoshannim—[R]Lilies (Ps 45; 69; 80; cp No. 21). Each of these expressions is preceded by the preposition *'al* (§ 86, No. 1), which J translates "upon"; R renders it here "according to," thus suggesting but not necessarily implying that what follows is the name of the tune. Cp (16) *'al-tašḥēt:* [J]*Altaschith* [Or, *Destroy not*]—[R]according to Do Not Destroy (Ps 57–9; 75—here R inserts "according to"; *'al,*

cp § 92, No. 3, is a negative particle). So too with several expressions which both J and R transliterate, because their meaning is unknown or at best uncertain: (17) *šmīnīt* (Ps 6; 12; 1 Chron 15.21); (18) *gittīt* (Ps 8; 81; 84); (19) *'almūt labbēn* (Ps 9; cp No. 20); (20) *'lāmōt* (Ps 46; 1 Chron 15.20; cp No. 19 and see § 75); (21) *šūšan 'ēdūt* (Ps 60; cp No. 15); (22) *moḥlat (l'annōt)* (Ps 53; 88); (23) *šigyōnōt* (Hab 3.1; cp No. 5).

§ 70 Still other terms indicate the musical instruments used to accompany the psalms. The prepositions used in such cases are usually different from the one noted in the preceding paragraph.

(1) *ngīnāh.* With *b-* (§ 82, No. 2), *bingīnōt:* [J]on Neginoth—[R]with stringed instruments (Ps 4; 6; 54f; 67; 76); cp *bingīnōtay:* [J]on my stringed instruments [Heb. *Neginoth*]—[R]with stringed [Heb *my stringed*] instruments (Hab 3.19); *ngīnōtay:* [J]my songs to the stringed instruments—[R]to stringed instruments [Heb *my stringed instruments*] (Is 38.20). (2) *nḥīlāh.* With *'el* (§ 82, No. 1), *'el-hannḥīlōt:* [J]upon Nehiloth—[R]for the flutes (Ps 5). An exception, using *'al,* is Ps 92.3 (see § 86, No. 1).

Other musical instruments are often mentioned both in Ps and in other parts of the OT. Several of them can now be identified more accurately than was possible when J was made, though R itself is not entirely consistent in two or three instances. The Hebrews' instruments, of course, did not always correspond exactly to ours; any English word may therefore be somewhat misleading.

(3) *kinnōr:* [J]harp—[R]lyre (33 times; cp Ps 150.3; Is 23.16, [JR]harp). (4) *nēbel:* [J]psaltery—[R]harp (often), lute (Ps 150.3); [J]viol—[R]harp (Is 5.12; 14.11; Amos 5.23; 6.5). (5) *'āsōr:* [J]instrument of ten strings—[R]harp of ten strings (Ps 33.2), lute (92.3). With No. 4: [J]upon a psaltery and an instrument of ten strings—[R]Upon a ten-stringed harp (Ps 144.9). (6) *šālīš:* [J]instruments of musick [Heb. *three-stringed instruments*]—[R]instruments of music [Heb *triangles,* or *three-stringed instruments*]. (7) *mēn:* [J]whereby—[R]stringed instruments (Ps 45.8); [J]stringed instruments—[R]strings (150.4).

(8) *'ūgab:* [J]organ—[R]pipe. (9) *ḥalīl:* [J]pipe—[R]flute. Cp (10) *neqeb:* [J]pipes—[R]engravings [Heb *uncertain*] (Ezek 28.13). (11) *šōpar:* [JR]trumpet; [J]cornet; [R]horn, trumpet blast. (12) *mna'na':* [J]cornet—[R]castanet.

J and R agree in the translation of two Hebrew words for "cymbals," and differ only in the choice of English words for another percussion instrument,

(13) *tōp:* [JR]timbrel; [J]tabret; [R]tambourine. Cp (14) *tōpet:* [J]a tabret—[R]men spit (Job 17.6, lit. a spitting). Note also (15) *šiddah:* [J]musical instruments, and that of all sorts [Heb. *musical instruments and instruments*]—[R]many concubines [The meaning of the Hebrew word is uncertain] (Eccles 2.8).

In addition to these Hebrew terms there are the Aramaic words in Dan 3.5, 7, 10, 15.

(16) *qeren:* [J]cornet—[R]horn. (17) *mašroqī:* [J]flute—[R]pipe (18) *qīytrōs̀:* [J]harp—[R]lyre. (19) *sabkā', s̀abkā':* [J]sackbut—[R]trigon. (20) *ps̀antērīn:* [J]psaltery—[R]harp. (21) *s̀ūmpōnyāh:* [J]dulcimer [Or, *singing*. Chald. *symphony*]—[R]bagpipe. Note also (22) *daḥwān:* [J]instruments of music [Or, *table*]—[R]diversions (6.18).

Chapter XVII

GEOGRAPHICAL AND BIOLOGICAL TERMS

§71 The meanings of Hebrew geographical terms have been considerably clarified by comparison with corresponding words in the cognate languages (§§ 38f) and by intensive study of the geography of Palestine and neighboring lands. There is much overlapping of meaning among them, however, so that the same English words may often be used for several Hebrew words. In general J and R use much the same words for each Hebrew term, but they frequently do not use the same words in the same places. Only occasionally is there a real difference of interpretation.

(1) For example, Hebrew and Aramaic, like many other languages, have words which may mean earth, ground, land, country, or world (*'ereṣ, 'dāmāh,* etc.). The question for the translator is just what is meant in each place where one of these words occurs. Only the context can tell in many instances which of the possible meanings is intended. Another example is (2) *ŝādeh* (JRusually "field," but used often for open and even wild country): Jcountry; Restate, forest, land, mainland, open, open country, region, soil. Note also (3) *gā'ōn,* used in a special sense in connection with the Jordan River; Jpride, swelling; Rjungle.

The word "city," for (4) *'īr,* is usually kept by R, but is changed to "town" 33 times because the places to which it is applied were not what we now call cities. In Jer 15.8 J mistakes for this word another, spelled and pronounced the same, which means anguish: paraphrasing the supposed meaning, "city and terrors," J reads "terrors upon the city"; R "anguish and terror."

Two geographical terms used often in the OT are especially

confusing. One is (5) *'ī,* translated "country" by J once, elsewhere "island" or "isle." R keeps "island" once and "isle" four times; usually, however, the word refers to coastal regions, and R renders it "coast," "coastland," or "land." In three places what appears to be this noun is actually the name of a wild animal (§ 73, No. 13). In Job 22.30 still another word, spelled and pronounced just like these two but meaning "not," has produced a curious mistranslation in J, "the island of the innocent," which means nothing in the context. Following the Versions, R omits the word and reads "the innocent man" (see § 140).

The other term referred to has caused confusion because of the range of meanings it covers. It is (6) *gbūl,* which means primarily a boundary or limit or a circumscribed area. It has many renderings: [JR]border, bound, coast, place; [J]limit, quarter; [R]area, barrier, boundary, coast-line, country, extent, frontier, land, landmark, region, rim, territory, wall.

(7) In addition to their standard terms for what we call the cardinal points of the compass, the Hebrews had other ways of indicating directions. One was to designate them in relation to a person facing east; e.g., [J]on the left hand of Damascus—[R]north of Damascus (Gen 14.15); [J]on the right hand—[R]southward (Josh 17.7); [J]before . . . behind—[R]on the east . . . on the west (Is 9.12). Since the Mediterranean Sea lies west of Palestine, it was sometimes mentioned to indicate the west; e.g., [J]from the sea—[R]from the west (Is 24.14); [J]toward the sea—[R]westward (Josh 19.11). So JR understand the Hebrew word for "sea" in Ezek 41.12, but cp Deut 33.23, [J]the west—[R]the lake (meaning here the Sea of Galilee). In Job 37.9 J erroneously interprets two expressions as indicating direction: [J]Out of the south [Heb. *Out of the chamber*]—[R]From its chamber; [J]out of the north [Heb. *scattering* winds]—[R]from the scattering winds.

§ 72 In its identifications of plants and animals J was dependent on traditional interpretations, many of which were erroneous and have been corrected by R, though scholars are not even now agreed on all points. The extent of improvement in this matter can be seen from the following changes in the identification of trees:

(1) *t'aššūr:* [J]box—[R]pine. (2) *šemen* (cp § 68, No. 26): [J]oil tree, pine—[R]olive, wild olive. (3) *tidhar:* [J]pine—[R]plane. (4) *brōt:* [J]fir—[R]pine. (5) *brōš:* [J]fir—[R]cypress. (6) *tirzah:* [J]cypress—[R]holm. (7) *rō'š:* [J]hemlock—[R]poisonous weeds. (8) *la'nāh:* [J]hemlock—[R]wormwood (so usually J). (9) *bākā':* [J]mulberry—[R]balsam. (10) *'armōn:* [J]chestnut—[R]plane. (11) *lūz:* [J]hazel—[R]almond. (12) *'ēlāh:* [J]elm, teil—[R]terebinth. (13) *'ayil:* [J]grove, tree—[R]tamarisk tree, oak. (14) *'ēšel:* [J]tree—[R]tamarisk tree. (15) *tōmer:* [J]palm tree—[R]scarecrows. (16) *ṣe'el:* [J]shady tree—[R]lotus plant, lotus tree. (17) *šiṭṭāh:* [J]shittah, shittim—[R]acacia.

Similar differences appear in the names of shrubs and other plants or parts of plants, or what either J or R undertands as such:

(18) *gōme':* [J]bulrush, rush—[R]papyrus. (19) *'ārāh:* [J]paper reed—[R]bare place. (20) *kōper:* [J]camphire [Or, *cypress*]—[R]henna blossoms, henna. (21) *qeṣaḥ:* [J]fitches—[R]dill. (22) *kuššemet:* [J]fitches [Or, *spelt*], rie—[R]spelt. (23) *qīqāyōn:* [J]gourd [Or, *palm-crist.* Heb. *Kikajon*]—[R]plant [Heb *qiqayon,* probably the castor oil plant]. (24) *'eseb:* [JR]grass, herb; [R]herbage, plant, vegetation. (25) *deše':* [JR]grass; [J]tender grass, herb; [R]new growth, vegetation. (26) *'ōr:* [J]upon herbs [Or, *after rain*]—[R]in sunshine (Is 18.4, lit. on light). (27) *'ōrāh:* [J]herbs—[R]light. (28) *'ar'ār:* [J]heath—[R]shrub. (29) *nahlōl:* [J]bushes [Or, *commendable trees*]—[R]pastures. (30) *rōtem:* [J]juniper—[R]broom, broom tree. (31) *ḥbaṣṣelet:* [J]rose—[R]crocus; cp Song 2.1, [J]rose—[R]rose [Heb *crocus*] (an example of R's reluctance to change expressions that have become a part of our language).

Note also the following: (32) *maṭṭā':* [J]plant—[R]plantation, place of planting. (33) *neṭa':* [J]plant—[R]planting; cp Is 17.11, [J]thy plant—[R]that you plant them. (34) *sārūq:* [J]principal plant—[R]branch. (35) *štil* and (36) *šelaḥ:* [J]plant—[R]shoot. (37) *salšillāh:* [J]basket—[R]branch. (38) *nṭīšāh:* [J]battlement, plant—[R]branch. (39) *šōkah:* [J]bough—[R]bundle. (40) *'āleh:* [J]branch—[R]green leaf. (41) *yōneqet:* [J]branch—[R]shoots (Job 8.16); [J]tender branch—[R]shoots (14.7); [J]branches—[R]shoots (Job 15.30; Ps 80.11; Hos 14.6); [JR]young twigs (Ezek 17.22). (42) *nēṣer:* [J]BRANCH—[R]branch (Is 11.1). In Jer 23.5; 33.15; Zech 3.8; 6.12; Dan 11.7 the Hebrew has another noun, *ṣemaḥ*). (43) *'ēb:* [J]fruit—[R]blossom. (44) *šāqām:* [J]sycamore fruit [Or, *wild figs*]—[R]sycamore trees (Amos 7.14; so J elsewhere). (45) *bikkūr:* [J]hasty fruit—[R]first-ripe fig.

An especially significant change is (46) *geza':* [J]stem—[R]stump (Is 11.1). The importance of this word here lies in its implication that the Davidic monarchy has been cut off. Cp 40.24, ^{J}stock—^{R}stem.

§ 73 Modern research has clarified many names of animals, birds, reptiles, and insects mentioned in the OT. Among domestic animals the following may be noted:

(1) *par:* ^{J}bullock, ox—^{R}bull (especially with reference to sacrifice, for which a castrated animal was not acceptable; but cp Is 34.7, ^{J}bullock—^{R}young steer). (2) *šōr:* ^{J}bullock—^{R}bull, ox, herd; ^{J}oxen—^{R}cattle. (3) *'abbīr* (lit. strong; § 47, No. 3; cp *'ābīr,* § 43, No. 5): ^{JR}bull; ^{J}mighty one, strong one, valiant man; ^{R}mighty bull, stallion, steed. (4) *pārāš:* ^{J}horseman—^{R}war horse. (5) *rekeš:* ^{J}mule—^{R}swift horse; ^{J}swift beast—^{R}steed. (6) *yēm:* ^{J}mules—^{R}hot springs (Gen 36.24). (7) *'ḥaštrān:* ^{J}camels—^{R}that were used in the king's service (Esther 8.10, 14). (8) *rammāk:* ^{J}young dromedaries—^{R}bred from the royal stud (v. 10). (9) *beker, bikrah:* ^{J}dromedary—^{R}young camel. (10) *karkārāh:* ^{J}swift beast—^{R}dromedary.

The following are a few of the terms applied to wild animals:

(11) *ḥayyāh:* ^{J}beast—^{R}living creature, living thing, wild beast. With *sādeh* (§ 71, No. 2): ^{JR}beast of the field, wild beast; ^{R}wild animal. (12) *zīz,* with *sādeh* (cp No. 11): ^{J}wild beast of the field—^{R}all that moves in the field. (13) *'ī* (cp § 71, No. 5): ^{J}wild beast of the island—^{R}hyena, jackal. (14) *tannīn* (§ 46, No. 9): ^{J}dragon—^{R}jackal, monster, sea monster, serpent; ^{J}sea monsters [Or, *sea calves*]—^{R}jackals; ^{J}whale—^{R}sea monster; ^{J}whale [Or, *dragon*]—^{R}dragon. (15) *t'ō, tō':* ^{J}wild bull, wild ox—^{R}antelope. (16) *r'ēm:* ^{J}unicorn—^{R}wild ox.

Several new identifications of birds appear in the parallel lists of "unclean" birds in Lev 11.13–19 and Deut 14.12–18, and in other places where the same words occur.

(17) *nešer:* ^{JR}eagle, but R sometimes vulture. (18) *pereṡ:* in Lev ^{JR}ossifrage; in Deut ^{J}ossifrage—^{R}vulture. (19) *dā'āh:* ^{J}vulture—^{R}kite. (20) *rā'āh:* ^{J}glede—^{R}buzzard (omitted by Lev; possibly confused in copying with No. 19, which Deut omits). (21) *'ayyāh:* in Deut ^{JR}kite; in Lev ^{J}kite—^{R}falcon; cp Job 28.7, ^{J}vulture—^{R}falcon. (22) *dayyāh:* Lev omits; in Deut ^{J}vulture, R omits with 5 Hebrew manuscripts (probably=No. 19); cp Is 34.15, ^{J}vultures—^{R}kites. (23) *bat ya'nāh:* ^{J}owl—^{R}ostrich (J mg in 2 places, Or, *ostriches;* also twice Heb. *daughters of the owl*). (24) *šaḥap:* ^{J}cuckow—^{R}sea gull. (25) *yanšūp:* Deut ^{JR}great

owl; Lev [J]great owl—[R]ibis. (26) *tanšemet:* [J]swan—[R]water hen (cp No. 35). (27) *qā'at:* [JR]pelican; cp [J]pelican—[R]vulture [The meaning of the Hebrew word is uncertain] (Ps 102.6); [J]cormorant—[R]vulture [same note] (Zeph 2.14); [J]cormorant—[R]hawk (Is 34.11). (28) *rāḥām:* [J]gier eagle—[R]vulture (Lev), carrion vulture (Deut). (29) *ḥsīdāh:* [JR]stork; cp [J]ostrich —[R]love [Heb obscure] (Job 39.13). (30) *dūkīpat:* [J]lapwing—[R]hoopoe.

Reptiles and insects, being both sometimes designated by such names as "creeping things," cannot always be easily distinguished. Like the unclean birds, the unclean "swarming things" in Lev 11.29f have some new identifications in R.

(31) *ṣāb:* [J]tortoise—[R]great lizard. (32) *'nāqāh:* [J]ferret—[R]gecko. (33) *kōaḥ:* [J]chameleon—[R]land-crocodile. (34) *ḥōmeṭ:* [J]snail—[R]sand-lizard. (35) *tanšemet:* [J]mole—[R]chameleon (cp No. 26).

Note also (36) *smāmīt:* [J]spider—[R]lizard. (37) *'akšūb:* [J]adder—[R]viper. (38) *ṣepa'* and (39) *ṣip'ōnī:* [J]cockatrice [Or, *adder*]—[R]adder. (40) *sārāp m'ōpēp:* [J]fiery flying serpent—[R]flying serpent (Is 30.6; cp Num 21.6–9, *sārāp* and *nāḥāš sārāp,* [JR]fiery serpent; Is 6.2, 6, *sārāp,* [JR]seraph, § 47, No. 5). (41) *ḥargōl:* [J]beetle—[R]cricket. (42) *'luqāh:* [J]horseleach—[R]leech [The meaning of the Hebrew word is uncertain] (Prov 30.15). (43) *kēn:* [J]lice—[R]gnats; cp Is 51.6, [J]in like manner—[R]like gnats [Or *in like manner*] (J and R mg take the word here as the adverb *kēn,* "so"). (44) *qereṣ:* [J]destruction—[R]gadfly.

In Joel 1.4 and other places where the same words occur the translator's vocabulary is taxed by the characteristically Semitic profusion of names for the locust, representing probably different phases of its life-cycle. J and R meet the problem in somewhat different ways.

(45) *gāzām:* [J]palmerworm—[R]cutting locust, cutter, locust. (46) *'arbeh:* [J]locust, grasshopper—[R]swarming locust, locust, grasshopper. (47) *yeleq:* [J]cankerworm, caterpiller—[R]hopping locust, hopper, locust, young locust. (48) *ḥāsīl:* [J]caterpiller—[R]destroying locust, destroyer. Cp (49) *gōb:* [J]grasshopper—[R]locust. (50) *'ōkēl* (participle of *'KL,* eat): [J]devourer—[R]devourer [Or *devouring locust*].

Chapter XVIII

MISCELLANEOUS WORDS

§74 Many other categories of terms used in the OT might be presented in the same way as those treated in the foregoing chapters. Social relations and institutions, ranks and titles, minerals and metals, clothing and ornaments, colors, commerce, weights and measures, the calendar, money, vessels and implements, tools and weapons, vehicles, animal husbandry, and architecture are all subjects dealt with more or less directly in words involving innumerable questions of interpretation. Limitations of space, however, preclude discussion of these matters, though they may be no less important than some of those already covered. Only a few selected items, which can hardly be classified except as miscellaneous, can be mentioned in this chapter. For the rest the reader must be referred to the commentaries and dictionaries, especially IB and IBD.

Ambiguity and overlapping of meanings in both Hebrew and English words cause much difficulty. Our word "abide," for example, may mean "stay" or "endure"; the latter word, indeed, may mean either "continue to exist, last," or "bear, stand"—and these last two words also have many meanings. So the Hebrew verb (1) *YŠB* may mean either "sit" or "dwell." Only the context or comparison with similar passages can determine the exact meaning intended in a particular place. Did Deborah, for example, "dwell" (J) or "sit" (R) under the palm tree (Judg 4.5)? Cp Ezek 2.6, [J]dwell among scorpions—[R]sit upon scorpions (see §82, No. 1). Both J and R translate this verb in many ways. Its interpretation is especially important where the subject is God; e.g., [J]dwellest (or dwelleth) between the cherubims—[R]is enthroned on the cherubim (1 Sam 4.4), art enthroned upon the cherubim (Ps 80.1), art enthroned above the cherubim (2 Kings 19.15; Is 37.16), sits enthroned on the cherubim (2 Sam 6.2), sits enthroned above the cherubim (1 Chron 13.6; in all these places in the Hebrew "the cherubim" is the direct object of the verb, lit. sits or sittest the cherubim). Cp [J]abideth—[R]is enthroned (Ps 55.19; 61.7); [J]dwellest in the heavens—[R]art enthroned in the heavens (Ps 123.1); note also [J]endure—[R]art enthroned (Ps 102.12), [J]sit enthroned—[R]sits enthroned (9.7); [J]inhabitest—[R]enthroned on (22.3).

A noun of broad meaning is (2) *ḥayil:*

[JR]riches; [J]forces, power, strength, substance; [R]full yield, goods, profit, wealth; cp [J]do thou worthily [Or, *get thee riches,* or, power]—[R]may you prosper (Ruth 4.11). In combinations, (a) *'īš ḥayil:* [JR]able man, valiant man; [J]man of activity, man of might, man of strength, strong man; [R]mighty man, man of war, soldier. (b) *'ēšet ḥayil:* [J]virtuous woman—[R]woman of worth, good wife. (c) *ben ḥayil:* [JR]man of valour (R valor): [J]strong man, valiant man; [R]able man, man of ability. (d) *gibbōr ḥayil:* [JR]mighty man of valour (R valor), mighty man of wealth; [J]valiant man, valiant man of might, mighty valiant man, mighty man of power [Or, *substance*]; [R]man of valor, mighty warrior, seasoned warrior, wealthy man. (e) *'īš gibbōr ḥayil:* [J]mighty man of valour—[R]mighty warrior.

Until fairly recently a similar confusion prevented the right understanding of a common idiom, (3) *ŠWB šbūt.* J takes *šbūt* to mean "captivity" (from *ŠBH,* take captive), and translates the verb in six ways: bring again, return, cause to return, turn, turn back, turn away. It is now widely recognized that *šbūt* in this idiom means "turning" (from *ŠWB*), so that the expression means literally "turn the turning," i.e., bring about a reversal of one's circumstances or condition; hence [R]restore the fortunes (Deut 30.3 etc., 29 times).

Conspicuous, if not startling, because the story of Joseph is so familiar, is the difference between J's and R's renderings of (4) *ktōnet paššīm:* [J]coat of many colours [Or, *pieces*]—[R]long robe with sleeves (Gen 37.3, and without J's note vv. 23, 32); [J]garment of divers colours—[R]long robe with sleeves (2 Sam 13.18), long robe (v. 19; in early printings of R, long-sleeved robe). The word *paš* (plural *paššīm*) occurs only in these places. Many scholars now understand it to mean the palms of the hands and soles of the feet, from a root meaning "flat." The whole expression thus means literally "robe of palms and soles," i.e., reaching to the hands and feet.

Inevitably rather distressing is the change (following EA) in the rendering of (5) *hadrat-qōdeš:* [J]the beauty of holiness—[R]holy array (1 Chron 16.29; 2 Chron 20.21; Ps 29.2). It is hard to lose from our Bible an expression which has become a part of the familiar language of prayer and praise, but the translator can consider only what the Hebrew really means. The first noun, with the single exception of Prov 14.28, is used only in this expression. It means adornment, i.e., the sacred vestments of the temple worship. The other noun is here an "adjectival genitive"; J too renders it holy in many places (e.g., Ex 3.5, holy ground, lit. ground of holiness; see § 101, No. 3).

§ 75 Of all the changes introduced by R, the one which has aroused most criticism, resentment, and even slander and attempted suppression, is the change from "virgin" to "young woman" in Is 7.14. The facts concerning this change must therefore be reviewed in some detail, though of course without any attempt to discuss all their possible implications or explanations. Many problems of interpretation are involved in this verse and the rest of the chapter. Just what the sign was that was given to King Ahaz in 735 B.C. and just how it was fulfilled in the birth of Christ (Mt 1.22f) are questions on which commentators may never entirely agree. They are not, however, questions of translation. The only question before us here is what the word *'almāh* means, and not what it has been taken to mean or what we want it to mean.

The word "virgin" is used by J to translate two Hebrew nouns, one of them 38 times and the other four times. The former, *btūlāh,* is translated as follows in various connections:

[J]maid—[R]maiden (Jer 51.22; Ezek 9.6; Zech 9.17), virgin (Ex 22.16; Job 31.1; Lam 5.11); [J]virgin—[R]maiden (1 Kings 1.2; Jer 31.13; Lam 1.4, 18; 2.10, 21); [JR]virgin (Gen 24.16; Ex 22.17; Lev 21.3, 14; Deut 22.19, 23, 28; 32.25; Judg 21.12; 2 Sam 13.2, 18; 2 Kings 19.21; Esther 2.3, 17, 19; Ps 45.14; Is 23.4, 12; 37.22; 47.1; 62.5; Jer 14.17; 18.13;

31.4, 21; 46.11; Lam 1.15; 2.13; Joel 1.8; Amos 5.2; 8.13). There is a related abstract noun, *btūlīm:* [JR]virginity (Lev 21.13); [J]I found her not a maid—[R]I did not find in her the tokens of virginity (Deut 22.14; cp vv. 15, 17, 20, [JR]tokens of virginity).

Quite clearly *btūlāh* means virgin.

The noun used in Is 7.14 is (2) *'almāh;* cp Gen 24.43, [J]virgin—[R]young woman; Song 1.3; 6.8, [J]virgins—[R]maidens. Elsewhere we have the following renderings: [J]damsels—[R]maidens (Ps 68.25); [J]maid—[R]girl (Ex 2.8), maiden (Prov 30.19). The word *'lāmōt,* left untranslated by JR in the title of Ps 46 and in 1 Chron 15.20 (§ 69, No. 20), may be the plural of *'almāh,* quoted from the beginning of a song to whose tune the psalm was sung, but this is not certain; cp *'almūt* ([R]according to Muth–) in the title of Ps 9 (§ 69, No. 19), which possibly should be read *'lāmōt.*

The masculine form *'elem* occurs twice in the OT: [JR]stripling (1 Sam 17.56); [J]young man—[R]youth (20.22). There is also an abstract noun, *'lūmīm:* [JR]youth (Ps 89.45; Is 54.4); [J]youth—[R]youthful vigor (Job 20.11; 33.25). Masculine and feminine nouns from the same root, meaning respectively "young man" and "young woman," are found in cognate languages (Ugaritic, Phoenician, Aramaic, and Arabic).

From all these facts it is clear that *'almāh* refers to the fresh maturity and strength of youth, with no implication as to sexual experience one way or the other. Why the Septuagint, which is quoted in Mt 1.23, translates it "virgin" (*parthenos*) here and in Gen 24.43, but "young woman" (*neanis*) in Ex 2.8; Ps 68.25; Song 1.3; 6.8, and "youth" (*neotēs*) in Prov 30.19, is a question into which we cannot go here.[1] The Standard Bible Committee, considering only the meaning of the Hebrew word in Is 7.14, could not honestly translate it as anything else than "young woman." The footnote, "Or virgin," was added, not to indicate that this might be the meaning, but because it was felt that in view of the use of this verse in the New Testament the traditional interpretation should in some way be recognized. (For JR "a" instead of "the" see § 91.)

[1] In Gen 34.3 the Septuagint uses *parthenos* for Dinah after the loss of her virginity (Hebrew *na'rā,* [J]damsel, [R]maiden).

§ 76 Four other important and rather difficult words must be noted briefly. One with a wide range of meaning is (1) *šālōm,* which means primarily "wholeness." In this case J and R do not differ in their understanding of the possible meanings of the word, but they sometimes interpret it differently in particular connections:

[JR]peace, prosperity, welfare; [J]rest; [R]health, safety, weal; note also [J]an answer of peace—[R]a favorable answer (Gen 41.16); [J]counsellors of peace—[R]those who plan good (Prov 12.20); [J]such as be at peace with him—[R]his friends (Ps 55.20); [J]the men that were at peace with thee—[R]your confederates (Obad 1.7); [J]there is peace to thee—[R]it is safe for you (1 Sam 20.21); [J]Is he well?—[R]Is it well with him? (Gen 29.6); [J]He is well—[R]It is well (same v.); [J]All is well [Or, *Peace* be to thee. Heb. *Peace*]—[R]All is well (2 Sam 18.28); [J]Is . . . safe? [Heb. Is there *peace?*]—[R]Is it well with . . . ? (vv. 29, 32); [J]Art thou in health?—[R]Is it well with you? (2 Sam 20.9); [J]Ye shall have peace—[R]It shall be well with you (Jer 4.10; 23.17); [J]to enquire of his welfare—[R]to greet him (1 Chron 18.10); [J]saluted him [Heb. *asked him of peace*]—[R]asked him of his welfare (Judg 18.15); [J]to salute [Heb. *to the peace of &c*]—[R]to visit (2 Kings 10.13); [J]the land of peace—[R]a safe land (Jer 12.5); [J]return in peace—[R]return victorious (Judg 11.31); [J]the chastisement of our peace—[R]the chastisement that made us whole (Is 53.5); [J]the seed shall be prosperous [Heb. *of peace*]—[R]there shall be a sowing of peace (Zech 8.12).

One of the most characteristic Hebrew words in the OT is (2) *'ōlām* (primarily an indefinite but very long time, past or future; hence remote antiquity or the remote future):

[JR]ancient, eternal, eternity, for ever, everlasting, of old, perpetual; [J]ever, of old time, from of old; [R]all future, long ago, of long ago, never-ending, primeval. Also in various phrases and combinations; e.g., [J]he shall serve him for ever—[R]he shall serve him for life (Ex 21.6); [J]his long home—[R]his eternal home (Eccles 12.5).

In later Hebrew *'ōlām* came to mean "world" or "universe"; J assumes this meaning in a few places in the OT:

[J]in the world—[R]always (Ps 73.12); [J]he hath set the world in their heart—[R]he has put eternity into man's mind (Eccles 3.11); [J]since the beginning of the world—[R]From of old (Is 64.4); [J]world without end—[R]to all eternity (Is 45.17).

§77 Among the most meaningful and at the same time difficult words of the OT is *ḥeseḏ,* translated by J in a dozen ways but most often as kindness (40 times), lovingkindness (30 times), or mercy (120 times). Recent studies have shown that none of these renderings conveys the basic meaning of the word, which is "fidelity to the requirements of a particular personal relationship, a loyal devotion grounded in love which goes beyond legal obligation and can be depended upon to the utmost" (*Introd RSVOT,* p. 61). It is not a feeling or a general attitude, but something that is "done": the verb most frequently used with *ḥeseḏ* is *'SH* (do, make, etc.).

After much study and discussion, the Standard Bible Committee decided that no one English noun could do justice to this word. For the *ḥeseḏ* of God the expression "steadfast love" was adopted as the principal rendering (cp J's occasional use of "tender mercies" or "tender love" for *raḥmīm,* the word usually translated "mercy" or "compassion").

Thus, to cite only a few examples, R reads steadfast love instead of favour (Job 10.12), goodness (Ps 33.5; 107.8, 15, 21, 31), kindness (Gen 24.12; Is 54.10; Joel 2.13; Jon 4.2), merciful kindness (Ps 117.2; 119.76), lovingkindness (Ps 63.3; Hos 2.19), lovingkindnesses (Ps 25.6; Is 63.7 twice), mercy (Gen 39.21; Ex 15.13; 34.7; Num 14.18f; 1 Kings 3.6; 2 Chron 1.8), mercies (Lam 3.22, 32; cp Is 55.3, [J]the sure mercies of David—[R]my steadfast, sure love for David). Cp Ruth 2.20, [JR]kindness (probably of God though possibly of Boaz); Jer 9.24, [J]lovingkindness—[R]steadfast love; 31.3, [J]lovingkindness—[R]faithfulness; Gen 19.19, [J]mercy—[R]kindness (addressed to angels); Job 37.13, [J]mercy—[R]love.

Only in Ps 23.6 does R keep "mercy" for *ḥeseḏ,* an example of conservatism in a familiar passage. In Ruth 1.8 the combination *'SH ḥeseḏ* is rendered "deal kindly" by both J and R.

With reference to man's *ḥeseḏ* toward God or man "steadfast love" is rarely used;

note, however, Hos 6.6, [J]mercy—[R]steadfast love (what God demands, cp the parallel, knowledge of God; but perhaps referring to right human relations, and clearly so understood when translated "mercy" by J, following the Greek, cp Mt 9.13; 12.7; note also Hos 10.12, [J]mercy—[R]steadfast love, presumably of man's *ḥesed,* parallel "righteousness"). Cp Hos 6.4, [J]your goodness [Or, *mercy,* or, *kindness*]—[R]your love (i.e., Ephraim's, which is not steadfast but should be); Jer 2.2, [J]kindness—[R]devotion (i.e., Israel's as a bride); Jon 2.8, [J]mercy—[R]true loyalty (contrasted with idolatry).

For man's *ḥesed* to man the following examples may be noted:

[J]favour—[R]favor (Dan 1.9); [J]goodness [Or, *bounty*]—[R]loyalty (Prov 20.6); [J]kindness—[R]loyalty (1 Sam 20.15; 2 Sam 16.17; Prov 19.22; cp Ps 141.5; Prov 31.26, [JR]kindness); [J]shew kindness—[R]show kindness (2 Sam 9.1, 3, 7), do me the kindness (Gen 20.13; 40.14), show loyal love (1 Sam 20.14, "of the LORD" but to be shown by David), deal loyally (2 Sam 10.2 twice, 1 Kings 2.7; 1 Chron 19.2 twice), keep showing loyalty (2 Sam 3.8); cp [J]shewed more kindness in the latter end—[R]made this last kindness greater (Ru 3.10); [J]deal kindly—[R]deal loyally (Gen 24.49); [J]according to the kindness that I have done unto thee—[R]as I have dealt loyally with you (21.23); [J]merciful men—[R]devout men (Is 57.1); [J]the merciful man—[R]a man who is kind (Prov 11.17); [J]mercy—[R]kindness (Ps 109.12; Prov 21.21; Hos 4.1; Mic 6.8; Zech 7.9), loyalty (Ps 101.1), love (Hos 12.6); [J]pity—[R]kindness (Job 6.14); [J]goodliness—[R]beauty (of "all flesh," i.e., humanity, Is 40.6); [J]goodness [Heb. *kindnesses*]—[R]good deeds (2 Chron 32.32).

§78 Another common word, often combined with *ḥesed* (see below), is *'met.* J most often translates it "truth," but primarily it means truth only in the sense of being true to a person or group, or to a commitment or responsibility; hence R usually changes to "faithfulness" (20 times, Gen 24.27 to Zech 8.8).

Cp [J]truth—[R]faithful (2 Chron 31.20), true (Mal 2.6), trustworthy (Ex 18.21; cp Neh 7.2, [JR]faithful); [J]in truth—[R]in good faith (Judg 9.15), faithfully (Is 61.8), a sure oath (Ps 132.11); [J]unto truth—[R]faithfully (Is 42.3); [J]in the truth of thy salvation—[R]With thy faithful help (Ps 69.13); [J]keepeth truth—[R]keeps faith (Ps 146.6); [J]truth—[R]true (Ps 119.142, 151; Is 43.9); [J]true—[R]truth (Ps 119.160); [J]faithfully—[R]with equity (Prov 29.14); [JR]the right way (Gen 24.48); [J]right seed—[R]pure seed (Jer 2.21); [J]truly—[R]in good faith (Judg 9.16, 19). Note also [J]establishment—[R]acts of faithfulness (2 Chron 32.1); [J]truth—[R]security (Is 39.8; Jer 33.6); [J]verity—[R]faithful (Ps 111.7).

As mentioned above, *ḥesed* and *'met* are often combined. Note the following renderings:

[J]kindly and truly—[R]loyally and truly (Gen 47.29); also [J]goodness and truth (Ex 34.6), kindness and truth (2 Sam 2.6), lovingkindness and truth (Ps 40.10f; 138.2), mercy and truth (Gen 24.27; Ps 25.10 and often); [R]loyalty and faithfulness (Prov 3.3; 14.22; 16.6; 20.28), steadfast love and faithfulness (Gen 24.27; Ps 25.10 etc.).

Chapter XIX

CONJUNCTIONS

§79 Translation is concerned not only with verbs, nouns, adjectives, and adverbs, but also with such minor parts of speech as conjunctions and prepositions, pronouns, and particles. Turning first to the conjunctions, we note at once that Hebrew does not have such an abundance of conjunctions as we have in English, but makes a few do duty for many meanings. Every reader of the Bible is familiar with its (from our point of view) excessive use of "and." In Hebrew this is quite normal and idiomatic; in fact, the conjunction so translated, *w-*, occurs much more frequently than one might infer from any but the most literalistic English translation.

To express the variety of ways in which this Hebrew conjunction is used both J and R use a number of different English conjunctions, frequently differing in their choice of the ones used in particular places:

[JR]again, also, although and though, because, but, even, for, if, now, or, seeing (that), so, so that, that, then, therefore, thus, to (with infinitive), when, with, yea, yet; [J]after, afterward, albeit, furthermore, howbeit, likewise, moreover, neither, nevertheless, notwithstanding, where, whereas, wherefor, which, who, whose; [R]and after, and as, as, both . . . and, lest, meanwhile, till, together with, whenever, while.

R goes considerably farther than J in the effort to vary the translation; in Gen 1f, e.g., we have [J]And—[R]So (1.21; 2.3); [J]And—[R]Then (1.26; 2.7); [J]And—[R]Thus (2.1). J sometimes and R much more often simply omit the conjunction, especially at the beginning of a sentence; e.g., Gen 1.2, 5, 10, 12; 2.10f, 13, 15, 20. In Gen 8.22 R drops the "and" between the successive pairs of nouns, reducing the number from seven to four. The genealogy of chapter 10 is both simplified and clarified by the omission of many "ands." Once J omits the conjunction by mistake, supposing it to be a part of the mysterious word: [J]Upharsin—[R]and Parsin (Dan 5.25; cp v. 28 Peres).

In Hebrew the conjunction is often used to connect two nouns in apposition; translating it then creates the false impression that two things or persons are referred to instead of one. J often reads "even" in such places. R sometimes follows but more often omits the conjunction; e.g., [J]the God of forces: and a god—[R]the god of fortresses . . . ; a god (Dan 11.38; both clauses refer to the same god). The most famous example of this is Zech 9.9, [J]riding upon an ass, and upon a colt—[R]riding on an ass, on a colt (cp Mt 21.5; Jn 12.15).

Equally alien to our idiom is the Hebrew use of the conjunction to introduce the final clause after a subordinate clause, with the result that it is sometimes difficult to tell where the final clause begins:

e.g., [J]And it shall come to pass, when I bring a cloud over the earth, that the bow shall be seen in the cloud: And I will remember my covenant—[R]When I bring clouds over the earth and the bow is seen in the clouds, I will remember my covenant (Gen 9.14f); [J]and the bow shall be in the cloud; and I will look upon it, that I may remember—[R]when the bow is in the clouds, I will look upon it and remember (9.16); [J]If thy brother be waxen poor, and hath sold away some of his possession, and if any of his kin come to redeem it, then shall he redeem that which his brother sold—[R]If your brother becomes poor, and sells part of his property, then his next of kin shall come and redeem what his brother has sold (Lev 25.25).

Frequently, where the Hebrew has simply a series of coordinate clauses joined by "and," the thought requires subordination of one clause to another. Sometimes J and R both do this but in different ways;

e.g., [J]When I remember these things, I pour out my soul—[R]These things I remember, as I pour out my soul (Ps 42.4, lit. These things I remember, and . . .). In Job 12.14f J has a long succession of clauses beginning with "and"; R has a series of conditional clauses, each with its final clause (cp 22.23–6). The understanding of the conjunction makes quite a difference in the interpretation of 1 Sam 17.34f, what J takes as a single incident being seen in R as one that is recurrent: [J]and there came a lion, and a bear, . . . : And I went out after him—[R]and when there came a lion, or a bear, . . . I went after him.

§ 80 An adverb which, like its English counterpart "also," is often used practically as a conjunction is (1) *gam:* [JR]also, even. R sometimes omits it;

e.g., [J]Drink, and I will give thy camels drink also—[R]drink, and I will water your camels (Gen 24.14). For other renderings cp Ps 52.5, [J]God shall likewise destroy thee—[R]But God will break you down; 95.9, [J]and saw my work—[R]though they had seen my work.

Used twice (*gam . . . gam . . .*), this word commonly means "both . . . and . . ."; but there are exceptions: e.g., [J]as Babylon hath caused . . . to fall, so at Babylon shall fall [Or, *Both Babylon* is *to fall, . . . and with Babylon, &c.*]—[R]Babylon must fall . . . , as for Babylon have fallen (Jer 51.49).

Another word for "also" is (2) *'ap,* often rendered "yea" in J, usually rendered "also" or omitted in R (see, e.g., Is 44.15f). This too is sometimes repeated; e.g., [J]yea, . . . ; yea, . . . ; yea, . . . : and—[R]Scarcely . . . , scarcely . . . , scarcely . . . , when (Is 40.24).

Also used both as adverb and as conjunction, and with a bewildering variety of meanings, is (3) *kī:*

[JR]although, because, but, even, for, if, surely, that, though, when, yet; [J]doubtless, forasmuch as, howbeit, nevertheless, therefore; [R]even though, even when, how, just as, nay, since, thus, which, yea.

The difficulty of choosing the right translation is illustrated by Ps 56.9, [J]this I know; for God is for me—[R]This I know, that [Or *because*] God is for me; cp 118.21, [J]I will praise thee: for—[R]I thank thee that. Occasionally *kī* serves, so to speak, as a quotation mark, introducing a direct quotation; e.g., [J]Thus ye speak, saying, If our transgressions—[R]Thus have you said, "Our transgressions . . ." (Ezek 33.10).

Even more ambiguous is (4) *'šer,* a connective particle which may serve either as a relative pronoun (§ 90) or as a conjunction;

e.g., [J]when the flocks came—[R]where the flocks came (Gen 30.38); [J]at Horeb, when [Or, *where*] the LORD made a covenant—[R]at Horeb, where . . . (1 Kings 8.9); [J]which went forth—[R]when they went forth (Num 33.1); [J]which overturneth them—[R]when he overturns them (Job 9.5); [J]all his days wherein—[R]all his days, because (2 Kings 12.2); [J]which have burned incense—[R]because they burned incense (Is 65.7); [J]which fear—[R]because they fear (Eccles 8.12; cp v. 13, [JR]because). Often used with prepositions, e.g., *ka'šer* (lit. according to what): [J]as—[R]when (Is 23.5); [J]as if—[R]when (51.13).

The Aramaic equivalent, (5) *dī,* is used in much the same ways and with the same ambiguity: e.g., [J]But—[R]that (Dan 2.9); [J]whereas—[R]as (vv. 41, 43).

Other words with the meaning "but" or the like are (6) *'bal,* e.g., [J]indeed—[R]No, but (Gen 17.19); [J]Verily—[R]No, for (1 Kings 1.43); (7) *'ūlām,* [J]But truly—[R]But (Mic 3.8); [J]But—[R]nevertheless (Ps 82.7); (8) *'ākēn,* [J]certainly—[R]But (Jer 8.8).

§ 81

The conjunction (1) *'im,* usually [JR]if, is sometimes rendered in other ways; e.g., [J]if—[R]when (Mic 5.8; cp Ps 94.18, [JR]When); [J]since—[R]if (Jer 23.38); [J]though—[R]If (Hab 2.3). A characteristic Hebrew idiom is the use of an if-clause in what was originally an oath-formula, but omitting the penalty; e.g., "If I do so," meaning "May I be accursed if I do so," i.e., "I certainly will not do so"; or, "If I do not," meaning "May I be accursed if I do not," i.e., "I certainly will." This idiom is not always recognized by J;

e.g., [J]if we do not so according to thy words—[R]we will surely do as you say (Judg 11.10); [J]Whereas our substance is not cut down—[R]Surely our adversaries are cut off (Job. 22.20; "adversary" is the meaning of the word rendered "substance" by J); cp (without the negative) [J]Surely the serpent will bite—[R]If the serpent bites (Eccles 10.11); [J]Surely thou wilt slay—[R]O that thou wouldst slay (Ps 139.19; lit. If thou wilt slay).

The adverb (2) *'ūlay* (perhaps) is sometimes translated by a conjunction;

e.g., [J]if so be (that)—[R]perhaps (Jer 21.2; 51.8), It may be (26.3), if it were to (Hos 8.7); cp Ezek 12.3, [J]it may be—[R]Perhaps.

The conjunction (3) *pen* (lest) sometimes idiomatically introduces a clause which has no main clause on which to depend;

e.g., [J]And lest [Or, *let not*] your heart faint—[R]Let not your heart faint (Jer 51.46); [J]Lest thou shouldest ponder—[R]she does not take heed (Prov 5.6; cp § 94); [J]Hear me, lest otherwise they should rejoice—[R]Only let them not rejoice (Ps 38.16).

The purpose and the result of actions are not so sharply distinguished in OT Hebrew as they are in English. The conjunction (4) *lma'an* (cp § 83, No. 2; actually a phrase, like our "in order that") expresses primarily purpose, but sometimes also result. In Gen 18.19 J does not recognize either meaning: [J]I know him, that he will—[R]I have chosen [Heb *known*] him, that he may (cp § 31, No. 3). In other places what J takes for an expression of purpose is seen by R as a statement of result:

e.g., [J]that thou mightest be justified—[R]so that thou are justified (Ps 51.4); [J]to the end that every one . . . may be cut off—[R]so that every man . . . will be cut off (Obad 1.9); [J]to remove you—[R]with the result that you will be removed (Jer 27.10; see also v. 15).

Other examples of conjunctions and their uses might be cited, but the foregoing will suffice to illustrate the relatively slight amount of divergence between J and R in this matter.

Chapter XX

PREPOSITIONS

§ 82 One of the hardest things to master in any language is its use of prepositions, and in this the Hebrew language reflects many ways of thinking that seem strange to the modern western mind. Again, however, it must be remembered that English as well as Hebrew prepositions may have more than one meaning: "above" and "over," for example, sometimes mean "more than" (cp "over and above"). The rendering, of course, must be in idiomatic English; it often depends also upon the context, as for example when a particular preposition is idiomatically used with a particular verb. Difference of rendering, therefore, does not always imply a difference of interpretation, but there are many places where misunderstanding is possible. The following instances show how some of the most common Hebrew prepositions are used, and how J and R sometimes differ in interpreting them:

(1) *'el* (basic meaning "to, toward," but often practically interchangeable with *'al,* § 86, No. 1):

JRagainst, at, by, for, in, into, on, over, to, toward, upon, with; Jby reason of, touching, unto; Rabout, adjoining, because of, concerning, of, opposite. Cp Ezek 2.6, Jdwell among scorpions—Rsit upon scorpions (see § 74, No. 1); 17.12, Jled them with him—Rbrought them to him (cp 26.20); Dan. 11.7, Jwith an army—Ragainst the army.

(2) *b-* (basic meaning "in," but used idiomatically in many ways):

JRagainst, among, at, because of, by, by reason of, for, in, into, of, on, over, through, under, upon, with; Jaccording to, after, before, between, concerning, for the sake of, throughout, toward, unto; Ralong, along with, amid, as, at the cost of, beside, by the help of, in accordance with, in connection with, in the midst of, in spite of, like, to the music of, to the sound of, within, worth. Cp Ex 6.3, [J]by the name of God Almighty—[R]as God Almighty; Ps 113.6, [J]to behold the things that are in heaven—[R]looks . . . upon the heavens (J fails to recognize the idiomatic use of *b-* with "see"); Is 63.1, [J]that speak in righteousness—[R]announcing vindication (idiomatic use with "speak"). For the use of *b-* with the infinitive see § 116.

(3) *blī* (without), used with a passive participle as object in Ps 19.3, [J]where their voice is not heard [Or, *without* these *their voice is heard.* Heb. *without their voice heard*]—[R]their voice is not heard (lit. without being heard is their voice).

(4) *ba'būr:* [JR]because of, for the sake of; [J]for; [R]on account of. In 1 Chron 14.2 J misses an important point: [J]his kingdom was lifted up on high, because of his people Israel—[R]his kingdom was highly exalted for the sake of his people Israel (cp 2 Sam 5.12, [J]for his people Israel's sake—[R]for the sake of his people Israel).

§ 83 (1) *l-* (to):

[JR]about, according to, against, as, at, by, concerning, for, for the sake of, in, of, on, to, upon, toward, with; [J]after, because of, beside, instead of, until, unto; [R]among, before, belonging to, on the side of, over, through.

Among the many idiomatic uses of this preposition, only a few can be noted.

(a) In psalm titles and the like:

[JR]A Psalm of David (Ps 3 etc.); [J]The writing of Hezekiah—[R]A writing of Hezekiah (Is 38.9). In these expressions "of," like the Hebrew, may mean "concerning," "belonging to," or "composed by"; but cp [J]to the chief musician—[R]To the choirmaster (Ps 4 etc.).

(b) Sometimes a phrase with *l-* is simply omitted by R where it is equivalent to an indirect object or the Latin dative of interest, advantage, or disadvantage: e.g., [J]heweth him down—[R]cuts down (Is 44.14); [J]strengtheneth for himself—[R]lets it grow strong (same v.); [J]get thee—[R]buy (Jer 13.1); [J]I bought her to me—[R]I bought her (Hos 3.2); [J]for his own behalf [Heb. *for him*] shall cause . . . to cease—[R]shall put an end to (Dan 11.18); [J]have done against themselves—[R]have done (Jer 11.17). In other places R translates the phrase; e.g., [J]for him—[R]to his advantage (Dan 11.17); [J]unto you—[R]for your profit (Ezek 13.18); [J]remember David—[R]Remember . . . in David's favor (Ps 132.1).

(c) Frequently this preposition means "belonging to," "in the possession of," or the like: e.g., [J]a shelter for me—[R]my refuge (Ps 61.3); [J]concerning Mahershalalhashbaz—[R]Belonging to Mahershalalhashbaz (Is 8.1); [J]unto the LORD—[R]the LORD's (44.5). This meaning is very common with the verb *HYH,* "be" or "become" (cp French C'est à moi, It is mine): e.g., [JR]she became my wife (Gen 20.12, lit. she became to me, i.e., became mine, for a wife); [J]This I had—[R]This blessing has fallen to me (Ps 119.56); [J]was in her and in her daughters—[R]she and her daughters had (Ezek 16.49); [J]shall also the Levites . . . have for themselves, for a possession—[R]shall be for the Levites . . . as their possession (45.5); [J]be for another man—[R]belong to another man (Hos 3.3). Often with this construction and meaning the verb is not expressed (cp § 108): e.g., [J]shall be for the prince—[R]to the prince shall belong (Ezek 45.7; cp 48.21f); [J]his seed is blessed—[R]his children become a blessing (Ps 37.26); [J]The preparations of the heart in man—[R]The plans of the mind belong to man (Prov 16.1); [J]the sword of the enemy—[R]the enemy has a sword (Jer 6.25); [J]The sword of the LORD—[R]the LORD has a sword (Is 34.6); [J]shall be toward the LORD—[R]to the LORD belong (Zech 9.1); [J]the day of the LORD of hosts shall be—[R]the LORD of hosts has a day (Is 2.12; cp 22.5; 34.8).

Note also the following idiomatic expressions:

[J]What hast thou here?—[R]What have you to do here? (Is 22.16); [J]What hath my beloved to do—[R]What right has my beloved (Jer 11.15); [J]What hast thou to do with me?—[R]What have you against me? (Judg 11.12; cp 1 Kings 17.18; lit. what to me and to you?); cp [J]what have ye to do with me?—[R]What are you to me? (Joel 3.4; here R translates literally); [J]What is the chaff to the wheat?—[R]What has straw in common with the wheat? (Jer 23.28; lit. what to the straw with the wheat?).

A few other uses of this preposition may be mentioned:

(d) [J]higher than the kings of the earth—[R]The highest of the kings of the earth (Ps 89.27; lit. high to . . .); (e) [J]How shall I pardon thee for this?—[R]How can I pardon you? (Jer 5.7; "for this" is part of an expression which means "How"). (f) In Aramaic *l-* is regularly used with the direct object of a verb, and this use appears occasionally in Hebrew, especially in Hosea: [J]Sow to yourselves in righteousness—[R]Sow for yourselves righteousness (10.12; cp 11.1, 3); note also 2 Chron 17.7, [J]sent to his princes—[R]sent his princes. See § 114 for *l-* with the infinitive.

There are several compound prepositional expressions or phrases formed with *l-:*

(2) *lma'an* (cp § 81, No. 4): [J]Because of the house of the LORD—[R]For the sake of the house of the LORD (Ps 122.9; cp v. 8); cp Prov 16.4, [J]for himself—[R]for its purpose. (3) *l'ummat:* [J]over against—[R]close to (Ex 37.14), along with (Ezek 1.20f), alongside (45.6; 48.13, 18 twice), corresponding to (40.18; 45.7), parallel to (42.7; 48.21). (4) *liqra't* (lit. at meeting, to meet): [J]fled against it—[R]fled into it (i.e., the sea, Ex 14.27); [J]at his coming [Heb. *meeting*]—[R]came to meet him (1 Sam 16.4); [J]at the meeting of David—[R]came to meet David (21.1). (5) *loqbēl* (Aramaic): [J]before—[R]in front of (Dan 5.1); [J]over against—[R]opposite (v. 5); [J]by reason of—[R]because of (v. 10).

§ 84

Equally versatile is the preposition *min* (from). As in many other cases, the interpretation of the preposition often depends on the interpretation of the verb or other word upon which the phrase is dependent;

e.g., [J]that appear from [Or, *that eat of &c*] mount Gilead—[R]moving down the slopes of Gilead (Song 4.1, lit. that move down from Mount Gilead; cp 6.5). In many instances R keeps closer than J to the primary meaning of the preposition; e.g., [J]by the mount Horeb—[R]from Mount Horeb (Ex 33.6); [J]shall comfort us concerning our work and toil—[R]shall bring us relief from our work and from the toil (Gen 5.29); [J]Concerning thy testimonies, I have known of old—[R]Long have I known from thy testimonies (Ps 119.152); [J]on this side—[R]from (2 Chron 20.2).

Like the others, however, this preposition also has many idiomatic uses; and J and R do not always agree as to which of these is intended.

(a) *Agent* (JR *by*): [J]Out of Jacob shall come he that shall have dominion—[R]By Jacob shall dominion be exercised (Num 24.19); [J]for the daughters of Jerusalem—[R]by the daughters of Jerusalem (Song 3.10); [J]Man's goings are of the LORD—[R]A man's steps are ordered by the LORD (Prov 20.24); [J]He was taken from prison and from judgment [Or, *He was taken away by distress and judgment*]—[R]By oppression and judgment he was taken away (Is 53.8); [J]by him [Or, *from him*] the daily sacrifice was taken away—[R]the continual burnt offering was taken away from him (Dan. 8.11); [J]coals were kindled by it—[R]glowing coals flamed forth from him (2 Sam 22.9; Ps 18.8).

(b) *Cause* (JR at, because of, before): [J]by thy covenant—[R]on account of the covenant with you (Ezek 16.61); [J]by reason of mine affliction [Or, *out of mine affliction*]—[R]out of my distress (Jon 2.2); [J]And of them shall be taken up a curse—[R]Because of them this curse shall be used (Jer 29.22); [J]afraid and ashamed of Ethiopia—[R]dismayed and confounded because of Ethiopia (Is 20.5); [J]ashamed of—[R]put to shame by (Jer 2.36 twice); cp [J]because of the ground—[R]Out of the ground (Gen 5.29); [J]strength because of the enemy—[R]refuge from the enemy (Nahum 3.11).

(c) *Part:* [J]taken . . . from off the sacrifices—[R]taken . . . out of the sacrifices (Lev 7.34); [J]offer a sacrifice of thanksgiving with leaven—[R]offer a sacrifice of thanksgiving of that which is leavened (Amos 4.5); [J]above all people—[R]out of all the peoples (Deut 7.6; cp 14.2); [J]all the beasts [Heb. . . . *from the beasts*]—[R]some of the animals (1 Kings 18.5); [J]will take thereof—[R]takes a part of it (Is 44.15); [J]reproach me so long as I live [Heb. *from my days*]—[R]reproach me for any of my days (Job 27.6); [J]of—[R]some of (Is 66.21; Jer 19.1; 39.10; cp 40.7); [J]certain of—[R]some of (Dan 1.3); [J]teach us of his ways—[R]teach us his ways (Is 2.3; Mic 4.2; lit. from his ways, implying but not emphasizing that not all of God's ways will be taught); [J]from men—[R]from among men (Aramaic, Dan 4.25, 32); [J]the workmen, they are of men—[R]the craftsmen are but men (Is 44.11, cp French Ce sont des hommes); [J]will he regard your persons—[R]will he show favor to any of you (Mal 1.9).

(d) *Comparison:* [J]above—[R]more . . . than (Neh 7.2; Eccles 2.7; Jer 15.8); [J]above the stars—[R]more than the stars (Nahum 3.16; J is ambiguous); [J]blessed with children—[R]Blessed above sons (Deut 33.24); [J]too narrow by reason of the inhabitants—[R]too narrow for your inhabitants (Is 49.19); [J]more and mightier than we—[R]too many and too mighty for us (Ex 1.9; cp Ps 142.6; Jer 31.11); [J]poorer than thy estimation—[R]too poor to pay your valuation (Lev 27.8); [J]more brutish than any man—[R]too stupid to be a man (Prov 30.2); [J]a full wind from those places [Or, *a fuller wind than those*]—[R]a wind too full for this (Jer 4.12); [J]a small thing for you—[R]too little for you (Is 7.13); [J]It is a light thing that thou shouldest be my servant [Or, *Art thou lighter than that thou shouldest, &c*]—[R]It is too light a thing that you should be my servant (Is 49.6, a very idiomatic and difficult but very important place, lit. light from your being to me a servant).

Note also the following: [J]more blameless than the Philistines [Or, . . . *blameless from the Philistines*]—[R]blameless in regard to the Philistines (Judg 15.3) [J]more honourable than the thirty [Or, *honourable among the thirty*]—[R]renowned among the thirty (2 Sam 23.23); [J]more just than God . . . more pure than his maker—[R]righteous before [Or *more than*] God . . . pure before [Or *more than*] his Maker (Job 4.17); [J]viler than the earth—[R]whipped out of the land (30.8, cp § 61); [J]fresher than a child's [Heb. *than childhood*]—[R]fresh with youth (33.25); [J]more desolate than the wilderness [Or, *desolate from the wilderness*]—[R]waste, . . . from the wilderness (Ezek 6.14); [J]he shall continue more years than the king of the north—[R]for some years he shall refrain from attacking the king of the north (Dan 11.8).

(e) *Separation:* [J]the fatness [Or, *of the fatness*] of the earth, and of the dew of heaven—[R]away from [Or *of*] the fatness of the earth . . . , and away from [Or *of*] the dew of heaven (Gen 27.39); [J]more than—[R]apart from (Eccles 2.25); [J]cast out of thy grave—[R]cast out, away from your sepulchre (Is 14.19).

Note especially the familiar but much debated verse, Job 19.26, [J]yet in my flesh [Or, . . . *yet out of my flesh*]—[R]then from [Or *without*] my flesh (in earlier printings R read without [Or *from*]; see note at end of v., The meaning of this verse is uncertain). With this cp the following: [J]from good—[R]to no avail (Ps 39.2); [J]from the vile—[R]and not what is worthless (Jer 15.19); [J]from thy fear—[R]so that we fear thee not (Is 63.17); [J]from the birth, and from the womb, and from the conception—[R]no birth, no pregnancy, no conception (Hos 9.11); [J]for glory [Or, *more . . . than with glory*]—[R]instead of glory (Hab 2.16); [J]from fear of evil—[R]without dread of evil (Prov 1.33); [J]by the archers [Heb. *of the bow*]—[R]without the bow (Is 22.3); [J]in his knowledge—[R]without knowledge (Jer 10.14; cp 51.17); [J]because of the force—[R]without strength (48.45); [J]that ye shall not have a vision [Heb. *from a vision*] . . . that ye shall not divine [Heb. *from divining*]—[R]without vision . . . without divination (Mic 3.6).

(f) Other idiomatic expressions: [J]of the mercy seat [Or, *of the* matter *of the mercy seat*]—[R]of one piece with the mercy seat (Ex 25.19; cp vv. 31, 35f; 28.8; 30.2; 37.8, 17, 21f, 25; 38.2; 39.5); [J]they call themselves of the holy city—[R]they call themselves after the holy city (Is 48.2) [J]to be no city—[R]is a city no more (25.2, lit. from a city); [J]because of him that passeth by, and because of him that returneth—[R]so that none shall march to and fro (Zech 9.8, lit. from passerby and from returner); [J]he looketh forth at the windows—[R]gazing in at the windows (Song 2.9; cp, same v., [JR]through the lattice); [J]thence—[R]in it (Is 65.20); [J]from thence—[R]there (Hos 2.15); [J]from the womb—[R]in the womb (Jer 20.17); [J]by reason of the cold—[R]in the autumn (Prov 20.4); [J]from the ends of the earth—[R]at the end of the earth (Ps 135.7); [J]From the north end—[R]Beginning at the northern border (Ezek 48.1); [J]from the south—[R]in the south (Josh 13.4); [J]from the north—[R]in a northerly direction (18.17); [J]if I be cleansed from my sin [Or, by it *more than by my sin*]—[R]than if I had sinned (Job 35.3, lit. from my sin, but this does not fit the context).

See also § 116 for *min* with the infinitive.

(g) The prepositions *min* and *l-* (§ 83, No. 1) are used together idiomatically with a meaning which J, translating too literally, fails to convey: [J]from the south to the ascent—[R]south of the ascent (Num 34.4); [J]on the south side unto Kadesh-barnea—[R]south of Kadesh-barnea (Josh 15.3, lit. from the south to K.); [J]northward at the gate of the altar—[R]north of the altar gate (Ezek 8.5); cp [J]from the appearance . . . even downward—[R]below what appeared to be (v. 2); [J]and from his loins even upward—[R]and above his loins (same v.).

§ 85 By combining two or more prepositions, or a preposition and a noun, adverb, or other word, Hebrew forms a number of compound prepositions which are sometimes hard to translate. A word often combined with *b-* (in) or *min* (from) is (1) *'ēber* (side, region across or beyond, and so simply across, beyond, on the other side of). It is often used alone;

e.g., [J]on this side Jordan eastward—[R]on the east side of the Jordan (Deut 4.49); [J]on the other side Jordan eastward—[R]eastward beyond the Jordan (Josh 13.27). Note also (cp § 42) [J]beyond the river—[R]the province Beyond the River (Neh 2.7, 9; also Aramaic, Ezra 4.17, 20; 6.6); [J]on this side the river—[R]the province Beyond the River (Neh 3.7; Aramaic, Ezra 4.10, 16; 5.3, 6; 6.6, 13).

J's oscillation between "this side" and "the other side" appears also in the translation of (2) *b'ēber* (lit. in-across), which occurs often in Deuteronomy and Joshua with confusing shifts between the point of view of Moses, speaking in the plains of Moab east of the Jordan, and that of the historian and his readers on the west side of the river. J's attempt to resolve the confusion by mutually contradictory renderings is abandoned by R;

e.g., [J]beyond Jordan—[R]beyond the Jordan (Deut 3.20, 25; Josh 9.10; 13.8); [J]on the other side Jordan—[R]beyond the Jordan (Deut 11.30;

Josh 12.1); Jon this side Jordan—Rbeyond the Jordan (Deut 1.1, 5; 3.8; 4.46f; Josh 9.1); Jon the side of Jordan westward—Rbeyond the Jordan to the west (Josh 5.1).

Similarly *'ēber* is combined with *min* (§ 84) to form (3) *mē'ēber:* e.g., Jfrom [Heb. *from aside*] the wilderness—Racross the wilderness (Job 1.19). This combination is sometimes followed by *l-* (§ 83, No. 1), lit. "from across (with reference) to," used in ways that create the same difficulty noted with No. 1:

Jon the other side Jordan—Rbeyond the Jordan (Josh 13.32; 1 Chron 6.78), on the other side of the Jordan (Josh 17.5); Jon this side Jordan westward—Rwestward of the Jordan (1 Chron 26.30).

Other compound prepositions also are formed with *min:*

(4) *lmin* (lit. to-from): Jfrom the day—RSince the day (Hag 2.18). (5) *mē'aḥar, mē'aḥrē* (lit. from after): Jfrom—Rfrom following (Jer 3.19; Zeph 1.6); Jas I followed [Heb. *from behind*]—Rfrom following (Amos 7.15); JFrom following [Heb. *from after*]—Rfrom tending (Ps 78.71). (6) *mē'ēt* (lit. from with): Jfrom—Ron behalf of (Lev 24.8); Jby—Rfrom (Num 7.84; 1 Sam 2.23; Is 54.15); Jof—Rfrom (2 Chron 11.4). (7) *mibblī* (lit. from-without): JRbecause there is not (2 Kings 1.3, 6, 16); Jbecause they have no—Rfor want of (Is 5.13); Jso that there is no—Rwithout (Zeph 3.6). (8) *mibba'ad* (lit. from-through): Jwithin thy locks—Rbehind your veil (Song 4.1, 3; 6.7). (9) *mē'ēn* (lit. from-not-being); Jtill there be no place—Rbecause there is no room elsewhere (Jer 7.32; cp 19.11); Jthat there shall be no inhabitant—Rtill no inhabitant is left (Zeph 2.5); Jthat there is none inhabitant—Rwithout an inhabitant (3.6); Jinsomuch that he regardeth not—Rbecause he no longer regards (Mal 2.13).

Other combinations with *min* will appear in §§ 86ff.

§ 86

Another hard-worked preposition of many meanings is *'al* (on):

JRabove, against, among, at, beside, by, by reason of, concerning, for, for the sake of, of, on, over, through, to, upon, with; Jaccording to, in, touching, toward, unto; Racross, adjoining, along, along with, because of, before, in addition to, in charge of, in front of, in spite of, on account of, on the ground of, rather than, together with, within.

Obviously the context often determines the particular meaning intended and governs the translation.

The following special cases may be mentioned;

[J]upon the heap—[R]by the heap (Gen 31.46; cp 24.11, 13 [JR]by); [J]upon a wall—[R]beside a wall (Amos 7.7); [J]upon the altar—[R]beside [Or *upon*] the altar (9.1); [J]strong above—[R]stronger than (Dan 11.5); [J]more than—[R]surpassing (Eccles 1.16); [J]heavier than—[R]heavy in spite of (Job 23.2); [J]not . . . for equity—[R]wrong (Prov 17.26). Occasionally, where a phrase is the equivalent of a "dative of interest" (cp § 83, No. 1), R omits it; e.g., [J]maketh idols against herself—[R]makes idols (Ezek 22.3); [J]his countenance was changed in him—[R]his color changed (Dan 5.9, Aramaic; so too 7.28; in 5.6,10 the Aramaic does not have the phrase).

The use of *'al* in psalm titles (§ 69, No. 15) may be recalled here.

Note also Ps 92.3, [J]Upon an instrument of ten strings, and upon the psaltery; upon the harp with a solemn sound—[R]to the music of the lute and the harp, to the melody of the lyre (cp § 70, Nos. 3–5).

In translating idiomatic phrases with *'al* both J and R sometimes paraphrase;

e.g., [J]Many days and years [Heb. *Days above a year*]—[R]In a little more than a year (Is 32.10); [J]hath been to me as a provocation of mine anger [Heb. *for my anger*] and of my fury—[R]has aroused my anger and wrath (Jer 32.31; lit. has been to me on my anger and on my wrath); [J]Rachel died by me—[R]Rachel to my sorrow died (Gen 48.7); [J]he shall make their habitations desolate with them—[R]their fold shall be appalled at their fate (Jer 49.20; cp 50.45); [J]the prince's part—[R]the prince's duty (Ezek 45.17; cp our colloquial "up to him"); [J]I have peace offerings with me [Heb. *Peace offerings* are *upon me*]—[R]I had to offer sacrifices (Prov 7.14; lit. sacrifices of peace offerings upon me); [J]a crying for wine—[R]an outcry . . . for lack of wine (Is 24.11; i.e., concerning wine); [J]are with me—[R]are a care to me (Gen 33.13); [J]when I am reproved [Or, *when I am argued with.* Heb. *upon my reproof,* or, *arguing*]—[R]concerning my complaint (Hab 2.1); [J]in the courts—[R]having the care of the courts (1 Chron 23.28); [J]whether it be done against a nation, or against a man only—[R]whether it be a nation or a man (Job 34.29). In Job 30.4 J takes a noun meaning "leaves" for a form of this preposition: [J]by the bushes—[R]the leaves of bushes.

The compound preposition *mēʿal* (*min* + *ʿal,* lit. from-on) causes no serious difficulty. A further elaboration is *mēʿal l-* (lit. from-on to, i.e., above with reference to);

e.g., ^{J}from beyond the tower—^{R}above the Tower (Neh 12.38; cp same v. ^{JR}upon the wall); ^{J}from above the gate—^{R}above the Gate (v. 39; the picture of the route of the procession in these verses depends largely on the meaning of this preposition); ^{J}from the firmament—^{R}from above the firmament (Ezek 1.25); ^{J}from [Or, *upon.* Heb. *from upon*] the border—^{R}beyond the border (Mal 1.5).

§ 87 Most of the other prepositions raise no questions of interpretation, but there are some exceptional instances worth mentioning.

(1) *ʿad:* ^{J}to—^{R}as far as, through; ^{J}toward—^{R}as far as, to; ^{J}unto—^{R}as far as, as far away as, as far over as, to, up to; cp ^{J}as yet—^{R}until now (2 Kings 13.23); ^{J}hitherto—^{R}still (Ps 71.17); ^{J}whilst it is yet morning—^{R}by morning (Judg 6.31); ^{J}How long shall be—^{R}For how long is (Dan 8.13, lit. until when; cp Ps 6.3 etc., ^{JR}how long); ^{J}until a time—^{R}for a time (Dan 7.25, Aramaic); ^{J}angry even unto death—^{R}angry enough to die (Jon 4.9).

(2) *ʿim* (^{JR}with, against): ^{J}before thee [Heb. *with thee*]—^{R}toward thee (Ps 73.22; cp v. 23, ^{JR}with thee); ^{J}in us—^{R}clear to us (Job 15.9); ^{J}in the tents—^{R}among the tents (Ps 120.5); ^{J}with him—^{R}among those (v. 6); ^{J}with—^{R}among (Ps 54, title; Is 38.11); ^{J}with her in the house—^{R}while she was in the house (1 Kings 3.17; J is literal but suggests an incongruous idea); ^{J}it is nothing with thee—^{R}there is none like thee (2 Chron 14.11); ^{J}are there not with you, even with you, sins—^{R}Have you not sins of your own (2 Chron 28.10); ^{J}there were many with me—^{R}many are arrayed against me (Ps 55.18); ^{J}be just with [Or, *before*] God—^{R}be just before God (Job 9.2; cp 25.4); ^{J}but it is not so with me [Heb. *but I* am *not so with myself*]—^{R}for I am not so in myself (9.35); ^{J}this is with thee—^{R}this was thy purpose (10.13); ^{J}this is done of thee [Heb. *is with thee*]—^{R}this has been your mind (1 Kings 11.11); ^{J}which I made with thee—^{R}which I made, as I made you (Job 40.15); ^{J}with him—^{R}he shall bring (Dan 11.17); ^{J}with—^{R}by the help of (v. 39).

(3) *taḥat* (^{JR}instead of, under): ^{J}for—^{R}in exchange for, in return for, in place of, instead of, under; ^{J}under—^{R}among; cp ^{J}under him—^{R}in his place (Is 25.10), where it stood (Ezek 17.6), His underparts (Job 41.30); ^{J}in myself—^{R}beneath me (Hab 3.16); ^{J}instead of thy husband

[Or, *being in the power of thy husband.* Heb. *under thy husband*]—[R]while you were under your husband's authority (Num 5.19; cp v. 20).

Again there is a compound preposition with *min, mittaḥat;* e.g., [J]out of his place [Or, . . . *from under him*]—[R]in his place (Zech 6.12); [J]under the rows—[R]at the bottom of the rows (Ezek 46.23); also *mittaḥat l-;* e.g., [J]And from under [Or, *from the place*] these chambers—[R]Below these chambers (42.9).

§ 88 Prepositions are often combined in Hebrew with the names of parts of the body, forming phrases which are used practically as propositions.

Thus with *yād* (hand) we have (1) *byad:* [J]into the hand of—[R]to (Jer 26.24, cp 38.19); [J]by the hand of Moses—[R]by Moses (with "command" or "speak," Lev 8.36; 10.11; Judg 3.4; Neh 9.14); [J]by the hand of the priests the Levites—[R]under the direction of the Levitical priests (2 Chron 23.18); [J]sent by the hand of Benaiah—[R]sent Benaiah (1 Kings 2.25; cp the rest of the v.); [J]by the ministry [Heb. *by the hand*] of the prophets—[R]through the prophets (Hos 12.10); [J]by the prophet [Heb. *by the hand of the prophet*]—[R]through the prophet (Jer 37.2; cp Zech 7.12); [J]to [Heb. *by the hand of*] Nebuzaradan—[R]through Nebuzaradan (Jer 39.11); cp [J]teach you by the hand [Or, being *in the hand*] of God—[R]teach you concerning the hand of God (Job 27.11).

(2) *lyad* (lit. to the hand of): [J]at the gates—[R]beside the gates (Prov 8.3). (3) *miyyad* (from the hand of): [J]out of the hand—[R]from (2 Kings 13.25, of capturing cities). (4) *'al-yad* or *'al-ydē* (on the hand or hands of): [J]as was ordained by David [Heb. *by the hands of David*]—[R]according to the order of David (2 Chron 23.18); [J]under the hand of—[R]under the direction of (26.11); [J]under their hand—[R]Under their command (v. 13).

So with *ṣad* (side), (5) *miṣṣad* (from the side of): [J]in the side of the ark—[R]by the side of the ark (Deut 31.26); cp [J]concerning—[R]with regard to (Dan 6.4, Aramaic).

Especially common are such phrases with *pnē* (face of). (6) *bipnē* (in the face of): [J]to his face—[R]against him (Hos 7.10). (7) *'el-pnē* (to the face of): [J]before, on the forepart of, over against; [R]alongside, beyond, facing, opposite, to the front of, extending from. (8) *lipnē* (to the face of): [JR]before, in the presence of, in the sight of; [J]before the face of, from the face of, with; [R]at the head of, in front of, for, in the way of, over, to, to the east of (cp § 71, No. 6), under, under the charge of. Cp [J]captain of the host before me—[R]commander of my army (2 Sam

19.13); [J]went out before the host—[R]went out to meet the army (2 Chron 28.9); [J]before I eat [Heb. *before my meat*]—[R]as [Heb *before*] my bread (Job 3.24); [J]of all that have been before them—[R]he was over all of them (Eccles 4.16, lit. to all over whom he was); [J]every man right forth—[R]every man straight before him (Jer 49.5). (9) *mippnē* (from the face of): [JR]from the face of, from, because of, before, by; [J]at, at the presence of, before the face of, by reason of, for, for fear of, in the sight of, of, out of the sight of, toward; [R]against, at the approach of, at the sight of, away from, for defense against, from the presence of, in the face of, to, to escape, to make way for. Cp [J]because of the famine—[R]victims of famine (Jer 14.16); [J]the LORD could no longer bear, because of the evil of your doings, and because of the abominations—[R]The LORD could no longer bear your evil doings and the abominations (44.22; R omits "because of" for the sake of smoother English). (10) *millipnē* (from to the face of): [JR]before, from; [J]from the face of, at the presence of; [R]in the presence of, from the presence of. (11) *'al-pnē* (on the face of): [JR]in, upon; [J]before the face of, before, from the face of, unto the face of, upon the face of, in the sight of, over against; [R]against, east of, on the east of, to the east of, from, from the front of, on, in the lifetime of, on the face of, on the surface of, opposite, over the face of, to the end of. Cp [J]that lieth before—[R]that overlooks (Josh 18.16); [J]in the open firmament of heaven [Heb. *face of the firmament of heaven*] —[R]across the firmament of the heavens (Gen 1.20).

In the same way prepositional phrases with *'ēnē* (eyes of) are used as prepositions. (12) *b'ēnē* (in the eyes of); [JR]in the sight of; [J]before; [R]in the eyes of. Cp [J]it seem—[R]it seems (Jer 40.4 twice); [J]it seemeth—[R]you think it (same v., lit. in your eyes). (13) *l'ēnē* (to the eyes of): [JR]before the eyes of; [R]in the presence of.

So too with *pī* (mouth of), (14) *kpī* (as the mouth of): [J]according to thy wish [Heb. *according to thy mouth*]—[R]as you are (Job 33.6). Cp *kpī 'šer* (lit. as the mouth of which): [J]according as—[R]inasmuch as (Mal 2.9). (15) *lpī* (to the mouth of): [J]at the entry of the city—[R]in front of the town (Prov 8.3); [J]according to the inheritance of them—[R]with a view to their inheritances (Josh 18.4). See § 115 for *lpi* with the infinitive.

Chapter XXI

PRONOUNS AND SUFFIXES, THE DEFINITE ARTICLE, PARTICLES

§ 89 Personal pronouns are not used in Hebrew as much as they are in English. As in Latin *amo* means not simply "love" but "I love," so in Hebrew a pronoun is not needed to indicate the person, number, and gender of the subject, which are shown by the form of the verb. Consequently, when a pronoun is used there is some special reason for it, and this must if possible be represented somehow in the translation.

The most common reason for using a pronoun is to express emphasis, and there are several ways of bringing this out in English;

e.g., [J]And thou shalt go—[R]As for yourself, you shall go (Gen 15.15; see also 17.9; Jer 7.16; Mic 3.8; 7.7; but cp Gen 17.4, [J]as for me, behold, my covenant—[R]Behold, my covenant); [J]For, behold, I have made thee—[R]and I, behold, I make you (Jer 1.18); [J]moreover take thou up—[R]And you, take up (Ezek 19.1); [J]Now, thou son of man—[R]And you, son of man (22.2); [J]I have commanded—[R]I myself have commanded (Is 13.3; see also Ezek 17.22, twice); [J]time for you, O ye, to dwell—[R]a time for you yourselves to dwell (Hag 1.4); [J]and he fought—[R]and himself fought (Is 63.10); [J]for themselves are separated—[R]for the men themselves go aside (Hos 4.14); [J]I, even my hands—[R]it was my hands that (Is 45.12); [J]now also will I—[R]now it is I who (Jer 4.12; see also 27.5; Hos 11.3; 12.10; 13.5; 14.8; Zech 6.13); [J]did ye at all fast unto me, even to me?—[R]was it for me that you fasted? (Zech 7.5); [J]the very time of his land—[R]the time of his own land (Jer 27.7).

In a "nominal sentence" (cp § 108), where no verb is expressed, a pronoun may be needed if the subject is not otherwise indicated;

e.g., [J]This is one thing—[R]It is all one (Job 9.22, lit. One it). A very idiomatic use of the pronoun appears in Ezek 33.5; [J]But he that taketh warning—[R]But if he had taken warning (lit. But he being warned). In the next verse the pronoun is demonstrative in effect, avoiding ambiguity as to the subject of the verb: [J]if the sword come, and take any person from among them, he is taken—[R]and the sword comes, and takes any one of them, that man is taken away.

Demonstrative pronouns and adjectives are sometimes used idiomatically in ways that require more or less free translation;

e.g., [J]Now by this—[R]Now (1 Kings 17.24, lit. now this); [J]at that time—[R]in its time (2 Chron 30.3); [J]in that time—[R]in such a time (Amos 5.13); [J]this—[R]such a thing (Joel 1.2); [J]we will give thee this also—[R]we will give you the other also (Gen 29.27); [J]according to these measures—[R]they had the same size as the others (Ezek 40.24); [J]like those windows—[R]like the windows of the others (v. 25); [J]This is—[R]Here shall be (1 Chron 22.1); [J]and this is—[R]and here (same v.); [J]and this is—[R]and there was (Zech 5.7); [J]So is this great and wide sea—[R]Yonder is the sea, great and wide (Ps 104.25).

In Daniel 2.38 J has a demonstrative adjective where there is none in the Aramaic: [J]this head—[R]the head. In 6.2, on the other hand, J uses only a definite article where there is a demonstrative adjective in the Aramaic: [J]the princes—[R]these satraps. The pronoun in 4.24 may be either personal or demonstrative: [J]and this is the decree—[R]It is a decree.

An interrogative pronoun in Amos 7.2, 5 is hard to translate: [J]by whom shall Jacob arise? [Or, *who* of (or, *for*,) *Jacob shall stand?*]—[R]How can Jacob stand? (lit. who shall Jacob stand?). Three pronouns—interrogative, personal, and demonstrative respectively—form a question in Jer 30.21: who is this that—[R]who would. Here R is less literal than J, but in Jon 1.10 it is more literal: [J]why hast thou done this?—[R]What is this that you have done?

§ 90 The relative pronoun is sometimes used in Hebrew in ways that cannot be literally rendered in English; in fact, what is ordinarily called a relative pronoun (*'šer*) is more exactly described as an indefinite connective particle, which can serve as a conjunction (see § 80, No. 4), as a relative pronoun, or as something which is too indefinite to be called either the one or the other.

It is not surprising, therefore, that J and R do not always translate or even understand this word in the same way;

e.g., [J]They did not destroy the nations, concerning whom the LORD commanded them—[R]They did not destroy the peoples, as the LORD commanded them (Ps 106.34, lit. which the LORD . . .); [J]That our sons may be as plants—[R]may our sons . . . be like plants (Ps 144.12, lit. which our sons like plants; J treats *'šer* here as a conjunction of purpose, going back to v. 11, Rid me, but in the Hebrew it begins a new stanza, apparently unconnected with what precedes it); [J]it is known that it is man—[R]it is known what man is (Eccles 6.10).

A common Semitic idiom, not always recognized by J, is the use of both a relative pronoun and a pronominal suffix to express the object of a verb or preposition; e.g., "which I bought it" instead of "which I bought," or "the house which I lived in it" instead of "the house in which I lived." It is sometimes easy to miss the intended connection; e.g., [J]every one that maketh mention thereof shall be afraid in himself—[R]everyone to whom it is mentioned will fear (Is 19.17, lit. everyone whom one mentions it to him will fear); [J]whose seed is in itself—[R]in which is their seed (Gen 1.11f, lit. which its seed is in it). The same usage appears with a different form of the relative pronoun (*še-*): [J]his bed, which is Solomon's—[R]the litter of Solomon (Song 3.7).

It may be noted also that a relative pronoun may be appropriate in English where the Hebrew uses a different construction; e.g., [J]He looketh—[R]who looks (Ps 104.32, lit. the one looking).

§ 91 The Hebrew language has no indefinite article, though the tendency to create one appears in an occasional use of the numeral one;

e.g., [JR]a man (Ezek 33.2, lit. one man); [JR]a woman (Zech 5.7, lit. one woman); cp [J]one saint—[R]a holy one (Dan 8.13; cp same v., with the same Hebrew, [J]another saint—[R]another holy one); [J]a certain man [Heb. *one man*]—[R]a man (Dan 10.5); [J]one stick—[R]a stick (Ezek 37.16).

The use of the definite article in Hebrew exhibits several peculiarities which occasion some differences of interpretation between J and R. J frequently inserts "the" where there is no article in the Hebrew;

e.g., [J]the fifth son—[R]a fifth son (Gen 30.17; cp v. 19); [J]all the fat—[R]All fat (Lev 3.16); [J]the great [Or, *much*] transgression—[R]great transgression (Ps 19.13); [J]the son of man—[R]a son of man (Ps 146.3; cp 8.4, [JR]the son of man, an example of R's conservatism in familiar passages); [J]The woman—[R]A woman (Deut 22.5; cp same v., [JR]a man).

In Aramaic there is no definite article; its force is represented by a special ending which marks the noun as "determined" or "emphatic" instead of "absolute" (i.e., indefinite). Here too J sometimes uses "the" where the Aramaic noun is not determined; e.g., [J]the great God—[R]a great God (Dan 2.45); [J]like the Son of God—[R]like a son of the gods (3.25, lit. like a son of gods; J inserts "the" with "Son," R with "gods"; cp. § 53). R too sometimes inserts the article where the Hebrew does not have it; e.g., [J]an everlasting king—[R]the everlasting king (Jer 10.10); [J]one among a thousand—[R]one of the thousand (Job 33.23). So too where Aramaic nouns are not "determined": [J]times and laws—[R]the times and the law (Dan 7.25, lit. times and law).

On the other hand, where the Hebrew has the definite article J sometimes omits it. It is a rule of Hebrew grammar that when two nouns are in the "construct" relation (see § 100), corresponding to the connection with "of" in English (e.g., the throne of the king), the first noun does not have an article even though it is definite in meaning (i.e., Hebrew must say "throne of the king"; cp English "the King's throne"). Consequently the presence or absence of an article with the second noun is often all that there is to show whether the first noun should have one in English. In Ex 31.18 J ignores this rule: [J]two tables of testimony—[R]the two tables of the testimony (lit. two tables of the testimony).

A proper name is of course definite without an article, and thus may make definite the noun preceding it in the "construct" relation;

e.g., [J]a voice of the LORD—[R]The voice of the LORD (Is 66.6); [J]an angel of the LORD—[R]the angel of the LORD (Judg 6.11, 22; 13.21; cp vv. 3, 16–21, [JR]the angel of the LORD, six times; v. 20, [JR]the angel of God).

In some places where no special grammatical construction is involved J omits the article;

e.g., [J]a great city—[R]the great city (Gen 10.12); [J]a bullock—[R]the bull (1 Sam 1.25); [J]a pomegranate tree—[R]the pomegranate tree (14.2); [J]all nations—[R]all the nations (Is 2.2); [J]King of nations—[R]King of the nations (Jer 10.7; cp 1.10; 3.17, see next paragraph); [J]like a wilderness—[R]like the desert (Zeph 2.13); [J]Three shepherds—[R]the three shepherds (Zech 11.8).

But, again, sometimes R omits the article where J keeps it:

[J]the perverse rebellious woman [Heb. . . . *perverse rebellion*]—[R]a perverse, rebellious woman (1 Sam 20.30); [J]this woman—[R]a woman (2 Sam 3.8, lit. the woman); [J]the tower of Lebanon—[R]a tower of Lebanon (Song 7.4, lit. tower of the Lebanon; in Hebrew Lebanon is regularly called "the Lebanon"); [J]over the nations and over the kingdoms—[R]over nations and over kingdoms (Jer 1.10); [J]all the nations—[R]all nations (3.17; cp Is 2.2; Jer 10.7, see last paragraph); [J]the wall [Or, . . . *a wall*]—[R]a wall (Ezek 43.8); [J]to the wood . . . to the dumb stone—[R]to a wooden thing . . . to a dumb stone (Hab 2.19; here R omits the article with "wood," J inserts it with "stone").

The fact is, as the foregoing instances may have led the reader to suspect, that Hebrew and English differ somewhat in their use of the definite article. There is no article in the Hebrew where R has one and J two in Eccles 8.10: [J]the place of the holy—[R]the holy place. In a number of instances both J and R read "a" instead of "the"; e.g., [J]a valley—[R]a ravine (Josh 8.11); [JR]a young man (Num 11.27); [JR]a lad (1 Sam 20.21); [J]a wench—[R]a maidservant (2 Sam 17.17).

One of the most notable places, and perhaps the most important, where both J and R do not translate the Hebrew definite article, is Is 7.14: [J]a virgin—[R]a young woman (see § 75). Various explanations of the Hebrew definite article in this crucial verse are offered by different scholars, but whatever view may be adopted, few, if any, would translate "the virgin," or "the young woman."

A few other special cases may be noted. The Hebrew nouns

'ēl and *'lōhīm* (§ 43), when used to mean simply "God," often have the article.

Cp [J]God—[R]This God (2 Sam 22.31, 33; Ps 18.30; lit. the God); [J]he is the God—[R]he is God (1 Kings 18.39); [J]It is God that girdeth me—[R]the god who girded me (Ps 18.32); [J]God that is holy [Or, *the holy God.* Heb. *the God the holy*]—[R]the Holy God (Is 5.16; J mg reproduces literally the normal Hebrew construction for an adjective modifying a noun with the article); [J]the God of our salvation—[R]God is our salvation (Ps 68.19); [J]He that is our God is the God of salvation—[R]Our God is a God of salvation (v. 20).

An exceptional and puzzling use of the article appears in 1 Chron 15.27: [J]the master of the song with the singers—[R]the leader of the music of the singers (lit. the leader the music the singers).

In Ps 51.4 J sees a specific reference to the sin of David mentioned in the title of the psalm: [J]and done this evil—[R]and done that which is evil (lit. the evil; Hebrew regularly uses the article with an abstract noun).

§ 92 Many things for which we use nouns, verbs, or other parts of speech are expressed in Hebrew by words which can most conveniently be regarded as particles, though they may actually be (or have been originally) nouns. Like words of other kinds, they are occasionally taken in different ways by J and R.

(1) *yēš* (lit. existence of, i.e., there is or are):

[J]he is a God that judgeth—[R]there is a God who judges (Ps 58.11); [J]there is a man—[R]sometimes a man (Eccles 2.21). With *'šer* (§ 80, No. 4; § 90): [J]and so it was, when the cloud—[R]Sometimes the cloud (Num 9.20, lit. there was when; cp v. 21). In such variations of rendering there is no essential difference of interpretation, and this is usually true also with (2) *'ayin, 'ēn* (lit. nonexistence of, i.e., there is not, etc.). There is at least a slight difference in meaning, however, in such instances as the following: [J]none can deliver—[R]there is none to deliver (Mic 5.8); [J]and none did search or seek—[R]with none to search or seek (Ezek 34.6, lit. and there was none searching and there was none seeking); [J]there is no throne—[R]without a throne (Is 47.1). Occasionally the divergence goes deeper. In Gen 39.9, e.g., J misunderstands a common use of *'ēn* with a personal suffix instead of a simple negative: [J]There is none greater in this house than I—[R]he is not greater in this house than I am.

Instead of the word for "not" (*lō'*) commonly used in declarative statements, Hebrew uses in hortatory sentences (3) *'al;* e.g., [JR]Let there be no strife (Gen 13.8). J apparently ignores this distinction in Job 36.18, treating a verb with *'al* as a simple negative statement: [J]a great ransom cannot deliver thee [Heb. *turn thee aside*]—[R]let not the greatness of the ransom turn you aside. The word "cannot," however, shows that this is a paraphrase rather than a careless mistake; the real difference in interpretation lies in J's rendering "a great ransom" for "the greatness of the ransom" (lit. muchness of ransom). R too on occasion translates verbs with *'al* freely;

e.g., [J]Let not the swift flee away, nor the mighty man escape—[R]The swift cannot flee away, nor the warrior escape (Jer 46.6, i.e., let them not try to get away); [J]do no more—[R]you will not do it again (Job 41.8, lit. do not add, i.e., repeat the attempt to lay hands on Leviathan).

Hebrew has no case-endings to distinguish subject from object, etc. (§ 99), but the direct object of a verb is normally indicated by the particle (4) *'ēt* (or *'et-*, or *'ōt-*). Now and then this is used in ways that are confusing.

Note, e.g., Is 53.8, [J]and who shall declare his generation? for he was cut off—[R]and as for his generation, who considered that he was cut off . . . ? Since "his generation" is preceded by *'ēt,* J takes it as the object of "declare" (R consider); but sometimes *'ēt* is used without a verb in the sense "as regards" or "as for" (cp § 80, No. 3, on "for" vs "that").

A much more difficult instance is Num 35.6, [J]And among the cities which ye shall give unto the Levites there shall be six cities for refuge—[R]The cities which you give to the Levites shall be the six cities of refuge. Here there is no verb to which "cities" and "six cities" can be objects, yet both are preceded by *'ēt.* The case is too complicated to be discussed here; possible explanations may be found in the commentaries. J and R simply try in different ways to give the general meaning.

In Zech 7.7 also *'ēt* is used where there is no verb: [J]Should ye not hear the words [Or, *Are not these the words*]—[R]were not these the words. The Hebrew says only, "not the words." J inserts "Should ye" and "hear," so that "the words," following *'ēt*, can be the object; J mg and R, in spite of the *'ēt*, take "the words" as the predicate of a nominal sentence (§ 108) and insert "there" for a subject.

§ 93 Several prefixes and suffixes are used in Hebrew for various purposes. (1) *h-* prefixed to a word, usually at the beginning of a clause, serves as a question-mark. J, following an old tradition, mistakes this interrogative prefix for a part of the verb in Job 34.31, [J]it is meet to be said—[R]has any one said. In Jer 12.9 J twice ignores the interrogative *h-*, treating two questions as declarative clauses: [J]mine heritage is . . . , the birds . . . are—[R]Is my heritage . . . ? Are the birds . . . ?

(2) *-āh,* added to a verb, gives it something of the force we express in English by saying "let me" or "let us." J sometimes fails to reproduce this meaning; e.g., [J]we take up corn—[R]let us get grain (Neh 5.2); [J]Now will I sing—[R]let me sing (Is 5.1; cp No. 3); [J]We lie down—[R]Let us lie down (Jer 3.25). Sometimes *-āh* is affixed to a verb expressing purpose (see § 112).

Already mentioned briefly in § 15 as an example of frequent omission in R is the particle (3) *-nā',* which turns a command into a request or makes a request more polite and humble. J's "now," frequently used for this particle, is sometimes retained by R but often dropped, especially where it seems to mean "at this time."

To the examples of this omission given in § 15 may be added Gen 15.5; 18.21; 19.19f; 27.2, 9, 26; Song 7.8; Is 5.1 (cp No. 2); Jer 17.15; 28.15.

In many places J renders this particle "I beseech thee." Sometimes this too is kept by R (e.g., Num 12.13); elsewhere it is omitted (e.g., Neh 1.8, 11; Is 64.9; Jer 38.4). In Jer 38.20 R substitutes "now" for "I beseech thee." Another rendering often used by J is "I pray thee." R changes this to "now" (e.g., Gen 27.19), shortens it to "I pray" (e.g., 30.14), or omits it (e.g., 12.13; 13.8; 18.4; 27.21; 33.14).

Chapter XXII

GRAMMATICAL FORMS: PERSON, NUMBER, AND GENDER

§ 94 Not only the choice of words but also their forms convey meaning and must be duly considered by a translator. In Hebrew as in English special endings show whether a noun is singular or plural, masculine or feminine. Ordinarily these are quite clear, but there are places where J and R go different ways in interpreting them.

In some cases the ambiguity of a Hebrew form has made possible a difference of interpretation. In certain forms of the Hebrew verb the second person masculine and the third person feminine are indistinguishable; only the context can show which is intended. J and R sometimes differ in such cases;

e.g., [J]when it shall come—[R]when you come (Gen 30.33; J understands a third person feminine, used for the impersonal neuter, see § 95); [J]Lest thou shouldest ponder—[R]she does not take heed to [The meaning of the Hebrew word is uncertain] (Prov 5.6; see § 81, No. 3 on "Lest"); [J]thou canst not know—[R]she does not know (same v.); [J]Thou shalt be inhabited—[R]She shall be inhabited (Is 44.26; cp v. 28); see also Is 54.6; Zeph 3.7, twice. Cp Ezek 14.17, [J]Sword, go through—[R]Let a sword go through; here J apparently takes the verb as second person masculine singular (lit. thou shalt go through), and translates it as imperative; but the Hebrew word for "sword" is feminine.

In the plural the second person feminine and the third person feminine are the same in certain forms and are sometimes confused;

e.g., [J]Ye shall be built—[R]They shall be built (Is 44.26); [J]ye have sent—[R]They even sent (Ezek 23.40).

What J takes as the first person singular is understood by R in a few places as an archaic or dialectical form of the second person feminine singular:

Juntil that I Deborah arose, that I arose—Runtil you arose, Deborah, arose (Judg 5.7); JI have broken thy yoke, and burst thy bands—Ryou broke your yoke and burst your bonds (Jer 2.20); JI have not found—Ryou did not find (v. 34).

A participle is sometimes used in Hebrew in place of a finite verb, and unless the subject is plainly expressed this may be ambiguous;

e.g., JI was astonished at the vision, but none understood it—RI was appalled by the vision and did not understand it (Dan 8.27; J and R differ also in their understanding of the negative particle *'ēn,* as used with the participle, see § 92, No. 2).

A common cause of difficulty for the interpreter is the fact that the Hebrew language has a way of shifting suddenly from the third to the second person, or from the second to the third, without rhyme or reason so far as we can see. Translators often smooth out such incongruities by changing one or more words to fit the context. In Is 33.1, for example, J reads "and they dealt not treacherously with thee," though the Hebrew says "with him"; in this case R evades the difficulty by rendering "with whom none has dealt treacherously" (cp, later in the same verse, Jthey shall deal treacherously with thee—Ryou will be dealt with treacherously).

R frequently resorts to such "smoothing," with a note giving the literal meaning;

e.g., Jhis shoulder . . . his hands—Ryour [Heb *his*] shoulder . . . your [Heb *his*] hands (Ps 81.6; cp v. 7, JThou calledst—Ryou called, etc.). In other instances no note is given. Several examples may be seen in Ps 104: Jwho layeth the beams of his chambers . . . who maketh the clouds his chariot: who walketh—Rwho hast laid the beams of thy chambers . . . who makest the clouds thy chariot, who ridest (v. 3; R continues the second person from the preceding v., J shifts to the third person with the Hebrew); see also vv. 4f, 10, 13f, 19. Most of the verbs in these verses represent Hebrew participles, which might be used for either the third or the second person; the verbs in vv. 5 and 19 are exceptions, but both might be read as participles with other vowels. The personal suffixes, however, definitely indicate the third person ("his," not "thy"). The Hebrew shifts back to the second person in vv. 6–9, but returns in v. 13 to the third person. This is a very common phenomenon in the OT.

§ 95 J and R sometimes differ as to the gender of words, now one and now the other being more literal. In Job 39.27–30, for examples, R translates literally the masculine pronouns of the Hebrew; J, for no obvious reason, makes them all feminine.

Like other Semitic languages, Hebrew has no neuter gender but uses the feminine for it. R therefore occasionally changes a feminine pronoun in J to the neuter;

e.g., [J]seekest her . . . searchest for her—[R]seek it . . . search for it (i.e., wisdom, Prov 2.4). Where poetic personification is involved the choice of genders may be difficult; thus J and R both say "it" in Prov 3.14, again referring to wisdom, but change to "she" and "her" in vv. 15ff, where wisdom is clearly personified. In 8.11, however, where J has "it," R changes to "her" because wisdom speaks in the preceding and following verses. Cp [J]her rivers . . . her little rivers—[R]its rivers . . . its streams (i.e., the deep's, Ezek 31.4); [J]she shall not stand—[R]it shall not stand (Dan 11.17; J assumes that the reference is to "the daughter of women," R understands the clause as impersonal, referring to the king's action). In Lam 1.17 a feminine adjective is interpreted by J as "a menstruous woman," by R as "a filthy thing."

On the other hand, what J takes as neuter is sometimes regarded by R as feminine;

e.g., [J]in the forest thereof . . . round about it—[R]in her forest . . . round about her (Jer 21.14; i.e., the "inhabitant of the valley," v. 13); [J]it—[R]she (Jer 50.13 twice, referring to "the last of the nations," personified as "your mother" in v. 12).

Occasionally what is masculine in J becomes neuter in R. In Song 2.7; 3.5; 8.4 J quite gratuitously translates feminine forms as masculine and inserts "my": [J]stir not up, nor awake my love, till he please—[R]stir not up nor awaken love until it please. Cp

3.6, [J]Who is this—[R]What is that (referring to Solomon's litter, v. 7). In Is 6.2 J translates a masculine personal suffix as neuter: [J]above it—[R]above him (i.e., the Lord).

In a number of places a form which is masculine in Hebrew, because it agrees with a masculine noun, is rendered literally by J, though the equivalent English noun is neuter;

e.g., [J]he shall come up over all his channels—[R]it will rise over all its channels (i.e., the River, Is 8.7; note also v. 8); [J]him . . . his . . . he—[R]it . . . its . . . it (46.7 repeatedly, referring to the idol made by the goldsmith, not to the goldsmith himself); [J]that devour him—[R]who ate of it (Jer 2.3, meaning Israel but not as a person); [J]cutteth him out windows—[R]cuts out windows for it (i.e., the house, Jer 22.14).

Since J uses "his" as the possessive form of "it" (§ 11), what now seems to be masculine may sometimes have been intended as neuter;

e.g., [J]in his time—[R]in its time (Eccles 3.11, referring to "everything"); [J]his plants—[R]the place of its planting (i.e., the cedar's, Ezek 31.4).

Sometimes, indeed, J has the neuter gender where R keeps the masculine gender of the original;

e.g., [J]it shall bruise thy head—[R]he shall bruise your head (Gen 3.15; the subject is the "seed" of the woman); [J]it had brightness round about—[R]there was brightness round about him [Or *it*] (Ezek 1.27); [J]concerning it—[R]concerning him (i.e., God, Job 36.33; J assumes an antecedent something like thunder, which is not in the Hebrew); [J]for it is holy—[R]Holy is he (Ps 99.3; cp v. 5, same Hebrew, [J]for he is holy [Or, *it is holy*]—[R]Holy is he; v. 9, [JR]for the LORD our God is holy); note also Dan 9.26, [J]the end thereof—[R]Its [Or *his*] end. Also in Aramaic: [J]let it be wet—[R]Let him be wet (Dan 4.15, 23; here the immediate antecedent is "stump," but the following clauses make clear the personal reference).

§ 96 In numerous instances R has a plural form where J has the singular. Sometimes, to be sure, the difference is only apparent: what appears to be a singular form in J is or may be actually a plural.

Thus, as already noted in § 11, J uses "people" for the plural as well as the singular; e.g., Ps 2.1; 9.11; 67.3; but cp Is 25.3, where the Hebrew noun is in the singular, interpreted by R as collective (see below).

Note also Ps 105.6, 43, [J]his chosen—[R]his chosen ones. J's "his chosen" may be either singular or plural; in v. 6 it seems to mean Jacob, cp "Abraham his servant," but the Hebrew is plural (except in two manuscripts); in v. 43 there is no ambiguity. In v. 15 "mine anointed" is ambiguous; here too the Hebrew is plural ([R]my anointed ones; cp the parallel, my prophets). Cp Song 5.1, [J]O beloved—[R]O lovers.

A frequent use of the singular in J where we normally expect the plural in English reproduces an idiomatic Hebrew use of the singular;

e.g., [J]our heart—[R]our hearts (Deut 1.28); [J]into the hand of the Chaldeans—[R]into the hands of the Chaldeans (Jer 32.28; cp same v., [JR]into the hand of Nebuchadrezzar); [J]they shall lay their hand upon their mouth—[R]they shall lay their hands on their mouths (Mic 7.16); [J]in their mouth [Heb. *in their throat*]—[R]in their throats (Ps 149.6); [J]a twoedged sword in their hand—[R]two-edged swords in their hands (same v.); [J]all their shoulder—[R]all their shoulders (Ezek 29.7). R is not always consistent, however, in this respect; e.g., [J]their mouth—[R]their mouths (Ps 73.9), but cp [JR]their tongue (same v.). In fact, following A too closely, R sometimes keeps the Hebrew singular where J changes to the more idiomatic plural; e.g., [J]The hands of the witnesses . . . the hands of all the people—[R]the hand of the witnesses . . . the hand of all the people (Deut 17.7); [J]by the hands of messengers—[R]by the hand of messengers (1 Sam 11.7).

Very often, where the singular is used in a collective sense, J translates literally but R uses the plural;

e.g., [J]the fruit tree—[R]fruit trees (Gen 1.11); [J]and the tree—[R]and trees (v. 12); [J]the living creature . . . and creeping thing, and beast—[R]living creatures . . . creeping things and beasts (v. 24; cp Ezek 1.20f; 10.15, 17, 20; 34.28). This kind of change from singular to plural in R is very common throughout the OT.

The indefinite third person masculine singular is used in Hebrew in an impersonal sense, where we often use the plural in English; e.g., [J]one saith—[R]they say (Is 65.8). J has not always recognized this idiom;

e.g., [J]He setteth an end to darkness, and searcheth—[R]men put an end to darkness, and search (Job 28.3, referring to miners working with lamps); ᴶshall he run—ᴿshall men leap (Is 33.4); ᴶhe made his grave—ᴿthey made his grave (53.9); ᴶhe will take you away—ᴿthey shall take you away (Amos 4.2); ᴶhe shall come—ᴿthey will come (Mic 7.12). See also § 107.

The same kind of "smoothing," which is sometimes found necessary as between the second and third person (§ 94), is also required on occasion with regard to the singular and plural. In Judg 14.3 R changes "my people" to "our people" to fit the context, following "his father and mother said to him." Singular pronouns are changed to plural in Job 21.19–21 to agree with the preceding verses. In Job 24.17 J inserts five words in a rather desperate attempt to do justice to the singular form of a Hebrew verb, though the context clearly calls for a plural: ᴶif one know them, they are in the terrors—ᴿfor they are friends with the terrors (lit. for he is acquainted with the terrors, but cp "them" earlier in the v. and "they" in v. 16). Of two words that belong together in Prov 3.18, one is plural and the other singular; J translates both as singular, R makes both plural: ᴶhappy is every one that retaineth her—ᴿthose who hold her fast are called happy. Many other instances of this kind might be cited, but they are usually fairly obvious efforts to smooth out a passage where J, translating literally, contains incongruities that are more disturbing to us now than they apparently were to the Hebrews.

Not all changes from singular to plural reflect less literal translation in R. Sometimes J's singular form is replaced with a plural by R to agree with the original.

So, e.g., ᴶan handbreadth—ᴿa few handbreadths (Ps 39.5); ᴶher waves—ᴿTheir waves (Jer 51.55); ᴶthe camp—ᴿcamps (Ezek 4.2); ᴶmore than any living—ᴿmore than all the living (Dan 2.30, Aramaic); ᴶthe greatness of the kingdom—ᴿthe greatness of the kingdoms (7.27, Aramaic); ᴶfort—ᴿfortresses (11.19).

§ 97 Plural forms in J are changed to singular forms in R about as often as the opposite change, and for much the same reasons. Certain nouns sometimes occur in the plural in Hebrew where we normally use the singular, and J's overliteral translations are often changed by R to conform to our English idiom;

e.g., [J]mercies—[R]mercy (2 Sam 24.14 etc., 11 times; also Dan 2.18, Aramaic; but cp Neh 9.19, 27f, 31, [JR]mercies); [J]tender mercies—[R]mercy (Ps 25.6 etc., 11 times); [J]compassions—[R]mercies (Lam 3.22), mercy (Zech 7.9); [J]lovingkindnesses—[R]steadfast love (Ps 25.6; 89.49; Is 63.7 twice; cp § 77); [J]mercies—[R]steadfast love (Gen 32.10; 2 Chron 6.42; Ps 89.1; 106.7, 45; 119.41; Is 55.3; Lam 3.22, 32); [J]righteousnesses—[R]righteousness (Dan 9.18), righteous deeds (Is 64.6; Ezek 33.13; cp § 57, No. 11); [J]loves—[R]love (Prov 7.18; Song 7.12; for two different Hebrew words); [J]recompences—[R]recompense (Jer 51.56); [J]desolations—[R]desolation (Ezek 35.9); [J]his hairs—[R]his hair (Dan 4.33, Aramaic); [J]the matters [Or, *words*]—[R]the matter (7.1, Aramaic); [J]booties—[R]booty (Hab 2.7).

A somewhat different case is the Hebrew word for "heaven" or "heavens," which is used only in the plural. J and R alike use both the singular and the plural of the English word, but they differ sometimes in their choice of the one or the other;

e.g., [J]the heaven—[R]the heavens (Gen 1.14f); [J]the new heavens—[R]the new heaven (Is 66.22; cp 65.17, [JR]new heavens).

In other places the singular is more appropriate or more in accord with normal English usage in the context;

e.g., [J]they shall make thee to eat grass as oxen—[R]you shall be made to eat grass like an ox (Dan 4.32, Aramaic; cp v. 33; 5.21); [J]no beasts might stand before him—[R]no beast could stand before him (8.4); [J]between the seas in the glorious holy mountain—[R]between the sea and the glorious holy mountain (11.45).

The impersonal use of a verb in the third person masculine singular was noted in § 96. Hebrew uses also the plural, as we do (e.g., they say). Where J uses "men" or "they" in this connection, R sometimes uses "one" or "no one";

e.g., [J]men have not heard, nor perceived—[R]no one has heard or perceived (Is 64.4); [J]neither shall men lament for them, nor cut themselves, nor make themselves bald for them—[R]and no one shall lament for them or cut himself or make himself bald for them (Jer 16.6; cp v. 7); [J]they shall not prophesy—[R]One should not preach (Mic 2.6). See also § 107.

Here too J and R sometimes resort to "smoothing" (§§ 94, 96), changing in this case from plural to singular forms to remove discrepancies or incongruities. In Prov 4.22, where the Hebrew says literally, "life are they to those who find them, and to all his flesh healing," J and R both smooth out the incongruity but in opposite ways: [J]they are life unto those that find them, and health to all their flesh—[R]they are life to him who finds them, and healing to all his flesh. In another place J changes a singular to a plural to prevent misunderstanding; R keeps the singular but inserts a proper name: [J]hell hath enlarged herself . . . : and their glory, and their multitude, and their pomp . . . shall descend—[R]Sheol has enlarged its appetite . . . and the nobility of Jerusalem [Heb *her nobility*] and her multitude go down, her throng . . . (Is 5.14). In Obad 1.6 the Hebrew means literally "How are searched Esau"; J follows the plural of the verb, R the singular of the noun: [J]How are the things of Esau searched out—[R]How Esau has been pillaged.

§98 Singular nouns are sometimes translated by J as plural, being apparently understood as collective;

e.g., [J]oxen and fatlings—[R]an ox and a fatling (2 Sam 6.13); [J]chariots—[R]a chariot (15.1); [J]lions—[R]a lion (Is 15.9); [J]palaces—[R]palace (Is 32.14); [J]the forts and towers—[R]the watchtower (same v.); [J]high places—[R]high place (Jer 48.35); [J]cedars . . . masts—[R]a cedar . . . a mast (Ezek 27.5); [J]the open fields [Heb. *face of the field*]—[R]the open field (29.5); [J]the chambers and the entries thereof—[R]a chamber with its door (40.38); [J]and laws—[R]and the law (Dan 7.25, Aramaic; lit. and law); [J]the most fenced cities—[R]a well-fortified city (11.15); [J]floods—[R]flood (Jon 2.3); [J]borders—[R]border (Mic 5.6); [J]thresholds—[R]threshold (Zeph 2.14); [J]bowls—[R]a bowl (Zech 9.15). In Eccles 7.12 R translates a plural noun by a collective singular: [J]them that have it—[R]him who has it (i.e., wisdom; lit. her possessors).

A complicated case is Ezek 43.8, where the Hebrew has four singular nouns in succession (lit. their threshold, my threshold, their doorpost, my doorpost). J and R both translate the first literally as singular; J renders the second as plural and the third as singular; R renders the second as singular and the third as plural; both render the fourth as plural.

J's reason for translating a singular form as plural is not clear in some instances;

e.g., [J]their villages—[R]its villages (Neh 11.31; the Hebrew singular suffix refers only to the last named city, Bethel); [J]all thine iniquities—[R]all your iniquity (Ps 103.3); [J]unto them—[R]for it (Is 5.26); [J]they shall come—[R]it comes (same v.; in vv. 28–30 R shifts to the plural with J); [J]in the midst of them—[R]in the midst of it (25.11); [J]the ends of the earth—[R]the end of the earth (43.6); [J]toward all winds—[R]to every wind (Ezek 17.21); [J]when they shall be in the siege [Or, . . . shall he be *which shall be in siege*]—[R]it will be . . . in the siege (Zech 12.2).

The word *'lohīm* (God, god, gods, § 43, No. 1) is plural in form but more often than not singular in meaning. In at least two places J takes it as plural where the context shows that the singular is intended: [J]gods—[R]a god (1 Sam 28.13, cp v. 14); [J]your gods —[R]your god (1 Kings 18.25, cp vv. 26f). Either interpretation is possible in Jer 48.35, [J]his gods—[R]his god.

A few special cases remain to be mentioned:

[J]in the congregations—[R]in the great congregation (Ps 26.12, lit. in congregations; R's "great" represents the plural form, understood as "intensive"); [J]their masters' houses—[R]their master's house (Zeph 1.9, lit. their masters' house, the plural form of "master" being an "intensive plural of rank").

Hebrew and Aramaic have not only singular and plural but also dual forms. Usually the dual is clearly recognized by J and R alike, but it is at least more clearly represented by R in Dan 7.4 (Aramaic), [J]upon the feet—[R]upon two feet.

Chapter XXIII

THE CASES

§ 99 With one exception (for which see §§ 100–102), there are no case endings or other special forms to indicate what we call the "case" of a noun, pronoun, or adjective. The names used for the cases in Indo-European languages can be applied only in an approximate way to Hebrew words; in general, however, the relations of words to one another and their functions in the sentence correspond to those of Indo-European grammar. The use of our names for the cases is therefore justified as a convenient way of indicating the places words have in a sentence.

The lack of distinctive case forms sometimes makes possible in Hebrew, as in English, ambiguity and confusion. In English, while we still have case inflections for pronouns, we depend largely upon the order of words in the sentence to show whether a noun is the subject or object. The normal order, however, is not rigidly followed, and ambiguity is not always avoided (cp Chapter VI). This is perhaps even more so in Hebrew. There is thus some occasion for differences of interpretation.

J and R sometimes differ as to what is the subject of a sentence; e.g., [J]the street shall be built again, and the wall [Or, *breach,* or *ditch*]—[R]it shall be built again with squares and moat (i.e., Jerusalem, Dan 9.25; lit. it shall be built again, square and moat). A somewhat similar instance of a noun in apposition with the subject is Lev 6.16, [J]with unleavened bread shall it be eaten —[R]it shall be eaten unleavened (lit. unleavened bread it shall be eaten).

In § 15 the idiomatic construction known as "prolepsis" has been noted as one which R often simplifies in translation. The examples given there illustrate one form of this idiom; another consists of the use of the "hanging nominative," i.e., a noun or pronoun standing by itself before a sentence in which it is repeated by a pronoun or the like. In English we often use the expression "As for . . . " in this way, and R sometimes adopts this way of representing the Hebrew idiom where J simplifies the construction.

So, e.g., [J]And the cities which ye shall give shall be of the possession of the children of Israel—[R]And as for the cities which you shall give from the possession of the people of Israel (Num 35.8); [J]The fourth beast shall be the fourth kingdom—[R]As for the fourth beast, there shall be a fourth kingdom (Dan 7.23, Aramaic; cp v. 24); [J]Also I in the first year . . . , even I, stood—[R]And as for me, in the first year . . . I stood up (11.1); [J]And both these kings' hearts [Heb. *their hearts*] shall—[R]And as for the two kings, their minds shall (v. 27).

In other places both J and R smooth out the idiom but in different ways, without any basic difference of interpretation (e.g., Is 34.3; Ezek 11.5; 42.7; 47.12; Hos 8.6; Zech 3.9).

Sometimes a noun or name which J understands as in the vocative case (i.e., in direct address) is taken by R as the subject of the sentence;

e.g., [J]O God, thou art terrible—[R]Terrible is God (Ps 68.35); [J]Thou art my portion, O LORD—[R]The LORD is my portion (Ps 119.57); [J]I will destroy thee, O covering cherub—[R]the guardian cherub drove you out (Ezek 28.16). In Prov 24.15 what J takes as a vocative is treated by R as a nominative, in apposition with the subject: [J]Lay not wait, O wicked man—[R]Lie not in wait as a wicked man.

The opposite change also occurs, what J takes as the subject of a sentence becoming in R a term of direct address;

e.g., [J]Thou art our sister, be thou—[R]Our sister, be (Gen 24.60); [J]for the righteous God trieth . . .—[R]thou who triest . . . , thou righteous God (Ps 7.9); [J]God is—[R]thou, O God, art (Ps 59.9, 17); [J]The inhabitants . . . brought [Or, *bring ye*]—[R]bring . . . , O inhabitants . . . (Is 21.14); [J]as he [Or, *O he*] that heweth . . . and that graveth—[R]you who hew . . . and carve (22.16); [J]And when thou art spoiled—[R]And you, O desolate one (Jer 4.30); [J]the Great, the Mighty God, the LORD of hosts, is his name—[R]O great and mighty God whose name is the LORD of hosts (32.18). See also Jer 47.5; Ezek 21.10; Zeph 3.16.

§ 100 What in Hebrew corresponds to our possessive or genitive case has several peculiarities of usage which are sometimes hard to translate or even to understand. Where in English we use a possessive pronoun, the Hebrew has a suffix; where both the possessor and the thing possessed are indicated by nouns, they appear in the "construct relation" mentioned in § 91, which must now be briefly explained. Instead of using as we do the possessive case or a preposition, or having a special ending for the possessor, Hebrew uses a special (usually shorter) form of the word for the thing possessed; i.e., instead of saying "the man's house" or "the house of-the-man," it says "house-of the man."

J sometimes fails to recognize this construction;

e.g., [J]king Arad—[R]the king of Arad (Num 21.1); [J]his bones are moistened with marrow—[R]the marrow of his bones is moistened (Job 21.24; the singular verb should have prevented J's mistake here); [J]strength and wisdom [Heb. *heart*]—[R]strength of understanding (36.5); [J]at the time appointed the end shall be—[R]it pertains to the appointed time of the end (Dan 8.19). In 1 Chron 4.19 two nouns in succession are in the "construct state"; J reproduces the first correctly but not the second: [J]And the sons of his wife Hodiah—[R]The sons of the wife of Hodiah.

Both J and R paraphrase the construct relation sometimes in particular connections;

e.g., [J]the land is worth four hundred shekels—[R]a piece of land worth four hundred shekels (Gen 23.15, lit. land of four hundred shekels). R occasionally replaces "of" with some other preposition to represent this construction: among (Ezek 32.2; Dan 11.14), from (Mal 4.2), in (Is 45.3; Hab 2.16), on (1 Kings 12.31). More elaborate forms of paraphrase are used in a few places; e.g., [J]the abomination of his eyes—[R]the detestable things your eyes feast on (Ezek 20.7, cp v. 8; R's "your" is an example of "smoothing," § 94).

Either the construct relation or a possessive suffix may represent a "subjective" or an "objective" genitive, just as we might say "the love of a man" either for the love he feels for another person or for the love someone else feels for him. In Zech 14.13 J and R both say "from the Lord" instead of "of the Lord" to make it clear that God is the subject who causes the panic (J tumult), not the object whom others frighten. R uses various forms of expression to avoid J's frequent ambiguity in this respect.

The following examples may serve to illustrate the "subjective genitive":

[J]the oppression of man—[R]man's oppression (Ps 119.134); [J]the God of my mercy—[R]the God who shows me steadfast love (Ps 59.17); [J]The fear of the wicked—[R]What the wicked dreads (Prov 10.24); [J]their calamity—[R]disaster from them (24.22); [J]the ruin of them both—[R]the ruin that will come from them both (i.e., God and the king, same v.); [J]the sighing thereof—[R]the sighing she has caused (Is 21.2); [J]I heard the defaming of many—[R]I hear many whispering (Jer 20.10); [J]Thy terribleness—[R]The horror you inspire (49.16); [J]her blood—[R]the blood she has shed (Ezek 24.7f). Sometimes R translates literally a subjective genitive which has been paraphrased by J; e.g., [J]the man that executeth my counsels—[R]the man of my counsel (Is 46.11); [J]the reproach offered by him [Heb. *his reproach*]—[R]his insolence (Dan 11.18; cp, later in the v., [J]his own reproach—[R]his insolence).

In some places J takes as an objective genitive what R understands as subjective;

e.g., [J]for fear of thee—[R]for your fear of him (Job 22.4); [J]for this a man is envied [Heb. *this is the envy of a man*]—[R]come from a man's envy (Eccles 4.4); [J]when I am reproved [Or, *when I am argued with.* Heb. *upon my reproof,* or, *argument*]—[R]concerning my complaint (Hab 2.1).

In other instances R sees an objective genitive where J either is ambiguous or represents the genitive as subjective;

e.g., [J]to my wounding . . . to my hurt . . .—[R]for wounding me . . . for striking me (Gen 4.23); [J]My wrong—[R]the wrong done to me (16.5; Lam 3.59; cp Obad 1.10; Hab 2.8, 17); [J]the cry of Sodom and Gomorrah—[R]the outcry against Sodom and Gomorrah (Gen 18.20; cp 19.13); [J]their evil report—[R]an ill report of them (37.2; cp Is 23.5; Hab 3.2);

[J]the days of his mourning—[R]the days of weeping for him (Gen 50.4; cp Zech 12.11).

Somewhat more elaborate ways of representing the objective genitive may be seen in Ps 39.11; 106.4; 132.1; Prov 19.22; Is 53.5; Jer 33.20 (cp v. 25); Nahum 2.3; Zech 11.4; 14.1, 15.

In 2 Sam 5.6, an extremely idiomatic and difficult verse, an infinitive with a personal suffix is followed by two nouns. The suffix is interpreted by J as a subjective genitive and by R as objective; the two nouns are taken by J as objective and by R as subjective genitives: [J]Except thou take away the blind and the lame—[R]but the blind and the lame will ward you off (lit. except the turning away of you of the blind and the lame).

§101 Frequent use is made in OT Hebrew of the "adjectival genitive," i.e., a noun in the genitive case instead of an adjective. Thus, for instance, the Hebrew says, literally, "flies of death," meaning "dead flies" ([JR]Eccles 10.1). This usage is well recognized by J and frequently translated, as it is here, by an adjective, but by no means always; in fact neither J nor R is entirely consistent, and in some places it is debatable whether the adjectival meaning was intended. Out of countless examples that might be cited, only a limited number can be presented here, involving a few important nouns which are used especially often in the "adjectival genitive."

(1) *kābōd* (glory): [J]the eyes of his glory—[R]his glorious presence (Is 3.8); [J]the chariots of thy glory—[R]your splendid chariots (22.18); [J]the throne of thy glory—[R]thy glorious throne (Jer 14.21; but cp Is 22.23, [J]a glorious throne—[R]a throne of honor).

(2) *tip'eret* (beauty, glory); [J]a crown of glory—[R]a beautiful crown (Prov 4.9; cp Is 28.5, [JR]a crown of glory . . . a diadem of beauty; here "glory" represents *ṣbī*); [J]the house of my glory—[R]my glorious house (Is 60.7).

(3) *qōdeš* (holiness, sanctuary): [J]from the habitation of thy holiness and of thy glory—[R]from thy holy and glorious habitation (Is 63.15, with No. 2; in the context JR both recognize several other adjectival genitives); [J]the mountain of his holiness—[R]His holy mountain (Ps 48.1); [J]mountain of holiness—[R]holy hill (Jer 31.23); [JR]the glorious holy mountain (Dan 11.45; J mg, Heb. *mountain of delight of holiness;* "glorious" here too represents *ṣbī*); see also Ps 47.8; Is 35.8; 63.18; Jer 23.9. Cp

[J]the stones of the sanctuary—[R]the holy stones (Lam 4.1; cp Num 31.6, [J]the holy instruments—[R]the vessels of the sanctuary). See also § 74, No. 5, on *hadrat qōdeš:* [J]the beauty of holiness—[R]holy array.

(4) *mamlākāh* and *malkūt* (kingdom, kingship, royalty): [J]royal cities [Heb. *cities of the kingdom*]—[R]royal cities (Josh 10.2); [J]the throne of the kingdom—[R]the royal throne (1 Kings 1.46; cp 9.5; 1 Chron 22.10; 28.5; 2 Chron 23.20); [J]the sceptre of thy kingdom—[R]Your royal scepter (Ps 45.6); see also Dan 4.29 (Aramaic); 6.26 (Aramaic); 11.21 for "kingdom" as an adjectival genitive, meaning "royal."

(5) *ṣedeq* and *ṣdāqāh* (§ 57, Nos. 10f): [J]the Branch of righteousness—[R]the righteous Branch (Jer 33.15); [J]thy righteous judgments [Heb. *judgments of thy righteousness*]—[R]thy righteous ordinances (Ps 119.7; without note v. 62); [J]the word of thy righteousness—[R]thy righteous promise (v. 123); [J]the right hand of my righteousness—[R]my victorious right hand (Is 41.10); [J]sacrifices of righteousness—[R]right sacrifices (Deut 33.19; Ps 4.5; 51.19); [J]the habitation of justice—[R]their true habitation (Jer 50.7).

Closely related to the adjectival genitive, or a variety of it, is the use of a noun to describe or qualify another, just as we use the prepositions "of" and "with" (e.g., a man of great wisdom, The House of Seven Gables);

e.g., [J]a little chamber . . . on the wall—[R]a small roof chamber with walls (2 Kings 4.10, lit. upper chamber of wall, i.e., not merely an open arbor or shelter); [J]like clay to the seal—[R]like clay under the seal (Job 38.14, lit. like clay of seal, i.e., sealing clay).

§ 102 Another use of the construct relation may be called for convenience the "genitive of specification," as in our English "long of limb" for "long-limbed." Sometimes two nouns are so combined;

e.g., [J]uprightness of heart—[R]an upright heart (Ps 119.7); [J]of perfect beauty—[R]perfect in beauty (Ezek 27.3, lit. completeness of beauty); [J]of low stature—[R]low (17.6, lit. lowness of height).

More often the word modified by the genitive is an adjective;

e.g., [JR]perfect in knowledge (Job 36.4; 37.16; lit. perfect of knowledge); [J]one that hath a pleasant voice—[R]with a beautiful voice (Ezek 33.32, lit. beautiful of voice); [J]the undefiled [Or, *perfect,* or, *sincere*] in the way—[R]those whose way is blameless (Ps 119.1, lit. perfect of way; cp Prov 11.20, same Hebrew, [J]upright in their way—[R]of blameless ways).

The adjectives "long" and "short" are frequently used in this way;

e.g., [J]longwinged—[R]of long pinions (Ezek 17.3); [J]of few days [Heb. *short of days*]—[R]of few days (Job 14.1); cp [JR]slow to anger (Neh 9.17; Ps 103.8; 145.8; Prov 15.18; 16.32; Joel 2.13; Jon 4.2; Nahum 1.3); [J]slow to wrath—[R]slow to anger (Prov 14.29); [J]longsuffering—[R]slow to anger (Ex 34.6; Num 14.18; Ps 86.15; lit. long of anger); [JR]the patient in spirit (Eccles 7.8, lit. long of spirit); [J]He that is soon angry—[R]A man of quick temper (Prov 14.17, lit. short of anger); [J]he that is hasty of spirit [Heb. *short of spirit*]—[R]he who has a hasty temper (Prov 14.29).

There is also in Hebrew what we may call the "genitive of apposition," by which two nouns referring to the same person or thing are stated in the construct relation, as though one modified the other (an idiom found also in English);

e.g., [J]a wild man—[R]a wild ass of a man (Gen 16.12); [J]the border of Arnon—[R]the boundary formed by the Arnon (Num 22.36); [J]the virgin of Israel—[R]The virgin Israel (Jer 18.13, cp 31.4, 21; Amos 5.2); [J]the joy of their glory—[R]their joy and glory (Ezek 24.25); [J]The strong among the mighty—[R]The mighty chiefs (Ezek 32.21, lit. mighty ones of mighty men; see § 43, No. 2; but cp, with the same two nouns in the singular, Is 9.6, [J]The mighty God—[R]Mighty God); [J]the star of your god—[R]your star-god (Amos 5.26).

Just as a noun in the construct state does not have a definite article, so too it does not take a possessive suffix; a suffix which belongs to it is therefore attached to the noun which follows and modifies it. Thus "the holy spirit" is in Hebrew (§ 101) "Spirit of holiness," but "his holy Spirit" is "Spirit of his holiness," not "his Spirit of holiness" (so, e.g., Is 63.10f). So too [JR]his glorious arm (v. 12) is in the Hebrew "arm of his glory." J often renders this idiomatic construction too literally, suggesting sometimes meanings not intended by the Hebrew writers;

e.g., [J]the head of his consecration—[R]his consecrated head (Num 6.9, 18); [J]the raiment of her captivity—[R]her captive's garb (Deut 21.13); [J]make the habitation of thy righteousness prosperous—[R]reward you with a rightful habitation (Job 8.6); ^{J}the border of his sanctuary—^{R}his holy land (Ps 78.54, cp § 71, No. 5); ^{J}the bill of your mother's divorcement—^{R}your mother's bill of divorce (Is 50.1); ^{J}the year of my redeemed—^{R}my year of redemption [Or *the year of my redeemed*] (63.4; R understands the second Hebrew word as an abstract noun); ^{J}the chambers of his imagery—^{R}his room of pictures (Ezek 8.12); ^{J}the occupiers of thy merchandise—^{R}your dealers in merchandise (27.27); ^{J}the pleasant places [Heb. *the desire*] for their silver [Or, *their silver shall be desired*]—^{R}their precious things of silver (Hos 9.6); ^{J}the wife of thy covenant—^{R}your wife by covenant (Mal 2.14).

A few apparent exceptions to this rule have caused much perplexity. In Song 1.15; 4.1 the Hebrew reads literally, "your eyes doves." J translates this, "thou hast doves' eyes," presupposing the meaning, "your eyes are (eyes of) doves." R reads more literally here, "your eyes are doves." Cp Mal 2.5, ^{J}My covenant was with him of life and peace—^{R}my covenant with him was a covenant of life and peace (lit. my covenant was with him life and peace; here R sees a meaning like that assumed by J in Song 1.15; 4.1).

Most difficult of all is Ps 45.6, ^{J}Thy throne, O God—^{R}Your divine throne [Or *Your throne is a throne of God,* or *Thy throne, O God*]. The Hebrew here reads literally, "your (or thy) throne God." R assumes in this case an exceptional use of the personal suffix with a noun in the construct state, lit. your throne of God, i.e., your divine throne. Such an exception to the rule might be justified by the fact that the more normal form of expression, lit. "throne of your God," would convey a meaning different from what was intended. R mg recognizes, however, the possibility of other interpretations, including (in printings from 1960 on) that of J. The variation between "your" and "thy," of course, reflects the differing interpretations of the whole Psalm as "messianic" or addressed to the reigning king (cp § 43, No. 1).

Like the personal suffix, a demonstrative pronoun must be attached to the second noun in the construct relation, even though it belongs properly to the first. Here again J sometimes ignores the idiom and conveys the wrong meaning by translating too literally;

e.g., [J]the year of this jubile—[R]this year of jubilee (Lev 25.13); [J]the book of this covenant—[R]this book of the covenant (2 Kings 23.21); [J]the wine cup of this fury—[R]this cup of the wine of wrath (Jer 25.15).

§ 103 There is no special form for the accusative (objective) case, aside from the use of the particle *'ēt* to designate the direct object of a verb (§ 92, No. 4). In general the accusative case is used much as in other languages, but some ways of using it are much more common in Hebrew than in English and must often be translated more or less freely.

Among these is the "cognate accusative," using for the object a noun from the same root as the verb, as in "dream a dream" or "fight a fight." Only rarely is any serious problem of interpretation involved; a few examples of this idiom and of J's and R's ways of handling it will therefore suffice for our purpose.

(a) *Breach a breach:* [J]had made a breach—[R]had broken forth (1 Chron 13.11). (b) *Capture a captivity:* [J]thou hast led captivity captive—[R]leading captives in thy train (Ps 68.18; cp Amos 1.6, 9); cp Is 22.17, [J]the LORD will carry thee away with a mighty captivity [Or, *the* LORD *who covered thee with an excellent covering*]—[R]the LORD will hurl you away violently (lit. hurl you a hurling). (c) *Devise a device:* [J]devise a device—[R]devising a plan (Jer 18.11; cp v. 18). (d) *Judge a judgment:* [J]Execute true judgment [Heb. *Judge judgment of truth*]—[R]Render true judgments (Zech 7.9; cp 8.16). (e) *Sacrifice a sacrifice:* [J]let them sacrifice the sacrifices of thanksgiving—[R]let them offer sacrifices of thanksgiving (Ps 107.22; cp Ezek 39.17, 19). (f) *Serve service:* [J]my service which I have done thee—[R]the service which I have given you (Gen 30.26); [J]caused his army to serve a great service—[R]made his army labor hard (Ezek 29.18); [J]for the service that he had served—[R]for the labor that he had performed (same v.). (g) *Sin a sin:* [J]the sins . . . by which they sinned, and by which they made Israel to sin—[R]the sins . . . which they sinned, and which they made Israel to sin (1 Kings 16.13; cp v. 26; 2 Kings 10.29, 31; 13.2 etc.); note also transgress a transgression, trespass a trespass (§ 84, Nos. 7, 9). (h) *Smite a smiting:* [J]smote . . . with the stroke of the sword—[R]smote . . . with the sword (Esther 9.5); [J]wounded thee with the wound—[R]dealt you the blow (Jer 30.14). (i) *Spoil a spoiling (rob a robbery*): [J]hath spoiled none by violence—[R]commits no robbery (Ezek 18.7; cp v. 16); [J]have used oppression, and exercised robbery—[R]have practiced extortion and committed robbery (22.29); [J]To take a spoil [Heb. *To spoil the spoil*]—[R]to seize spoil (38.12; cp v. 13; note also, same vv., [J]take a prey [Heb. . . . *prey the prey*]—[R]carry off plunder). (j) *Swarm a swarm:* [J]bring forth abundantly—[R]bring forth swarms (Gen 1.20; cp v. 21). (k) *Trust a trust:* [J]What confidence is this wherein thou trustest?—[R]On what do you rest this confidence of yours? (2 Kings 18.19, lit. What is this trust which you trust?) (l) *Vow a vow:* [J]they shall vow a vow—[R]they will make vows (Is 19.21; cp Jer 44.25).

§ 104 Nouns appear also in what we may call the adverbial accusative, corresponding to a phrase without a preposition. J and R usually insert a preposition to convey the force of an adverbial accusative, but they frequently differ in their choice of the preposition, reflecting a difference of interpretation; in fact they do not always agree that the noun in question is in the accusative case at all. Only the context, of course, can determine the meaning in such instances.

Various connections are expressed in this way, including the end or direction of motion, place, time, manner, instrument or means, and specification. The following examples illustrate the varying interpretations and renderings of adverbial accusatives in J and R:

[J]Out of that land went forth Asshur—[R]From that land he went into Assyria (Gen 10.11); [J]he came with the heads of the people—[R]he came to the heads of the people (Deut 33.21); [J]went up toward Jerusalem—[R]came up to Jerusalem (Is 7.1); [J]through the wilderness—[R]to the desert (16.8); [J]at Gilgal—[R]to Gilgal (Amos 4.4); [J]in the midst of the river of Gad—[R]in the middle of the valley, toward Gad (2 Sam 24.5); [J]in the sanctuary—[R]to the holy place (Ps 134.2); [J]in the valley—[R]to the valley (Num 21.20); [J]to the top of Pisgah—[R]by the top of Pisgah (same v.); [J]near Jericho—[R]at Jericho (Num 26.3, 63; 31.12; 33.50); [J]even thine altars—[R]at thy altars (Ps 84.3; J takes "altars" as in apposition with "house" and "nest"); [J]the place of judgment . . . the place of righteousness—[R]in the place of justice . . . in the place of righteousness (Eccles 3.16; J takes "place" both times as object of "I saw"); [J]of the house—[R]in the house (Is 3.6; J translates as a genitive, which the form shows to be impossible); [J]the waste places—[R]among the ruins (Is 5.17; again J takes as object; cp v. 24, where J takes "flame" as subject); [J]and darkness shall pursue his enemies—[R]and will pursue his enemies into darkness (Nahum 1.8; cp the parallel, "he will make . . ."); [J]Deliver thyself, O Zion—[R]Escape to Zion (Zech 2.7); [J]these are the four spirits

[Or, *winds*] of the heavens, which go forth—[R]These are going forth to the four winds of heaven (6.5); [J]and there shall be a very great valley—[R]by a very wide valley (14.4); [J]which is thy sword [Or, by *thy sword*]—[R]by thy sword (Ps 17.13; cp v. 14); [J]the boughs thereof were like—[R]with its branches (80.10; cp the parallel, "with its shade"); [J]it shall be a kindness—[R]in kindness (141.5).

Chapter XXIV

VERB-FORMS: THE STEMS; ACTIVE AND PASSIVE

§105 Nothing is more characteristic of the Semitic languages than their method of modifying the meaning of a verb by changes in its form. Not only are person, number, and gender indicated by prefixes and endings, but from each "root" grow several "stems," marked by prefixes, vowel-changes, or the doubling of this or that consonant. Only in exceptional cases is there any difference between J and R in their understanding of the force of the stems, yet some of the differences are more or less important. A brief account of the stems is therefore necessary here. Reduced to the simplest terms they are as follows:

I. Simple narrative, active (*Qal*);
II. Simple narrative, passive (usually), or (sometimes) reflexive (*Niphal*);
III. Intensive, active (*Piel,* etc.);
IV. Intensive, passive (*Pual,* etc.);
V. Causative, active (*Hiphil*);
VI. Causative, passive (*Hophal*);
VII. Reflexive (*Hithpael,* etc.).

For the benefit of Hebrew students the conventional names of the stems are given in parentheses; but since these names mean nothing to readers who have not studied Hebrew, the Roman numerals in the foregoing list will be used to designate the stems in what follows.

Occasionally J and R differ in their identification of a stem, because at some points, in some classes of verbs, the corresponding forms of two stems happen to be the same. In Ezek 9.1, for example, J reads the verb as III (understood here as causative);

R reads it as I: [J]cause . . . to draw near—[R]Draw near (cp Is 41.21, where JR understand the same form as III). In Job 24.7 the verb "lodge" may be either I or V; J takes it as the latter, R as the former: [J]cause . . . to lodge—[R]lie all night. The form of a verb in Ps 109.19 may be either I or V; the former means "wrap oneself in," the latter "cover." J takes it as V, R as I: [J]which covereth him—[R]which he wraps round him. The form of "hear" in Eccles 12.13 may be either the first person plural of I (as J reads it) or the third person singular of II (so R): [J]Let us hear—[R]has been heard.

Stem II causes more trouble than any other, because it may be either passive or reflexive in meaning. Sometimes both J and R understand it as reflexive (e.g., Prov 6.3, 5; Is 48.2). The most conspicuous and perhaps most important example of disagreement between J and R at this point is the expression used in Gen 12.3, [J]in thee shall all families of the earth be blessed—[R]by you all the families of the earth shall bless themselves [Or *in you all the families of the earth shall be blessed*] (cp 18.18; 28.14). R recognizes here a real alternative, but the reflexive meaning is supported by the fact that Stem VII is used in the same formula in Gen 22.18 and 26.4 and in Ps 72.17. What is meant is made clear by Gen 48.20, [J]In thee shall Israel bless, saying, God make thee as Ephraim and as Manasseh—[R]By you Israel will pronounce blessings, saying, 'God make you as Ephraim and as Manasseh.'

Other places where Stem II is taken as passive by J and as reflexive (variously translated) by R include the following:

[J]was I not known—[R]I did not make myself known (Ex 6.3; cp Is 19.21; Ezek 38.23); [J]be defiled—[R]defile himself (Lev 21.1, 3; cp Ezek 20.30f, where J has both interpretations; v. 7, [J]defile not yourselves—[R]do not defile yourselves; note also 23.30; cp v. 7, [JR]she defiled herself); [J]he was sold—[R]he sold himself (Lev 25.50; cp v. 47, [J]sell himself—[R]sells himself; see also Is 50.1; 52.3); [J]I will be glorified—[R]I will manifest my glory (Ezek 28.22; cp 39.13); [J]and shall be sanctified—[R]and manifest my holiness (28.22, 25; cp 36.23; 39.27).

In Gen 17.11 J ignores the normal passive force of Stem II because it seems to have a direct object, but R recognizes this as an adverbial accusative of specification (§ 104): [J]ye shall circumcise the flesh of your foreskin—[R]you shall be circumcised in the flesh of your foreskins; cp v. 14, [J]whose flesh of his foreskin is not circumcised—[R]who is not circumcised in the flesh of his foreskin; vv. 24f, [JR]when he was circumcised in the flesh of his foreskin.

§ 106 Stems III and IV cause little difficulty, but their basic "intensive" force includes various shades of meaning. One of these is the "frequentative," indicating continued repetition of an act. Sometimes also they may have the causative meaning more often expressed by V and VI. In Job 24.10 J takes as causative a verb which R understands as frequentative: [J]They cause him to go naked—[R]They go about naked. The force of Stem III in Ps 30.1 is treated by R as permissive rather than strictly causative: [J]and hast not made my foes to rejoice—[R]and hast not let my foes rejoice.

With some verbs Stem I is never used and Stem III has only the simple narrative meaning. J fails to recognize this fact in Ezek 13.6, [J]they have made others to hope—[R]they expect (J here inserts "others"). In Deut 21.23 J translates Stem III as passive for no apparent reason: [J]that thy land be not defiled—[R]you shall not defile your land.

Similar fluctuations appear in the use of Stem V. The permissive meaning assigned by R to Stem III in Ps 30.1 is recognized by both J and R in Ezek 39.7 in Stem V: [J]I will not let them pollute my holy name—[R]I will not let my holy name be profaned. J and R interpret Is 29.21 somewhat differently: [J]make a man an offender—[R]make a man out to be an offender (lit. cause to sin; cp for a word—by a word).

Stem V sometimes indicates beginning or becoming rather than cause; e.g., [J]made him sick—[R]became sick (Hos 7.5).

The normal causative force is ignored by J in some places; e.g., [J]let righteousness spring up—[R]let it cause righteousness to spring up (Is 45.8); [J]are profound—[R]have made deep (Hos 5.2). On the other hand, verbs which are used regularly in Stem V in a simple narrative sense are occasionally treated as causative by J, even though this necessitates supplying an object: [J]they make the oppressed to cry—[R]people cry out (Job 35.9); [J]cause me to behold—[R]look upon (Hab 1.3). In Is 48.15 the difference between J and R is one of idiomatic translation rather than interpretation: [J]he shall make his way prosperous—[R]he will prosper in his way; cp Jer 5.28, [J]yet they prosper—[R]to make it prosper (i.e., the cause of the fatherless).

A verb which occurs nowhere else appears twice in Amos 2.13. Authorities differ as to its meaning, but JR accept an interpretation which in English is naturally rendered as passive: I, be pressed; V, cause to be pressed, i.e., press. The first occurrence is clearly V; the second may be I or V. J translates both as passive, with an active rendering in the margin; R reads both as active: [J]I am pressed under you [Or, *I will press your place*]—[R]I will press you down in your place (cp § 87, No. 3); [J]is pressed [Or, . . . *presseth*]—[R]presses down.

J often treats Stem VII as passive rather than reflexive;

e.g., [J]shall be shaven—[R]shall shave himself (Lev 13.33; cp context); [J]were purified—[R]purified themselves (Num 8.21); [J]shall be purified, and made white—[R]shall purify themselves, and make themselves white (Dan 12.10); [J]shall not be reckoned—[R]not reckoning itself (Num 23.9); [J]be sold—[R]offer yourselves for sale (Deut 28.68; cp but no man will buy you); [J]was strengthened—[R]established himself (2 Chron. 1.1); [J]were not sanctified—[R]had not sanctified themselves (30.17); [J]it is turned—[R]they turn (Job 37.12, lit. turn themselves; cp 38.14, [J]It is turned—[R]It is changed); [J]is known—[R]makes himself known (Prov 20.11; Stem I means "be known"); [J]will I be exalted—[R]will I lift up myself (Is 33.10; cp, same v. with Stem II of a different verb, [J]will I lift up myself—[R]I will be exalted); [J]be gathered together—[R]assemble (i.e., gather themselves, Is 44.11); [J]be avenged—[R]avenge myself (Jer 5.9, 29); [J]be polluted—[R]defile themselves (Ezek 14.11).

Very rarely R renders VII as passive:

[J]hath girded himself—[R]is girded (Ps 93.1); [J]glorified himself—[R]will be glorified (Is 44.23). Note also, as special cases, [J]maketh himself rich . . . maketh himself poor—[R]pretends to be rich . . . pretends to be poor (Prov 13.7); [J]maketh himself a prophet—[R]prophesies (Jer 29.26; cp v. 27).

§ 107 The fact that a verb is frequently used in Hebrew with an indefinite, unexpressed subject, much as we say in English "people say," "they say," "it is said," or the like, has already been pointed out (§§ 96f). The meaning in such cases is often best represented in English by changing the construction to the passive. The third person, masculine, singular form of the verb is sometimes used in this way;

e.g., [J]one told Joseph—[R]Joseph was told (Gen 48.1; cp v. 2); [J]shall one carry forth—[R]shall be carried forth (Lev 16.27); [J]that he may bring her forth without the camp, and one shall slay her before his face—[R]and she shall be taken outside the camp and slaughtered before him (Num 19.3; cp v. 5); [J]where he worshipped God—[R]where God was worshiped (2 Sam 15.32); [J]he hath broken . . . he hath despised . . . he regardeth no—[R]are broken . . . are despised, there is no regard for (Is 33.8); [J]he shall burn it—[R]it shall be burnt (Ezek 43.21); [J]one shall then open him the gate—[R]the gate . . . shall be opened for him (46.12); [J]one shall shut—[R]shall be shut (same v.); [J]when he hath taken away the multitude—[R]when the multitude is taken (Dan 11.12). In Ezek 11.7, where R uses a passive verb for an impersonal third masculine singular, J follows a different Hebrew text: [J]I will bring you forth—[R]you shall be brought forth.

Far more often than the singular, the third masculine plural is used impersonally;

e.g., [J]they shall afflict them—[R]they will be oppressed (Gen 15.13); [J]they watered the flocks—[R]the flocks were watered (29.2; cp v. 8); [J]if men should overdrive them—[R]if they are overdriven (33.13); [J]that they have laid privily—[R]which is hidden (Ps 31.4); [J]they have made void thy law—[R]thy law has been broken (119.126); [J]they shall call them—[R]they shall be called (Is 62.12; cp Jer 3.17); [J]they have offered . . . and poured out —[R]has been offered . . . have been poured out (Jer 32.29); [J]men shall buy fields—[R]Fields shall be bought (v. 44; cp v. 43, [JR]shall be bought). This construction appears very often in Ezekiel; see, e.g., 3.25; 22.7; 23.10, 49; 28.3, 16; 32.16; 39.11; 40.38, 41f; 43.22, 25; 46.15. It is found also many times in the Aramaic of Daniel; e.g., [J]but for their sakes that shall make known [Or, *but for the intent that . . . may be made known*]—[R]but in order that . . . may be made known (2.30); see also 4.25f, 32; 5.20f, 23, 29; 6.16, 24; 7.5, 13, 26. It is not absent from the Hebrew chapters of the same book; e.g., [J]let them give us—[R]let us be given (1.12); Jthey shall not give—Rhas not been given (11.21); Jthey shall forecast—Rshall be devised (v. 25). See also Hos 11.7; Nahum 3.10; Zeph 2.4; Zech 7.14; 10.11; 14.11; Mal 1.4.

With both singular and plural verbs used in this way J sometimes supplies definite subjects not expressed or implied in the Hebrew;

e.g., Jshall the priest make an atonement—Rshall atonement be made (Lev 16.30); JGod overthroweth—Rare cast down (Prov 21.12). The most conspicuous instance of this is undoubtedly the very difficult but important verse, Job 19.26, JAnd though after my skin worms destroy this body [Or, *After I shall awake, though this* body *be destroyed*]—Rand after my skin has been thus destroyed.

In a few places J uses a passive for an active verb, but R translates literally:

Jthe words that are spoken—Rthe things that men say (Eccles 7.21); JI should not be despised [Heb. *they should not despise me*]—Rnone would despise me (Song 8.1); Jare expired—Rthey have completed (Ezek 43.27); Jshall be confounded [Or, *they shall make . . . ashamed*]—Rthey shall confound (Zech 10.5).

A special form of impersonal verb which can be rendered as passive is an infinitive after the verb "command" or the like in Daniel, both Hebrew and Aramaic;

e.g., Jhad said he should bring them in—Rhad commanded that they should be brought in (1.18, lit. commanded to bring them in); Jcommanded to call the magicians . . .—Rcommanded that the magicians . . . be summoned (2.2); Jcommanded to destroy . . .—Rcommanded that . . . be destroyed (v. 12, Aramaic; cp vv. 13, 46; 3.13, 19; 4.6; 5.2; 6.23).

A passive verb may be used impersonally, with no subject expressed. In Ps 22.30, to avoid ambiguity, R renders a verb in Stem IV (§ 105) as an indefinite active plural: Jit shall be accounted—Rmen shall tell (lit. it shall be told, but the subject is not "Posterity" or, as J has it, "a seed").

Chapter XXV

TENSES

§ 108 Hebrew and Aramaic have no tenses as we know them. What are commonly called the tenses in these languages indicate only whether the action of the verb is complete and finished or incomplete and continuing or repeated. They are known therefore as the Perfect and Imperfect. Some of the various ways in which they are used seem strange to one accustomed to thinking in terms of past, present, and future, as the examples given in the following two section will show.

Meanwhile it is to be noted that these two languages make much use of "nominal sentences," consisting only of subject and predicate with some form of the verb "be" understood. Ordinarily such sentences make a statement concerning the present, but they may on occasion refer to past or present time. The translator must infer from the context and the situation whether this is so, and occasionally J and R draw different inferences;

e.g., [J]we were bondmen—[R]we are bondmen (Ezra 9.9, cp in our bondage, vv. 8 and 9); [J]were doorkeepers—[R]were to be gatekeepers (1 Chron 15.24); [J]their office was—[R]their duty shall be (23.28); [J]I was no prophet, neither was I a prophet's son; but I was an herdman—[R]I am no prophet, nor a prophet's son; but I am a herdsman (Amos 7.14); [J]Shall not the day of the LORD be darkness—[R]Is not the day of the LORD darkness (5.20); [J]shall be great . . . shall be offered . . . shall be great—[R]is great . . . is offered . . . is great (Mal 1.11); [J]for this time is evil—[R]for it will be an evil time (Mic 2.3).

§ 109 The perfect "tense," as has been said, expresses completed action. With it we shall consider here the idiomatic use of the imperfect with a special form of the conjunction "and" (§ 79) called the *w*-conversive, because it "converts" the imperfect into a perfect in meaning. "I said," for example, is expressed by the perfect, but "And I said" by the imperfect with the *w*-conversive. Since everything to be said of the one form applies also to the other, it is unnecessary for our purpose to distinguish them. In the same way the perfect becomes imperfect in meaning when it has the *w*-conversive; its use in that form will therefore be considered with the imperfect tense.

Since an act naturally falls into the past when it has been completed, verbs in the perfect tense usually refer to past action. J sometimes translates them as present or future where there is no apparent reason for so doing, and R more naturally uses the past tense;

e.g., [J]smiteth—[R]smote (Job 26.12); [J]turneth not . . . neither do they seek—[R]did not turn . . . nor seek (Is 9.13); [J]hunt . . . cannot . . . is near . . . are fulfilled . . . is come—[R]dogged . . . could not . . . drew near . . . were numbered . . . had come (Lam 4.18); [J]are swifter—[R]were swifter (v. 19); [J]thus saith—[R]thus said (Zech 2.8; 11.4; elsewhere often [J]saith—[R]says, but cp context here); [J]then shall the people of the LORD go down to the gates—[R]Then down to the gates marched the people of the LORD (Judg 5.11); [J]shall be full—[R]were full (Is 22.7); [J]shall smite—[R]smote (Jer 49.28); [J]it shall devour thee—[R]it consumed you (Ezek 28.18); [J]will . . . be jealous . . . and pity—[R]became jealous . . . and had pity (Joel 2.18).

Sometimes the perfect tense is used for something contrary to fact in the past. J so takes it in Lam 4.12, [J]would not have believed—[R]did not believe (cp Jer 40.14, same Hebrew, [J]believed them not—[R]would not believe them). In other places R understands the perfect tense in this way;

e.g., [J]For now I will stretch out my hand, that I may smite . . . ; and thou shalt be cut off—[R]For by now I could have put forth my hand and struck . . . and you would have been cut off (Ex 9.15); [J]If I say . . . I should offend—[R]If I had said . . . I would have been untrue (Ps 73.15); [J]I have purged thee—[R]I would have cleansed you (Ezek 24.13); [J]But he that taketh warning shall deliver—[R]But if he had taken warning, he would have saved (33.5). In Ezek 36.20 R interprets the verb from the situation and context as implying involuntary exile rather than voluntary emigration: [J]and are gone forth—[R]yet they had to go out.

Often the English present perfect tense best expresses the meaning of the Hebrew perfect. R so renders it in some places where J uses the past tense;

e.g., [J]which was shewed thee—[R]which has been shown you (Ex 26.30; cp 27.8); [J]thou satest—[R]thou hast sat (Ps 9.4); [J]that they might drink—[R]and have drunk it (Joel 3.3; here J ignores the force of the "*w*-conversive" with the imperfect); see also Mic 1.12; Mal 1.2f. So sometimes where J has the present; e.g., [J]Thou tellest—[R]Thou hast kept count (Ps 56.8); [J]Thou feedest them . . . and givest them—[R]Thou hast fed them . . . and given them (80.5); [J]when they hear—[R]for they have heard (138.4); [J]I travail not, nor bring forth children, neither do I nourish . . . nor bring up—[R]I have neither travailed nor given birth, I have neither reared . . . nor brought up (Is 23.4); see also Jer 15.9; Dan 2.28 (Aramaic; cp J mg); Mic 6.16.

So also in many places where J reads the future;

e.g., [J]shall hear . . . shall take hold on—[R]have heard . . . have seized (Ex 15.14); [J]Then shall the earth yield—[R]the earth has yielded (Ps 67.6); [J]our way that we should go—[R]the journey on which we have set out (1 Sam 9.6); [J]shall be—[R]has become (Is 49.5; cp Jer 48.39).

In other connections the past perfect tense may be used in English for the Hebrew perfect. So sometimes J where R prefers the past tense;

e.g., [J]had offended—[R]offended (Gen 40.1); [J]had fought . . . had taken—[R]fought . . . took (Judg 1.8).

Elsewhere R uses the past perfect where J has other tenses;

e.g., [J]went—[R]had gone (Gen 31.19); [J]did . . . borrowed—[R]had also done . . . had asked (Ex 12.35); [J]saw—[R]had seen (Ps 95.9); [J]sent—[R]had sent (105.17); [J]spake . . . did so—[R]had spoken . . . had done so (Is 20.2); [J]and he lay—[R]and had lain down (Jon 1.5); [J]is come—[R]had come (Lam 4.18).

§110 The perfect tense is used also in Hebrew to express a present, continuing activity or state resulting from something already done or achieved, something, so to speak, completed though still continuing.

Note, e.g., [J]sitteth—[R]sits enthroned (Ps 29.10, twice; cp 119.23, [J]did sit and speak—[R]sit plotting); [JR]I sojourn . . . I dwell (Ps 120.5); [JR]I trust (Ps 31.6; cp v. 14, [J]I trusted—[R]I trust; Zeph 3.2, [J]trusted not—[R]does not trust); [J]neither is there breath left—[R]no breath is left (Dan 10.17). The perfect tense of the verb "be" often stands for the present (lit. has become); see, e.g., Ps 55.18; 61.3; Is 30.4; Jer 14.4; Ezek 21.12 ([J]shall be).

This use of the perfect is especially common with verbs of knowing, perceiving, feeling, and the like;

e.g., [J]that have not known thee—[R]that do not know thee (Ps 79.6); [J]we saw—[R]we see (Gen 26.28; cp Ps 50.18; 55.9; 97.4; Zech 10.2); [J]Zion heard, and was glad; . . . rejoiced—[R]Zion hears and is glad, . . . rejoice (Ps 97.8; cp Jer 20.10; Hab 3.16); [J]were amazed—[R]are discomfited (Job 32.15); [J]were confounded . . . were ashamed—[R]are disappointed . . . are confounded (6.20; cp Is 30.5); [J]I desired—[R]I desire (Hos 6.6; cp Mic 7.1); [J]we feared not—[R]we fear not (Hos 10.3); [J]I have loved—[R]I love (Ps 26.8; cp 47.4; 78.68; Is 43.4; 48.14; Mal 2.11); [J]I have hated—[R]thou hatest [With one Heb Ms Gk Syr Jerome: Heb *I hate*] (Ps 31.6); see also Jer 12.8; but cp Hos 9.15, [J]there I hated them—[R]there I began to hate them (i.e., at Gilgal, referring to a particular time and place).

Similarly, although the imperfect is commonly used for repeated action, the perfect sometimes expresses an established, customary action; e.g., [J]backbiteth not—[R]does not slander (Ps 15.3). It may even appear in the same context with other verbs in the imperfect, as in Job 24.2, [J]remove . . . take away . . . feed—[R]remove . . . seize . . . pasture (here the first verb is imperfect, the second perfect, the third imperfect with *w*-conversive, and the next verse continues with imperfects). JR agree in so understanding many verbs in the perfect tense; see, e.g., Ps 63.8; 64.5; 119.136, 148, 157; 127.1; 129.8. In many places, however, R interprets verbs in this sense where J renders otherwise;

e.g., [J]slew . . . digged . . . [Or, *houghed* . . .]—[R]slay . . . hamstring (Gen 49.6; cp v. 7); [J]looked—[R]look (Job 6.19; cp Ps 14.2; 53.2, [J]looked down—[R]looks down).

The Hebrew perfect tense may even have future meaning, expressing certainty as to what is bound to happen. This is especially characteristic of prophetic utterances, where it is called the "prophetic perfect." JR often agree in so construing verbs;

e.g., ^{J}the altar shall be rent—^{R}the altar shall be torn down (1 Kings 13.3); ^{J}shall conceive and bear—^{R}shall conceive and bear [Or *is with child and shall bear*] (Is 7.14; see §120 for the second verb); ^{J}they shall remove, they shall depart—^{R}shall flee away (Jer 50.3).

R sees prophetic perfects also in many places where J uses the past or present perfect tense;

e.g., ^{J}I have left [Or, *I will leave*]—^{R}I will leave (1 Kings 19.18); ^{J}hath broken—^{R}will destroy (2 Chron 20.37; see the rest of the v. for the fulfilment); ^{J}were they in great fear—^{R}they shall be in great terror (Ps 14.5); ^{J}they are brought down and fallen: but we are risen, and stand upright—^{R}they will collapse and fall; but we shall rise and stand upright (20.8; cp 27.2; 53.5; 55.18; 85.10); ^{J}did more grievously afflict—^{R}will make glorious (Is 9.1; J understands the verb as lit. "make heavy" and paraphrases); ^{J}I have likened—^{R}I will destroy (Jer 6.2; J and R assume two different verbs which look and sound alike; in v. 3 JR interpret two perfects as future).

In Job 33.25, where J renders a Hebrew perfect as future, R takes it as expressing a command: ^{J}His flesh shall be fresher—^{R}let his flesh become fresh.

§ 111 The imperfect tense (or its equivalent, the perfect with *w*-conversive) is naturally used very often for the future. J and R both so understand it in many places, even when they use somewhat different renderings;

e.g., ^{J}Shall they therefore empty their net, and not spare continually to slay—^{R}Is he then to keep on emptying his net, and mercilessly slaying (Hab 1.17); ^{J}I will shake . . . ; and I will overthrow . . . ; and I will destroy . . . ; and I will overthrow—^{R}I am about to shake . . . , and to overthrow . . . ; I am about to destroy . . . , and overthrow (Hag 2.21f; the first verb is a participle, see § 120; the rest are in the perfect with *w*-conversive); ^{J}A thousand shall fall—^{R}A thousand may fall (Ps 91.7; cp Is 54.10; Jon 3.9; Mal 1.4); ^{J}Although the fig tree shall not blossom—^{R}Though the fig tree do not blossom (Hab 3.17).

R sometimes interprets the imperfect as future where J translates as present, optative or imperative, or even past;

e.g., [J]he seeth—[R]he shall see (Ps 49.10); [J]and turneth . . . and scattereth—[R]and he will twist . . . and scatter (Is 24.1); [J]That all flesh may know—[R]and all flesh shall know (Ezek 21.5); [J]The Lord be witness—[R]the Lord will be witness (Judg 11.10; cp 1 Sam 20.42); [J]let thy name be magnified—[R]thy name will be magnified (2 Sam 7.26); [J]let . . . be established—[R] . . . will be established (same v.; 1 Chron 17.24; cp Ps 6.10; Prov 1.14; 4.26); [J]Turn thou—[R]she will return (Jer 3.7; cp Lam 3.64–6); [J]I must die—[R]I will die (1 Sam 14.43); [J]hath chosen—[R]will choose (Deut 12.21); note also Mic 3.11, [J]can come—[R]shall come.

The imperfect tense often refers to the present, and is often so taken by R when J uses the future;

e.g., [J]I will establish—[R]I establish (Gen 9.11); [J]shall not lie down—[R]does not lie down (Num 23.24); [J]I shall see him . . . I shall behold him—[R]I see him . . . I behold him (24.17); [J]shall chase—[R]puts to flight (Josh 23.10); [J]shall they rehearse—[R]they repeat (Judg 5.11); [J]I will call . . . so shall I be saved—[R]I call . . . and I am saved (2 Sam 22.4; Ps 18.3).

So too R sometimes reads the present tense where J sees the idea of ability or possibility;

e.g., [J]Can two walk together—[R]Do two walk together (Amos 3.3); or where J sees a wish or command; e.g., [J]The Lord render to every man—[R]The Lord rewards every man (1 Sam 26.23); [J]Therefore shall a man leave . . . and shall cleave . . . and they shall be—[R]Therefore a man leaves . . . and cleaves . . . and they become (Gen 2.24); [J]therefore trust thou in him—[R]and you are waiting for him (Job 35.14); [J]let them return . . . let them make a noise—[R]they come back . . . howling (Ps 59.14; cp v. 6); [J]Let them wander up and down . . . and grudge [Or, . . . *they will stay all night*]—[R]They roam about . . . and growl (v. 15); [J]Let God be magnified—[R]God is great (70.4); [J]confounded be—[R]are put to shame (97.7).

J often uses the past or the present perfect tense for Hebrew imperfects which R renders as present;

e.g., [J]their south border was . . . it went out . . . and passed along . . . and ascended—[R]their south border ran . . . it goes out . . . , passes along . . . and goes up (etc., Josh 15.2–11); [J]For I have told him [Or, *And I will tell him*]—[R]And I tell him (1 Sam 3.13).

The connotation of ability to do something, already noted in J, is found in several other places in R as an interpretation of the imperfect tense:

[J]I have run . . . have I leaped—[R]I can crush . . . I can leap (2 Sam 22.30; Ps 18.29); [J]Hast thou with him spread out—[R]Can you, like him, spread out (Job 37.18); [J]payeth not again—[R]cannot pay back (Ps 37.21); [J]shall dwell—[R]can dwell (Is 33.14, twice); [J]shall not save them at all—[R]cannot save them (Jer 11.12); [J]should have entered—[R]could enter (Lam 4.12); [J]will feed them—[R]can . . . feed them (Hos 4.16); [J]what then should a king do to us?—[R]and a king, what could he do for us? (10.3).

§112 The imperfect tense is often used to express purpose, and it is often so taken by R where J understands it in some other way;

e.g., [J]and she shall bear—[R]that she may bear (Gen 30.3; cp the next clause); [J]and the King of glory shall come in—[R]that the King of glory may come in (Ps 24.7, 9); [J]and he gave ear unto me—[R]that he may hear me (77.1); [J]and we shall be saved—[R]that we may be saved (Ps 80.3, 7, 19; with *-āh,* § 93, No. 2); [J]and they walked in their own counsels—[R]to follow their own counsels (Ps 81.12); [J]that maketh glad . . . which strengtheneth—[R]to gladden . . . to strengthen (Ps 104.15; cp same v., [JR]to make . . . shine); [J]I will go into them—[R]that I may enter through them (118.19); [J]so will I keep—[R]that I may keep (119.134, with *-āh,* § 93, No. 2; cp vv. 146, 175).

Frequently the imperfect expresses a wish, a blessing, or a curse. Examples of its interpretation in this sense by J have appeared in the foregoing paragraphs. In many other places R so understands it where J does not;

e.g., [J]Canaan shall be—[R]and let Canaan be (Gen 9.26f; cp the rest of v. 27); [J]The Lord shall add—[R]May the Lord add (30.24); [J]and God shall be with thee—[R]and God be with you (Ex 18.19; cp 2 Chron 19.11; Ps 12.3; 29.11).

Commands also may be expressed by the imperfect tense as well as the imperative mood (§ 118). The most familiar instances are the Ten Commandments with their "Thou shalt" and "Thou shalt not" (R "You shall," "You shall not"). When used in this way the imperfect may be rendered also by an imperative (as in Ps 51.18, [J]build thou—[R]rebuild). R does this in many places, including not a few where J has a different interpretation;

e.g., [J]ye shall haste and bring—[R]Make haste and bring (Gen 45.13); [J]O my soul, thou hast trodden down strength—[R]March on, my soul, with might (Judg 5.21); [J]because thou defendest them—[R]and do thou defend them (Ps 5.11); [J]Thou shalt keep them, O Lord, thou shalt preserve them [Heb. *him*]—[R]Do thou, O Lord protect us, guard us (12.7; cp 51.6; 61.6); [J]and shalt see, and shalt read—[R]see that you read (Jer 51.61); [J]Then shalt thou say—[R]and say (v. 62).

Occasionally R uses the verb "must" in such cases;

e.g., [J]ye shall tell—[R]You must tell (Gen 45.13); [J]And as for my flock, they eat . . . and they drink—[R]And must my sheep eat . . . and drink (Ezek 34.19); [J]Judah shall plow, and Jacob shall break his clods—[R]Judah must plow, Jacob must harrow for himself (Hos 10.11).

Both J and R sometimes use "let" for the same purpose, but in different places;

e.g., [J]let him pay—[R]he shall pay (Ex 22.7); [J]Let favour be shewed—[R]If favor is shown (Is 26.10); [J]let them return unto thee—[R]They shall turn to you (Jer 15.19); but cp [J]hear, O earth—[R]let the earth hear (Deut 32.1); [J]he rewardeth him—[R]Let him recompense it to themselves (Job 21.19); [J]His eyes shall see . . . he shall drink—[R]Let their own eyes see . . . let them drink (v. 20). Cp [J]inhabiteth—[R]should inhabit (Job 15.28); [J]may walk . . . may do—[R]should go . . . should do (Jer 42.3); [J]they shall not prophesy—[R]One should not preach (Mic 2.6); [J]will not weary themselves—[R]none . . . need weary themselves (Jer 2.24); [J]shall be praised—[R]is to be praised (Prov 31.30).

§ 113 Even past actions may be indicated by the Hebrew imperfect tense, especially if they were continued or customary. In such instances as the following JR both recognize the reference to the past, but R brings out the implication of repeated, customary action by saying "used to" or "would":

[J]Moses took the tabernacle, and pitched it—[R]now Moses used to take the tent and pitch it (Ex 33.7; see also the rest of the v. and vv. 8–11);

[J]rose up early, and stood—[R]used to rise early and stand (2 Sam 15.2); [J]went and told them—[R]used to go and tell them (17.17); [J]did Solomon offer—[R]Solomon used to offer (1 Kings 3.4); [J]went and feasted—[R]used to go and hold a feast (Job 1.4); [J]who had come and gone—[R]they used to go in and out (Eccles 8.10); [J]when Moses went in—[R]whenever Moses went in (Ex 34.34); [J]and Moses put—[R]and Moses would put (v. 35); [J]he put forth his hand—[R]he would put out his hand (2 Sam 15.5); [J]and rose up early . . . and offered—[R]and he would rise early . . . and offer (Job 1.5; the preceding verbs are imperfects with *w*-conversive, equivalent to the perfect for customary action, § 110); [J]I caused it to rain . . . and caused it not to rain—[R]I would send rain . . . and send no rain (Amos 4.7). Cp [J]they sacrificed—[R]they kept sacrificing (Hos 11.2); [J]did eat up—[R]was eating (Amos 7.4).

In many places where J does not see a reference to the past in a verb in the imperfect tense, R so interprets it;

e.g., [J]Thou sellest . . . and dost not increase thy wealth by their price—[R]Thou hast sold . . . demanding no high price for them (Ps 44.12; cp v. 11, [J]Thou hast given us—[R]Thou hast made us); [J]shall pitch—[R]were to encamp (Num 3.23; cp vv. 24f, 29–32); [J]shall submit themselves . . . shall be obedient—[R]came cringing . . . obeyed (2 Sam 22.45; Ps 18.44; cp same v., [J]hear—[R]heard, where the construction is different); [J]they shall fall and perish—[R]they stumbled and perished (Ps 9.3).

The imperfect tense is sometimes used in the conditional or concluding clause of a condition contrary to fact; so JR in Job 16.5, [J]I would strengthen you—[R]I could strengthen you (cp v. 4); Ps 55.12, [J]I would have hid myself—[R]I could hide; 81.14, [J]I should soon have subdued . . . and turned—[R]I would soon subdue . . . and turn; Is 48.19, [J]should not have been cut off—[R]would never be cut off (cp v. 18). Again R often finds this meaning where J does not recognize it;

e.g., [J]I will stretch out my hand, that I may smite thee . . . and thou shalt be cut off—[R]I could have put forth my hand and struck you . . . and you would have been cut off (Ex 9.15); [J]Thou shalt call, and I will answer thee; thou wilt have a desire—[R]Thou wouldest call, and I would answer thee; thou wouldest long (Job 14.15; cp vv. 16f).

A passage worthy of detailed examination for the use of the tenses in Hebrew is Ps 107.16ff. In it will be found many variations among the English translations, with puzzling shifts in the Hebrew between perfect and imperfect, illustrating several of the usages mentioned in the foregoing paragraphs.

A word of caution may be in order here, though it applies equally well in other connections. No language which has grown naturally instead of being manufactured is entirely logical and consistent. The use of the Hebrew tenses is no exception. This does not mean that one translation is as good as another, or that renderings can be chosen casually or arbitrarily. It means that the translator must be all the more careful to determine, if at all possible, just what was in the writer's mind.

Chapter XXVI

INFINITIVE, PARTICIPLE, AND IMPERATIVE

§ 114 The Hebrew infinitive, in addition to being used much like the infinitive in English, has also several characteristic uses which are hard to represent in English. It is frequently combined with prepositions, especially the preposition "to" (*l-*, § 83, No. 1). This is very common, as in English, after certain verbs, such as "begin" (e.g., Gen 4.26, [J]began men to call—[R]men began to call; cp Mic 6.13, [J]will I make thee sick in smiting thee—[R]I have begun to smite you, see § 140), or "command" (e.g., Gen 3.11, [J]the tree, whereof I commanded thee that thou shouldest not eat—[R]the tree of which I commanded you not to eat).

The infinitive with *l-* is sometimes used idiomatically after the verb "be" (*HYH*);

e.g., [J]be for my comfort [Heb. *to comfort me*]—[R]be ready to comfort me (Ps 119.76); [J]help me—[R]be ready to help me (v. 173, lit. be to help me); [J]Whithersoever the spirit was to go—[R]Wherever the spirit would go (Ezek 1.20); so with *lma'an* (§ 83, No. 2), [J]were . . . to shed blood—[R]have been bent on shedding blood (22.6; cp v. 9).

The infinitive is often used with "to," as it is in English, as the equivalent of a clause of purpose. JR both translate it with a clause in some places;

e.g., [J]that he may do—[R]that we may do (Esther 5.5, lit. to do); [J]that he would shew—[R]that he might show (Dan 2.16, Aramaic); cp [J]To know . . . to perceive, etc.—[R]That men may know . . . understand, etc. (Prov 1.2–4); [J]that they may keep thee—[R]to preserve you (7.5; cp Jer 7.18); [J]to sin—[R]for sinning (Hos 8.11).

In a few places J takes such a phrase as expressing purpose where R does not, or vice versa;

e.g., [J]that I may . . . perform—[R]as I pay (Ps 61.8); [J]corrupting [Heb. *to corrupt*]—[R]to destroy (Dan 11.17); [J]. . . small, . . . great, and falsifying—[R]that we may make . . . small, . . . great, and deal deceitfully (Amos 8.5); [J]bowing down to the earth—[R]to cast me to the ground (Ps 17.11); [J]should come and smite—[R]the coming . . . to smite (Jer 46.13); [J]by promising him life [Or, *that I should save his life*. Heb. *by quickening him*]—[R]to save his life (Ezek 13.22). Cp [J]that God might manifest them [Or, *that they might clear God*]—[R]that God is testing them (Eccles 3.18, lit. to test them God.)

Sometimes the same construction represents not purpose but result, though J, like the Hebrew, does not distinguish the one from the other;

e.g., [J]and they entered into the land to destroy it—[R]so that they wasted the land as they came in (Judg 6.5); [J]that I might fall—[R]so that I was falling (Ps 118.13, lit. to fall); [J]that they should not give him—[R]so that he was not given over (Jer 26.24); [J]that I should remove it—[R]so that I will remove it (32.31); [J]to sanctify—[R]and so communicate holiness to (Ezek 46.20). So too with *lma'an* (§ 83, No. 2), [J]to profane my holy name—[R]so that my holy name is profaned (Amos 2.7).

§ 115 A characteristic Hebrew idiom is the use of the infinitive with *l-* where in English we use a participle to express an accompanying action or circumstance. The most common example is the expression "saying" (lit. to say) after "speak" or "spoke." Since this is redundant in English, R usually omits it (see § 15). With other verbs also both J and R recognize this idiom and represent it in some places by a participle, sometimes with "by" or "in";

e.g., [J]in not keeping—[R]by not keeping (Deut 8.11); [J]in giving him—[R]giving him (10.18); [J]speaking of them—[R]talking of them (11.19); [J]by taking heed thereto—[R]By guarding it (Ps 119.9). Note also Ezek 17.18, [J]by breaking—[R]and broke (cp 20.32, [J]to serve—[R]and worship).

More often J translates the infinitive literally and R uses a participle to convey the meaning more clearly;

e.g., [J]to do justice and judgment—[R]by doing righteousness and justice (Gen 18.19); [J]to observe the sabbath—[R]observing the sabbath (Ex 31.16); [J]to defile . . . to profane—[R]defiling . . . profaning (Lev 20.3).

In other places J uses a purpose-clause and R a participle;

e.g., [J]that he might fulfil—[R]thus fulfilling (1 Kings 2.27); [J]that I may publish . . . and tell—[R]singing aloud . . . and telling (Ps 26.7); cp [J]that I may not destroy—[R]and not destroy (Is 65.8); [J]neither obey—[R]disobeying (Jer 42.13); [J]He keepeth—[R]guarding (Prov 2.8). Cp § 114 on Dan 11.17 and Amos 8.5, where J uses participles for Hebrew infinitives which R takes as expressing purpose.

Occasionally the infinitive with *l-* is used as an expression of time. This meaning is very rarely recognized by J, but note Ex 5.19, [J]after it was said—[R]when they said (lit. to say); Jer 41.4, [J]after he had slain—[R]after the murder of (lit. to kill). R sees a temporal meaning in a few places where J has some other interpretation: [J]to offer all burnt sacrifices—[R]whenever burnt offerings are offered (1 Chron 23.31); [J]to make—[R]when he makes (Hab 2.18); [J]that he may know—[R]when he knows (Is 7.15). In Jer 29.10 the infinitive is used with *lpī* (§ 88, No. 15): [J]after seventy years be accomplished—[R]When seventy years are completed.

The infinitive with *l-* may also represent future time (cp English "about to," "is to," etc.);

e.g., [J]to be given—[R]was to be issued (Esther 3.14; 8.13); [J]to be laid in the balance—[R]in the balances they go up (Ps 62.9); [J]was ready to save me—[R]will save me (Is 38.20).

In a few instances the infinitive with *l-* is the equivalent of our "indirect discourse";

e.g., [J]I shall speak . . . to pluck up, and to pull down, and to destroy it—[R]I declare . . . that I will pluck up and break down and destroy it (Jer 18.7; cp v. 9); [J]how Nebuchadrezzar . . . should come—[R]about the coming of Nebuchadrezzar (46.13); [J]I said, I will pour out . . . , to accomplish—[R]I thought I would pour out . . . and spend (Ezek 20.8, 21); [J]whereof the word of the LORD came to Jeremiah the prophet, that he would accomplish—[R]which, according to the word of the LORD to Jeremiah the prophet, must pass (Dan 9.2).

A very idiomatic use of the infinitive, sometimes hard to translate into good English, indicates necessity, obligation, or duty (cp the obsolete English expression, "It is to laugh").

Note, e.g., [J]must be held in—[R]must be curbed (Ps 32.9, lit. to curb); [J]shall bring forth—[R]must lead forth (Hos 9.13, lit. to cause to go out); [J]they might not depart—[R]they did not need to depart (2 Chron 35.15, lit. it was not for them to depart). A complicated instance is 2 Chron 5.13, [J]as the trumpeters and singers were as one, to make one sound to be heard—[R]it was the duty of the trumpeters and singers to make themselves heard in unison (lit. it was as one for the trumpeters and for the singers to cause to hear one sound). Cp [J]it is that they shall be destroyed—[R]they are doomed to destruction (Ps 92.7); [J]hath caused . . . to fall [Or, . . . is *to fall*]—[R]must fall (Jer 51.49); [J]even without . . . to pluck it up—[R]It will not take . . . to pull it (Ezek 17.9, lit. And not with . . . to lift it); [J]to slay thereon—[R]on which . . . were to be slaughtered (40.39).

§ 116 The Hebrew infinitive is used also with other prepositions. With "in" (*b*-, § 82, No. 2), often of time, corresponding to a "when"-clause;

e.g., [J]as he was come over—[R]as he was about to cross (2 Sam 19.18, lit. in his passing over); [J]when it was in building—[R]When the house was built (1 Kings 6.7; cp, same v., [J]while it was in building—[R]while it was being built); [J]when the LORD would take up Elijah—[R]when the LORD was about to take Elijah up (2 Kings 2.1).

This construction occurs often, with variations in the tenses of the English verbs used for the Hebrew infinitives, to agree with the main verbs.

Note, e.g., [J]when thou judgest—[R]in thy judgment (Ps 51.4); [J]and when he had spoken—[R]While he was speaking (Dan 10.11); [J]And when the man . . . went forth . . . , he measured—[R]Going on . . . , the man measured (Ezek 47.3).

Other meanings too may be represented by the infinitive with *b*-, including cause;

e.g., [J]while he talked with him—[R]because he had been talking with God (Ex 34.29); [J]when God helped—[R]because God helped (1 Chron 15.26).

Other ways of representing this idiom in English are adopted by both J and R in one place or another, indicating sometimes different interpretations of its meaning;

e.g., [J]by casting up mounts—[R]when mounds are cast up (Ezek 17.17); [J]by taking vengeance—[R]revengefully (25.12); [J]for the avenging of Israel—[R]That the leaders took the lead in Israel (Judg 5.2; J and R obviously differ also as to the meaning of the verb and its cognate object); [J]when the people willingly offered themselves—[R]that the people offered themselves willingly (same v.); [J]for they shall see eye to eye, when the LORD shall bring again Zion—[R]for eye to eye they see the return of the LORD to Zion (Is 52.8; here R takes the preposition with the verb "see," as often, cp § 82, No. 2); [J]when God disposed them—[R]how God lays his command upon them (Job 37.15); [J]when they said to them—[R]in that men said of them (Ezek 36.20); [J]in that thou hast justified thy sisters—[R]for you have made your sisters appear righteous (16.52); [J]in that thou art a comfort—[R]becoming a consolation (v. 54); [J]In that ye say—[R]By thinking (Mal 1.7; cp v. 12; 2.17; Ezek 3.18; 33.8); [J]When I shall say—[R]Though I say (Ezek 33.13, cp v.14); [J]If he commit iniquity—[R]When he commits iniquity (2 Sam 7.14); [J]But if the wicked turn—[R]and when the wicked turns (Ezek 33.19; cp v. 18, [JR]When); [J]that ye may have—[R]When you have (6.8).

In much the same way the infinitive is used with "according to," "as," or "like" (*k*-); in fact *b* and *k* look so nearly alike in Hebrew that often some manuscripts have one and others the other (e.g., Dan 10.19, [JR]when).

Note, e.g., [J]when they saw—[R]whenever they saw (2 Kings 12.10); [J]when Ezra had prayed, and when he had confessed—[R]While Ezra prayed and made confession (Ezra 10.1; cp Ezek 11.13); [J]when Joshua had spoken—[R]as Joshua had commanded (Josh 6.8); [J]As the whirlwind passeth, so . . .—[R]When the tempest passes, . . . (Prov 10.25); [J]When the whole earth rejoiceth—[R]For the rejoicing of the whole earth (Ezek 35.14); [J]by his strength—[R]when he has become strong (Dan 11.2); cp [J]as when he fought—[R]as when he fights (Zech 14.3, lit. according to the day of his fighting).

The preposition "from" (*min,* § 84) with the infinitive has several shades of meaning corresponding to its use with nouns. Here too J and R occasionally differ in their interpretations, or at least in their renderings;

e.g., [J]at the hearing of it . . . at the seeing of it—[R]so that I cannot hear . . . so that I cannot see (Is 21.3); [J]after the league made with him—[R]from the time that an alliance is made with him (Dan 11.23); [J]from holding of . . . from hearing of . . . from seeing—[R]lest they hold . . . from hearing of . . . from looking upon (Is 33.15); [J]keepeth the sabbath from polluting it—[R]keeps the sabbath, not profaning it (56.2; cp v. 6); [J]who ceaseth from raising [Or, *from waking,* or, *the raiser will cease*] after he hath kneaded the dough, until it be leavened—[R]ceases to stir the fire, from the kneading of the dough until it is leavened (Hos 7.4); [J]I will not pity . . . , but destroy them [Heb. *from destroying them*]—[R]I will not pity . . . , that I should not destroy them (Jer 13.14); [J]a deeper speech than thou canst perceive—[R]an obscure speech which you cannot comprehend (Is 33.19); [J]It is a light thing that thou shouldest be—[R]It is too light a thing that you should be (49.6, an important but very difficult verse). Note also, with the compound form *middē,* [J]since I spake—[R]as often as I speak (Jer 31.20); [J]since thou spakest—[R]whenever you spoke (48.27).

Much less often the infinitive is used with "until" (*'ad,* § 87, No. 1),

e.g., [J]until he came—[R]by the time the man came (Ezek 33.22); or with "on" etc. (*'al,* § 86, No. 7), e.g., [JR]because they have threshed (Amos 1.3; cp vv. 6, 9, 11, 13; 2.1, 4, 6).

§ 117 In a number of the instances given in the foregoing sections the infinitive (like the English participle) is the equivalent of a noun. It is so also in other connections, and may often be so translated; e.g., [J]By swearing, and lying, etc.—[R]there is swearing, lying, etc. (Hos 4.2). Sometimes, however, J or R uses a finite verb to represent the infinitive;

e.g., [J]your treading is—[R]you trample (Amos 5.11); [J]before the coming of . . .—[R]before . . . comes (Mal 4.5); [J]the voice of them that shout . . . the voice of them that cry . . . the noise of them that sing—[R]the sound of shouting . . . the sound of the cry . . . the sound of singing (Ex 32.18); [J]when I begin, I will also make an end [Heb. *beginning and ending*]—[R]from beginning to end (1 Sam 3.12); [J]all the fruit to take away—[R]the full fruit of the removal (Is 27.9); [J]to give—[R]and the giving over of (Dan 8.13); [J]to do judgment—[R]When justice is done (Prov 21.15; cp Mic 6.8, same Hebrew, [J]to do justly—[R]to do justice); [J]we cannot stand—[R]none can stand (Ezra 9.15, lit. there is not to stand); [J]to him whom man despiseth—[R]to one deeply despised (Is 49.7, lit. to despising of soul); [J]that thou hast forsaken—[R]for you to forsake (Jer 2.19).

In Eccles 5.1, where the infinitive is used like a noun as the subject of a clause, J translates it as an imperative: [J]and be more ready to hear, than to give—[R]to draw near to listen is better than to offer. In Deut 12.5 J mistakes an infinitive for a noun: [J]even unto his habitation—[R]and make his habitation (lit. and to dwell).

Still another idiomatic use of the infinitive makes it the equivalent of a finite verb in narrative. J sometimes wrongly translates it in such places as an imperative;

e.g., [J]Hold up my goings—[R]My steps have held fast (Ps 17.5); [J]Prepare—[R]They prepare (Is 21.5); [J]watch—[R]they spread (same v.); [J]eat, drink—[R]they eat, they drink (same v.); [J]yet return again—[R]and would you return (Jer 3.1). Note also the following differences of interpretation: [J]is to depart—[R]turns aside (Prov 16.17; cp Dan 9.11, [J]even by departing—[R]and turned aside); [J]and to pour out—[R]and they pour out (Jer 7.18, not the same construction as [JR]to make, same v.); [J]to make all ready—[R]made all ready (Ezek 7.14). In other places JR both use finite verbs to translate the Hebrew infinitive; e.g., [J]And they gave them drink—[R]Drinks were served (Esther 1.7); [J]I will do—[R]have brought (Ezek 23.30); [J]thou puttest thy nest—[R]your nest is set (Num 24.21; cp, same Hebrew, Obad 1.4, [J]thou set thy nest—[R]your nest is set).

Of all the uses of the Hebrew infinitive, the most distinctively idiomatic is the addition of an infinitive to a finite verb to express emphasis, as in Gen 2.17 (and often), [J]thou shalt surely die—[R]you shall die (lit. to die you shall die). Many ways of translating this very common idiom are adopted by J and R. Space can be taken here for little more than a list of the most notable.

Adverbs and phrases are frequently used to stress the force of the verb;

e.g., [JR]at all, carefully, certainly, grievously, indeed, surely, utterly, very, wholly; [J]altogether, assuredly, clean, doubtless, earnestly, exceedingly, expressly, diligently, greatly, in any case, in any wise, sore, speedily, still, straitly, throughly, without fail; [R]be sure to, bitterly, by all means, by no means, continually, in any way, only, never, plainly, suddenly, truly, violently.

Occasionally J uses the present participle for the Hebrew infinitive; e.g., [J]in blessing I will bless thee, and in multiplying I will multiply thy seed—[R]I will indeed bless you, and I will multiply your descendants (Gen 22.17). J sometimes and R often omit any representation of the infinitive where the verb by itself seems sufficiently strong.

Note also the following special cases:

[J]shall surely make restitution—[R]shall make full restitution (Ex 22.6); [J]would fain flee—[R]flees . . . in headlong flight (Job 27.22); [J]Be thou diligent to know—[R]Know well (Prov 27.23); [J]Hear ye indeed [Or, *without ceasing, &c.* Heb. *hear ye in hearing &c*] . . . and see ye indeed [Heb. *in seeing*]—[R]Hear and hear . . . see and see (Is 6.9; cp 59.11); [J]utterly fall—[R]fall exhausted (40.30); [J]Ye shall certainly drink—[R]You must drink (Jer 25.28; cp 36.16; 49.12); [J]shall be utterly broken [Or, *made naked*]—[R]shall be leveled to the ground (51.58); [J]go speedily—[R]go at once (Zech 8.21).

Only rarely is any significant difference of interpretation involved in these various renderings; note, however, [J]I will not leave thee altogether unpunished—[R]I will by no means leave you unpunished (Jer 30.11; cp 46.28).

§ 118 The imperative form of the verb presents relatively few difficulties. Some confusion is caused by the fact that one form of the imperative and one form of the infinitive are the same; hence, e.g., [J]to take away [Or, *take thou away*]—[R]take away (Is 4.1); [J]I will pour it out—[R]Pour it out (Jer 6.11); [J]Remembering [Or, *Remember*]—[R]Remember (Lam 3.19). Usually, however, the context makes clear what is intended. In other forms of the imperative it is indistinguishable from the perfect tense; so, e.g., [J]worship him, all ye gods—[R]all gods bow down before him (Ps 97.7).

When two or more imperatives occur together (as in "come and see"), the later ones are sometimes treated, now by J and now by R, as future; e.g., [J]Seek ye me, and ye shall live—[R]Seek me and live (Amos 5.4; cp v. 6); see also 2 Kings 18.31 (Is 36.16); Jer 6.16; 29.6; 35.15. This, of course, is merely a matter of more or less literal translation, with the same understanding of the meaning. So too in Ps 128.5f, [J]thou shalt see—[R]May you see (lit. see). In Ps 130.7 and 131.3, however, J apparently takes the imperative for an imperfect: [J]Let Israel hope—[R]O Israel, hope.

§ 119 The use of participles in Hebrew is much more complicated, with many variations of meaning and consequently some differences of interpretation between J and R. In Nahum 1.2, for example, the participle "avenging" is used three times; J uses two ways of rendering it and R two other ways: [J]revengeth . . . revengeth . . . will take vengeance—[R]avenging . . . avenging . . . takes vengeance. When the participle is used, as it often is, for continuing action in the present, R frequently has the progressive present tense where J has the simple present;

e.g., [J]mustereth—[R]is mustering (Is 13.4); see also Jer 7.17 (cp v. 18); Mic 1.3; Zech 3.7. Cp [J]pray—[R]keep on praying (Is 45.20); [J]The city sheddeth blood—[R]A city that sheds blood (Ezek 22.3); [J]they afflict . . . they take . . . and they turn aside—[R]you who afflict . . . who take . . . and turn aside (Amos 5.12); [J]keeping the covenant—[R]who keepest covenant (Dan 9.4); [J]he shall make it desolate—[R]one who makes desolate (v. 27, cp § 21); [J]dwelling—[R]who dwell (Joel 3.17); cp [J]that I am the LORD that sanctify them—[R]that I the LORD sanctify them (Ezek 20.12).

With the definite article the participle is often the equivalent of a relative clause, as in Ps 145.14, [J]all that fall—[R]all who are falling; cp Ezek 3.27; Zeph 1.12; Zech 8.9. J does not always recognize this meaning where R sees it;

e.g., [J]He fashioneth . . . he considereth—[R]he who fashions . . . and observes (Ps 33.15); [J]They lavish—[R]Those who lavish (Is 46.6); [J]shall I cause to bring forth—[R]shall I, who cause to bring forth (66.9).

In many cases the active participle becomes practically a noun; in other words, many nouns are participles in form. The most familiar example, perhaps, is the word commonly rendered "judge" (§ 55, No. 2). Another is the term "Maker," used often for God; note also Gen 14.19, 22, [J]possessor of heaven and earth—[R]maker of heaven and earth. Cp [J]he fighting—[R]foemen (Ps 56.1).

A common idiom is the use of the participle with the particle *'ēn,* "there is not" (§ 92, No. 2). It occurs most often in the expression "none shall make you afraid" (Lev 26.6 etc.), rendered with slight variations by J and R but without any difference of meaning; see Deut 28.26 and Jer 7.33; Job 11.19; Is 17.2; Ezek 34.28; Mic 4.4; Zeph 3.13; Jer 30.10 (46.27); Ezek 39.26; Nahum 2.11. For the same construction with other Hebrew verbs note the following:

[J]that no man taketh up—[R]with none to gather them (Is 13.14); [J]and no man gathereth them—[R]with none to gather them (Nahum 3.18, same Hebrew); [J]but none shall look back [Or, *cause them to turn*]—[R]but none turns back (2.8).

R reads as present a number of participles which J treats as past;

e.g., [J]which was shewed thee—[R]which is being shown you (Ex 25.40, lit. which you are being caused to see); [J]saved—[R]saves (1 Sam 10.19).

Sometimes J translates a participle as future and R as present;

e.g., [J]I will stir up—[R]I am stirring up (Is 13.17; cp Jer 50.9). Cp Prov 31.6, [J]unto him that is ready to perish—[R]to him who is perishing (J is ambiguous, suggesting "who wants to die").

§ 120 The Hebrew participle is actually used for the future in many places. JR both interpret it sometimes in this sense; note especially Is 7.14, [JR]shall conceive, and bear [R mg, Or *is with child and shall bear*] ("shall conceive" represents an adjective, lit. pregnant; "bear" is a participle, lit. "bearing"; cp Gen 16.11, where the same adjective is used, but the verb is a perfect with *w*-conversive, § 109). Elsewhere R often changes to the future a present tense used in J for a Hebrew participle. Sometimes the expression "about to" is used; e.g., [J]that thing which I do—[R]what I am about to do (Gen 18.17); see also 1 Kings 2.2; Ezek 24.16; 36.22; cp Zech 11.9. R says "about to" in some places also where J has the future tense;

e.g., [J]I will judge—[R]I am about to punish (1 Sam 3.13); see also Jer 37.7; Ezek 37.19; Hag 2.21; Zech 12.2. Cp [J]Thus might we procure—[R]But we are about to bring (Jer 26.19).

In Jer 20.4, where J translates a participle as future, R treats it as expressing rather an attendant circumstance: [J]and thine eyes shall behold it—[R]while you look on. In 22.30 J and R understand differently the meaning of a participle following a verb in the imperfect tense: [J]no man of his seed shall prosper, sitting upon the throne—[R]none of his offspring shall succeed in sitting on the throne. Sometimes R uses the future tense for participles which J renders as present;

e.g., [J]maketh the earth empty, and maketh it waste—[R]will lay waste the earth and make it desolate (Is 24.1); [J]thou art greatly despised—[R]you shall be utterly despised (Obad 1.2; cp Jer 49.15).

R sees a present reference in some places where J understands a Hebrew participle as referring to the past; e.g., [J]Oh that my people had hearkened—[R]O that my people would listen (Ps 81.13). In Ex 13.4 a participle is translated in the past tense by J; R takes it as future with a suggestion of the imperative:

[J]This day came ye out—[R]This day you are to go forth (in v. 3 [JR]came out represents the Hebrew perfect tense). Cp [J]praised—[R]shall offer praises (1 Chron 23.5; R takes all of vv. 4f as direct discourse, J only the last clause of v. 5).

In other places the force of a participle referring clearly to the past is similarly expressed in R;

e.g., [J]which married—[R]who were to marry (Gen 19.14); [J]Asaph made a sound with cymbals—[R]Asaph was to sound the cymbals (1 Chron 16.5; cp 15.24, [J]did blow—[R]should blow); [J]that did the work—[R]that were to do the work (Neh 2.16); cp [J]their names being changed—[R]their names to be changed (Num 32.38).

In Is 32.12, following a series of imperatives in v. 11, a participle of accompanying action is translated as future by J but by R as another imperative: [J]They shall lament for—[R]Beat upon.

Similarly in 14.31, after two imperatives, J translates a participle as past, R as imperative: [J]art dissolved—[R]melt in fear. Passive participles translated by J in the present are understood by R in some cases as the equivalent of a third person imperative, or as expressing a wish; e.g., [J]Blessed is . . . cursed is—[R]Blessed be . . . cursed be (Num 24.9; cp Ps 115.15; 119.12; Is 12.5).

Participles sometimes refer clearly to the past and are so rendered by both J and R (e.g., Deut 33.3; 1 Sam 15.12; Jer 10.12; 51.15; Nahum 2.12). In such cases R often uses the English past progressive;

e.g., [J]did burn—[R]was burning (Deut 5.23); [J]formed—[R]was forming (Amos 7.1; see also vv. 4, 7; Zech 1.8, 10f; 3.3); cp [J]had called—[R]was calling (1 Sam 3.8); [J]had overflown [Heb. *filled over*]—[R]was overflowing (1 Chron 12.15). Note also 2 Chron 36.16, [J]mocked—[R]kept mocking; Neh 1.4, [J]fasted, and prayed—[R]continued fasting and praying; Dan 4.7 (Aramaic), [J]did not make known—[R]could not make known; Mic 2.11, [J]If a man walking—[R]If a man should go about.

In other places R has the past tense for a participle which J translates as present or future;

e.g., [J]gathereth . . . layeth up—[R]gathered . . . put (Ps 33.7); cp [J]shall eat—[R]ate (2 Sam 9.11); [J]shall be brought forth—[R]were being led out (Jer 38.22).

Corresponding exactly to our past progressive tense, the Hebrew participle is sometimes used with the perfect tense of *HYH* (be); R then uses the past progressive or present perfect progressive, while J may have the present, future, or past;

e.g., [J]do feed themselves—[R]have been feeding themselves (Ezek 34.2); [J]shall stand—[R]have been standing (Ps 122.2); [J]stood—[R]was standing (Ezek 43.6).

Some differences in the rendering of participles are merely matters of more or less literal translation (cp Chapter VII). J is more literal, for example, in Esther 3.14, [J]was published—[R]by proclamation; Prov 22.14, [J]he that is abhorred of the LORD—[R]he with whom the LORD is angry. R is more literal in Is 10.22, [J]the consumption decreed shall overflow—[R]Destruction is decreed, overflowing.

Chapter XXVII

SENTENCE STRUCTURE AND CONNECTION OF IDEAS

§121 The differences of interpretation between J and R in many cases are concerned not with the meaning of individual words, but with the relation between words and ideas, often involving the grammatical structure of the sentence.

J occasionally puts words in mistaken connections through ignoring rules of Hebrew syntax;

e.g., [J]the brother of Japheth the elder—[R]the elder brother of Japheth (Gen 10.21); [J]I being in the way, the LORD led me—[R]As for me, the LORD has led me in the way (24.27); [J]and a great stone was upon the well's mouth—[R]The stone on the well's mouth was large (29.2); [J]The priests the Levites, and all the tribe of Levi—[R]The Levitical priests, that is, all the tribe of Levi (Deut 18.1); [J]ere the lamp of God went out in the temple . . . , and Samuel was laid down—[R]the lamp of God had not yet gone out, and Samuel was lying down within the temple (1 Sam 3.3); [J]Thou sayest, (but they are but vain words,) I have counsel and strength for the war—[R]Do you think that mere words are strategy and power for war? (2 Kings 18.20; cp Is 36.5); [J]as the grass on the house tops, and as corn blasted before it be grown up—[R]like grass on the housetops; blighted before it is grown (2 Kings 19.26; J's insertion misses the point that grass on a clay roof has no depth of root and withers prematurely); [J]all that were strong and apt for war—[R]all of them strong and fit for war (2 Kings 24.16); [J]And he took Geshur, and Aram, with the towns of Jair—[R]But Geshur and Aram took from them Havvothjair (1 Chron 2.23); [J]That prepareth his heart to seek God, . . . though he be not cleansed according to the purification of the sanctuary—[R]who sets his heart to seek God, . . . though not according to the sanctuary's rules of cleanness (2 Chron 30.19); [J]I know it is so of a truth—[R]Truly I know that it is so (Job 9.2); [J]and they take away the sheaf from the hungry—[R]hungry, they carry the sheaves (24.10); [J]And moreover, because the preacher was wise [Or, *the more wise the preacher was, &c*], he still taught the people knowledge—[R]Besides being wise, the Preacher also taught the people knowledge (Eccles 12.9); [J]And further, by these, my son, be admonished—[R]My son, beware of anything beyond these (v. 12); [J]a cloud and smoke by day, and the shining of a flaming fire by night—[R]a cloud by day, and smoke and the shining of a flaming fire by night (Is 4.5); [J]the land that thou abhorrest shall be forsaken of both her kings—[R]the land before whose two kings you are in dread will be deserted (7.16); [J]the dimness shall not be such as was in her vexation—[R]there will be no gloom to her that was in anguish (9.1); [J]a name better than of sons and of daughters—[R]a name better than sons and daughters (56.5; J misses the point of this promise to the eunuchs); [J]So the king of the south shall come into his kingdom—[R]Then the latter (i.e., the king of the north, v. 8) shall come into the realm of the king of the south (Dan 11.9); [J]and one shall certainly come—[R]which shall come on (v. 10; the subject is the "multitude"); [J]lay themselves down upon clothes laid to pledge by every altar—[R]lay themselves down beside every altar upon garments taken in pledge (Amos 2.8); [J]to them that are at ease in Zion, and trust in the mountain of Samaria—[R]to those who are at ease in Zion, and to those who feel secure on the mountain of Samaria (Amos 6.1; i.e., two separate groups, in Judah and Israel respectively); [J]but he that remaineth, even he,—[R]it too shall be a remnant (Zech 9.7).

§ 122 In the poetic portions of the OT the metrical structure, which was not understood at the time when J was made (§ 5), is an important aid in establishing the right connections of ideas. The division of lines and the parallelism between lines often make clear what is easily misunderstood if the poetry is read as prose. As the following examples show, the rearrangement of sentences required by observing the metrical structure does not always seriously alter the meaning, but there are places where the difference is significant:

Num 21.27, [J]Come into Heshbon, let the city of Sihon be built and prepared—

> [R]Come to Heshbon, let it be built,
> let the city of Sihon be established.

2 Sam 1.23, [J]Saul and Jonathan were lovely and pleasant in their lives, and in their death they were not divided—

[R]Saul and Jonathan, beloved and lovely!
In life and in death they were not divided.

Job 4.6, [J]Is not this thy fear, thy confidence, thy hope, and the uprightness of thy ways?—

[R]Is not your fear of God your confidence,
and the integrity of your ways your hope?

Job 19.14f, [J]My kinsfolk have failed, and my familiar friends have forgotten me. They that dwell in mine house, and my maids, count me for a stranger—

[R]My kinsfolk and my close friends have failed me;
the guests in my house have forgotten me;
My maidservants count me as a stranger.

Ps 35.19, [J]Let not them that are mine enemies wrongfully rejoice over me—

[R]Let not those rejoice over me
who are wrongfully my foes.

Ps 48.1f, [J]Great is the LORD, and greatly to be praised in the city of our God, in the mountain of his holiness. Beautiful for situation, the joy of the whole earth, is mount Zion, on the sides of the north, the city of the great King—

[R]Great is the LORD and greatly to be praised
in the city of our God!
His holy mountain, beautiful in elevation,
is the joy of all the earth,
Mount Zion, in the far north,
the city of the great King.

Ps 72.16, [J]There shall be an handful of corn in the earth upon the top of the mountains; the fruit thereof shall shake like Lebanon—

[R]May there be an abundance of grain in the land;
on the tops of the mountains may it wave;
may its fruit be like Lebanon.

Ps 84.9, [J]Behold, O God our shield, and look upon the face of thine anointed—

> [R]Behold our shield, O God;
> look upon the face of thine anointed!

Is 35.1f, [J]The wilderness and the solitary place shall be glad for them; and the desert shall rejoice, and blossom as the rose. It shall blossom abundantly, and rejoice even with joy and singing—

> [R]The wilderness and the dry land shall be glad,
> the desert shall rejoice and blossom;
> like the crocus it shall blossom abundantly,
> and rejoice with joy and singing.

Is 40.3, [J]The voice of him that crieth in the wilderness, Prepare ye the way of the LORD, make straight in the desert a highway for our God—

> [R]A voice cries:
> "In the wilderness prepare the way of the LORD,
> make straight in the desert a highway for our God

(an outstanding instance of a change made reluctantly, because of the familiarity of the passage, but compelled by recognition of the poetic parallelism).

In the first chapter of Nahum, in spite of some confusion in the Hebrew text, the form of an alphabetic acrostic is clearly perceptible. It shows that not only a new line but a new stanza begins in the middle of v. 3: [J]The LORD is slow to anger, and great in power, and will not at all acquit the wicked: the LORD hath his way in the whirlwind and in the storm, and the clouds are the dust of his feet—

> [R]The LORD is slow to anger and of great might,
> and the LORD will by no means clear the guilty.
>
> His way is in whirlwind and storm,
> and the clouds are the dust of his feet.

§ 123 In many places J and R differ as to connections between words and ideas, not as a matter of Hebrew syntax or metrical structure but as a matter of interpretation. Some of the poetic passages cited in § 122 show that the division of the text into verses was not always made at the right place.

In prose passages too this occasionally happened, though it cannot be so easily demonstrated.

Thus J begins a new sentence with v. 6 of Gen 12, which R connects with the preceding clause: [J]and into the land of Canaan they came. And Abram passed . . .—[R]When they had come to the land of Canaan, Abram passed . . . (see § 79). Cp Num 24.2f, [J]and the spirit of God came upon him. And he took up his parable—[R]And the Spirit of God came upon him, and he took up his discourse. In Dan 11.6f R begins a new paragraph with a phrase (In those times) which J, following the traditional verse-division, attaches to the preceding sentence.

Not only the verse-division but the much older division between chapters was sometimes made at the wrong place. The second half of 2 Kings 24.20, for example, goes logically with what follows. R therefore begins here a new paragraph and includes in it the first seven verses of chapter 25.

Other differences of interpretation do not affect the division into chapters and verses. The following examples are more or less typical:

[J]the father of such as dwell in tents, and of such as have cattle—[R]the father of those who dwell in tents and have cattle (Gen 4.20; not two groups but the same); [J]And there came two angels—[R]The two angels came (19.1; J breaks the close connection with chap. 18); [J]and them which came out of the cities they destroyed—[R]and those who came out of the cities destroyed them (Judg 20.42; cp 2 Kings 17.33); [J]And Boaz said unto her, At mealtime come thou hither—[R]And at mealtime Boaz said to her, "Come here . . ." (Ru 2.14); [J]while the land is yet before us; because we have sought the LORD our God, we have sought him, and he hath given us rest—[R]the land is still ours, because we have sought the LORD our God; we have sought him, and he has given us peace (2 Chron 14.7); [J]Though I were perfect, yet would I not know my soul—[R]I am blameless; I regard not myself (Job 9.21); [J]His confidence shall be rooted out of his tabernacle—[R]He is torn from the tent in which he trusted (18.14); [J]Who maketh his angels spirits; his ministers a flaming fire—[R]who makest the winds thy messengers, fire and flame thy ministers (Ps 104.4; see §§ 47, 50, 94); [J]In my distress I cried unto the LORD, and he heard me. Deliver my soul—[R]In my distress I cry to the LORD, that he may answer me: "Deliver me . . ." Ps 120.1f); [J]and hath closed your eyes: the prophets and your rulers, the seers hath he covered—[R]and has closed your eyes, the prophets, and covered your heads, the seers (Is 29.10; J not only punctuates wrongly here but also misses the point by taking the common word for "head" as meaning "ruler").

In longer passages the connection between sentences is sometimes interrupted and obscured by digressions; the meaning may then be considerably clarified by putting the intervening matter in parentheses. Thus R encloses Nahum 2.2, making it clear that vv. 3ff go back to v. 1. In J "his mighty men" seems to mean Jacob's instead of the enemy's. For other examples see § 6.

§ 124

Another point of interpretation on which J and R sometimes part company is the distinction between statements and questions. In the absence of any punctuation in Hebrew to mark the difference, it is not always easy to tell the two apart. There is a Hebrew prefix which can be attached to the first word of a clause to indicate a question, but it is not always used. The interpretation of a sentence as declarative or interrogative sometimes affects the connection of ideas.

J sometimes treats as a question what R takes as a statement, exclamation, or command;

e.g., [J]art thou come . . . ?—[R]You have come (1 Kings 17.18); [J]Knowest thou . . . ?—[R]You know . . . ! (Job 38.21, ironical); [J]Art thou also become . . . ? art thou become . . . ?—[R]You too have become . . . ! You have become . . . ! (Is 14.10); [J]where is thy zeal and thy strength, the sounding of thy bowels and of thy mercies toward me? are they restrained?—[R]Where are thy zeal and thy might? The yearnings of thy heart and thy compassion are withheld from me (63.15); [J]wilt thou not hearken unto me?—[R]you will not listen to me (Jer 38.15); [J]What is thy mother? A lioness . . .—[R]What a lioness was your mother . . . ! (Ezek 19.2); [J]Shall I cause it to return . . . ?—[R]Return it (21.30); [J]Art thou that Daniel . . . ?—[R]You are that Daniel . . . (Dan 5.13, Aramaic); [J]Who is wise, and he shall understand these things? prudent, and he shall know them?—[R]Whoever is wise, let him understand these things; whoever is discerning, let him know them (Hos 14.9).

Occasionally a question is used idiomatically in Hebrew as the equivalent of a statement, and R translates it as a statement even though the Hebrew has the interrogatory prefix;

e.g., [J]Doth not David hide himself with us?—[R]David is in hiding among us (lit. with us, Ps 54 title); [J]thou hast delivered my soul from death: wilt not thou deliver my feet from falling . . . ?—[R]thou hast delivered my soul from death, yea, my feet from falling (56.13).

There are also places where J has a statement and R a question;

e.g., [J]then I restored that which I took not away—[R]What I did not steal must I now restore? (Ps 69.4); [J]unto the hills, from whence cometh my help—[R]to the hills. From whence does my help come? (121.1); [J]Let thy fountains be dispersed abroad . . .—[R]Should your springs be scattered abroad . . . ? (Prov 5.16); [J]Men do not despise—[R]Do not men despise . . . ? [Or *Men do not despise*] (6.30); [J]them that are weaned from the milk, and drawn from the breasts—[R]Those who are weaned from the milk, those taken from the breast? (Is 28.9; J takes this as the answer to the preceding question, R as a continuation of it); [J]Bread corn is bruised—[R]Does one crush bread grain? (v. 28); [J]they will destroy . . .—[R]would they not destroy . . . ? (Jer 49.9; cp the first half of the v.); [J]But thou hast utterly rejected us [Or, *For wilt thou utterly reject us?*]; thou art very wroth against us—[R]Or hast thou utterly rejected us? Art thou exceedingly angry with us? (Lam 5.22); [J]and thou shalt not commit this lewdness—[R]Have you not committed lewdness . . . ? (Ezek 16.43; R begins a new paragraph with this question); [J]For thy sister Sodom was not . . .—[R]Was not your sister Sodom . . . ? (v. 56); [J]And as for my flock, they eat . . . and they drink . . .—[R]And must my sheep eat . . . and drink . . . ? (34.19); [J]now the LORD will feed them—[R]can the LORD now feed them . . . ? (Hos 4.16); [J]the battle . . . did not overtake them—[R]Shall not war overtake them . . . ? (10.9); [J]I will ransom them . . . I will redeem them . . .—[R]Shall I ransom them . . . ? Shall I redeem them . . . ? (13.14); [J]Arise, it shall teach!—[R]Arise! Can this give revelation? (Hab 2.19); [J]yea, as yet the vine . . . hath not brought forth—[R]Do the vine . . . still yield nothing? (Hag 2.19). In Jer 12.9 J ignores the interrogative prefix: [J]the birds round about are against her—[R]Are the birds of prey against her round about?

Part Three

The Hebrew and Aramaic Text

Chapter XXVIII

TEXTUAL CHANGES WITHOUT FOOTNOTES

§125 As has been said already (§§ 4, 9), one of the three major reasons for revising the King James Version is that the Hebrew and Aramaic text which it represents is imperfect, and we are now able to correct it at many points. The means available for this purpose and the ways in which they have been used in the Revised Standard Version call for some explanation. They include older and better manuscripts than those underlying J, a more critical use of the ancient Versions (§ 135), and more scientific methods in the study of the text.

A sketch of the history of the text, necessarily brief and much simplified, may help to make these matters clear. The process of divine inspiration to which we owe the existence of the Bible was not one of dictating the whole text exactly as it now stands. The books of the OT were composed in the course of a thousand years or more, and during that period there was no systematic effort to keep the original words without change. Much of the material was passed on from generation to generation by word of mouth and preserved only by memory for a long time before it was written down at all. When the books as we now have them were put together, the editors who compiled them and the scribes who copied them felt free to introduce occasional words of explanation or transition, and to correct what seemed to them errors; they also sometimes made mistakes in copying.

In spite of all this, the distinctive ideas and even literary style and vocabulary of the different books show that the text was transmitted with extraordinary fidelity. That some mistakes were made, however, is shown by the fact that in the last few centuries before Christ there were manuscripts which differed among themselves in many particulars. Some of them have been found among the scrolls and fragments found in caves near the Dead Sea. Evidently, along with what was eventually recognized as the standard text, there were other lines of textual tradition with many variations in spelling, grammar, and wording.

As the Scriptures, especially the Law, came to be more and more highly revered and more thoroughly studied, the need for revision and standardization of the text was increasingly felt. In the first two centuries of our era this task was undertaken by rabbinical scholars, and from then on it was pursued with intense devotion by the men known as Masoretes, i.e., experts in the tradition (Hebrew *māsōrāh*).

For several centuries all this had to do only with the consonants of the text, which were all that the Hebrew alphabet included. Except for the occasional use of a few consonants for certain vowels, there was no way to indicate what vowels should be pronounced with the written consonants. Undoubtedly there was an oral tradition of the vowels, for the text could not be read without them, and writing was at first only an aid to memory. Differences of pronunciation, however, inevitably arose, sometimes seriously affecting the meaning of the words. The ancient Greek version (§ 135) shows that as early as the second or third century before Christ the Hebrew words were not always understood and pronounced as indicated in our printed Hebrew Bibles. Systems of marking the vowels began to be devised after A.D. 600, and by the year 1000 the system of "pointing" now used in the printed text had been developed.

In addition to all this the Masoretes made copious notes of variant readings, corrections, and many curious details of the text (see §§ 127–9). The result of their labor is that their standardized text has been preserved since the second century A.D. with remarkable uniformity. Even so, mistakes in copying were still made. Variations persist in late medieval manuscripts, and in the printed Bibles which began in the sixteenth century to take their place. Most of these variations are matters of relatively insignificant detail, but a translator must decide what text he is to translate.

The principles and procedures governing R in reaching this

decision will be explained in the following sections. In general, departures from the standard, Masoretic Hebrew text are made only when there is good reason to regard a different reading as more likely to be that of the original text. No one manuscript or group of manuscripts, to say nothing of any printed edition, is regarded as having superior authority. Where the manuscripts differ, each variant has to be judged on its own merits, in view of the context, parallel or similar passages, the style and vocabulary of the particular author or book, and any other available evidence. If no manuscript offers an acceptable reading, other means of finding a better one have to be used.

§ 126 As noted in § 9, some kinds of textual correction have been thought not to require footnotes to point them out or explain them. This is true, first of all, when a reading is attested by three or more Hebrew manuscripts, though occasionally R has notes even in such places. (There is no magic, of course, in the number three. The line might have been drawn at some other number, but notes on all the variant readings adopted would have multiplied beyond reason the number of footnotes.) The fact that a variant reading appears in a few manuscripts is in itself no reason to adopt it. A mistake in one manuscript may have been, and often was, faithfully copied in many others. Sometimes, indeed, an ancient mistake has been perpetuated in all of the extant manuscripts, and the original reading has been lost or has survived only in the ancient Versions. Sometimes, however, it is preserved in a few or only one of the Hebrew manuscripts. The reading of the few is therefore sometimes more ancient and correct than that of all the others.

Some of the places where R has adopted a textual variant attested by three or more (often a great many more) Hebrew manuscripts are the following:

[J]made as if they had been ambassadors—[R]made ready provisions (Josh 9.4); [J]the great stone of Abel—[R]The great stone (1 Sam 6.18; J inserts in the English what R reads in the Hebrew; cp § 131); [J]Syria—[R]Edom (2 Sam 8.12; Ezek 16.57; 27.16; cp 2 Kings 16.6; an instance of the very common confusion of *d* and *r* in Hebrew); [J]lavers—[R]pots (1 Kings 7.40); [J]saw—[R]was afraid (19.3; cp 2 Chron 26.5; Neh 6.16; Zeph 3.15).

In 2 Kings 7.13 the Hebrew text as J had it repeats several words. J incorporates the repetition, but in the attempt to make sense of it varies the translation and punctuation: [J]which are left in the city [Heb. *in it*], (behold, they are as all the multitude of Israel that are left in it: behold, I say, they are even as all the multitude of the Israelites that are consumed:). The text used by R does not have the repetition: [R]seeing that those who are left here will fare like the whole multitude of Israel.

Note also the following: [J]from the ark—[R]from the holy place (2 Chron 5.9); [J]dead bodies—[R]clothing (20.25); [J]Azariah—[R]Ahaziah (22.6); [J]the son of Jehoahaz—[R]son of Ahaziah (25.23); [J]in their rebellion—[R]in Egypt (Neh 9.17; J moves the phrase up to the beginning of the clause); [J]them—[R]us (Ps 12.7, twice); [J]I had fainted unless I had believed—[R]I believe (27.13; J has to insert three words to make sense of "unless," which is not in the manuscripts followed here by R); [J]of them that seek death—[R]and a snare of death (Prov 21.6); [J]forgotten—[R]praised (Eccles 8.10); [J]spring—[R]garden (Song 4.12); [J]A vineyard of red wine—[R]A pleasant vineyard (Is 27.2); [J]thy teachers—[R]your Teacher (30.20, twice); [J]my mouth—[R]the mouth of the LORD (34.16); [J]shall be there, and a way—[R]shall be there (35.8; J's text repeats a Hebrew word); [J]Moses, and his people—[R]Moses his servant (63.11); [J]brought them up . . . with the shepherd—[R]brought up . . . the shepherds (same v.); [J]pass with thine enemies—[R]serve your enemies (Jer 15.14; cp 17.4); [J]your altars—[R]their altars (17.1; about 170 manuscripts, as well as some of the Versions, support R here); [J]forget you—[R]lift you up (23.39); [J]Jehoiakim—[R]Zedekiah [Another reading is *Jehoiakim*] (27.1); [J]evil—[R]famine (28.8); [J]thither was their spirit to go; and the wheels were lifted up—[R]and the wheels rose (Ezek 1.20; there are many such instances in Ezekiel of repetitions not found in R's text); [J]be strong, yea, be strong—[R]be strong and of good courage (Dan 10.19); [J]assemble themselves—[R]gash themselves (Hos 7.14).

§127 Not only did the Masoretes establish a standard text and supply it with vowels; in many places, where they believed that what stood in the text was in some way unacceptable, they wrote in the margin the word they preferred, marking it "Read" (Aramaic *qrē*). They also gave the word which stood in the written text (Aramaic *ktīb*) the vowels of their preferred reading instead of its own (as was done with the divine name, § 44). Thus in Joshua 3.16 the *ktīb* (abbreviated K) has *b'dm,* i.e., *b'ādām* (Rat Adam). The Masoretes vocalized this, however, *bĕ'ādām,* and put in the margin as *qrē* (abbreviated Q) *mē'ādām* (Jfrom Adam).

Very often the Q is merely a correction of the spelling or grammatical form of a word. Even where the meaning is affected, moreover, it is not easy to tell whether the substitution represents a variant reading with tradition behind it, or merely expresses a preference or prejudice of the Masoretes themselves. That a real variant may be preserved in this way is shown by the fact that the Q of some manuscripts is often the K of others, with support also in some cases in the Versions (§ 135).

In the following places, for example, JR both follow the Q, which is the K of some manuscripts and also agrees with one or more of the Versions:

JRhis children (Deut 33.9, K his son); Jwere enlightened—Rbecame bright (1 Sam 14.27, K saw); JRat the river Euphrates (2 Sam 8.3, K omits Euphrates); JRMy son (1 Chron 22.7, K his son); JLet death sieze upon them—RLet death [Or *desolations*] come upon them (Ps 55.15, K Desolations upon them); JRbosom (74.11, K portion, or statute, doubtless the result of mistaking a *y* for a *w*); JRhis word (Jer 23.18, K my word); JRostriches (Lam 4.3, K because eyes, probably an accidental error in copying).

In some places also where J adopts the Q but R does not there is some support for the Q in manuscripts and in the Versions;

e.g., Jagainst mine own life—Ragainst his life [Another reading is *at the risk of my life*] (2 Sam 18.13); Jmy mercy—Rhis steadfast love (Ps 59.10); Jme—Rus (60.5); Jhave borne—Rshall forget (Ezek 39.26).

So also a number of places where the Q is adopted by R but not by J. Several of these involve confusion between *lō* (to him) and *lō'* (not):

Jand not we ourselves [Or, *and his we are*]—Rand we are his [Another reading is *and not we ourselves*] (Ps 100.3); Jand not [Or, *to him*] increased the joy—Rthou hast increased its joy (Is 9.3); JThough Israel be not gathered—Rand that Israel might be gathered to him (49.5). Cp Ex 21.8, where JR both follow the Q: Jwho hath betrothed her to himself—^{R}who has designated her for himself [Another reading is *so that he has not designated her*].

§ 128 Sometimes JR both adopt the Q where there is support in the Versions (§ 135) but not in the K of any Hebrew manuscripts;

e.g., ^{J}armies—^{R}ranks (1 Sam 17.23, K caves); ^{J}my way—^{R}my [Another reading is *his*] way (2 Sam 22.33; see also v. 34 and cp Ps 18.32f); ^{JR}my cord (Job 30.11, K his cord); ^{JR}me (Ps 71.20, twice, K us). Even without any support in manuscripts or versions JR sometimes both follow the Q; e.g., ^{J}his saints—^{R}his faithful ones (1 Sam 2.9, K reads the singular); ^{JR}Dodo (2 Sam 23.9, K Dodai); ^{JR}Segub (1 Kings 16.34, K Segib; cp 1 Chron 2.21f).

With or without support in manuscripts or versions, J frequently adopts the Q where R holds to the K;

e.g., ^{J}A troop cometh—^{R}"Good fortune!" (Gen 30.11); ^{J}the money of them that were redeemed—^{R}the redemption money (Num 3.51); ^{J}plain—^{R}fords (2 Sam 15.28; cp 17.16, where "plains" is the K and "fords" the Q of some manuscripts, while others have "fords" as K and "plains" as Q); ^{J}Ephrain—^{R}Ephron [Another reading is *Ephrain*] (2 Chron 13.19); ^{J}and they returned to Jerusalem—^{R}and from the inhabitants of Jerusalem (2 Chron 34.9); ^{J}and Ramoth—^{R}Jeremoth (Ezra 10.29); ^{J}yet will I trust in him—^{R}I have no hope (Job 13.15, another case of *lō* and *lō'*); ^{J}multitude—^{R}strife (33.19); ^{J}his soul . . . his life—^{R}my soul . . . my life (v. 28); ^{J}bring home—^{R}return (39.12); ^{J}that I should not go down—^{R}from among those gone down [Or *that I should not go down*] (Ps 30.3); ^{J}captivity—^{R}fortunes (85.1; 126.4; cp § 74, No. 3); ^{J}and those that have known—^{R}that they may know (119.79); ^{J}an excellent spirit [Or, *a cool spirit*]—^{R}a cool spirit (Prov 17.27); ^{J}and behold it together—^{R}and terrified (Is 41.23); ^{J}by myself—^{R}Who was with me? [Another reading is . . . *by myself*] (44.24); ^{J}transgress—^{R}serve (Jer 2.20); ^{J}be removed—^{R}a horror (15.4; 24.9; 29.18); ^{J}see—^{R}fear (17.8); ^{J}Sabeans [Or, *drunkards*]—^{R}drunkards [Heb uncertain] (Ezek 23.42); ^{J}return—^{R}be inhabited (35.9).

There are places, however, where J stays with the K but R follows the Q;

e.g., ^{J}renowned—^{R}chosen (Num 1.16); ^{J}emerods—^{R}ulcers (Deut 28.27), tumors (1 Sam 5.6, 12; 6.5f, cp vv. 11, 17); ^{J}He is the tower of salvation—

[R]Great triumphs he gives [Another reading is *He is a tower of salvation*] (2 Sam 22.51; cp Ps 18.50); [J]directeth [Or, *considereth*]—[R]considers [Another reading is *establishes*] (Prov 21.29); [J]his righteousness—[R]his righteous deeds (Ezek 3.20; cp 18.24).

§ 129 The Masoretic notes on the text (§ 125) record corrections of other kinds which are not, like the Q (§§ 127f), attached to the text itself. Some, called "scribal corrections" (*tiqqūnē s̀ōprīm*), consist of readings which stand in the text but are said to be alterations of expressions considered irreverent by the scribes. The value of these notes for restoring the correct text is very questionable, though it is hard to see why the Masoretes should have asserted the existence of irreverent readings unless they had evidence for them.

Even if there were such readings in old manuscripts, conceivably they and not the "corrections" were corruptions of the original text. In all but four of the eighteen verses in which corrections of this sort are recorded, both J and R accept the "corrected" Masoretic text rather than the alleged "original" reading. J, indeed, follows the Masoretic text in every instance; and where R adopts what the Masoretes call the original text, there is other evidence for it. In two cases some Hebrew manuscripts support R's reading: [J]to myself—[R]to thee (Job 7.20); [J]you have snuffed at it—[R]you sniff at me [Another reading is *it*] (Mal 1.13). In the former of these instances the Greek (§ 135) also has R's reading. In the two remaining places also there is support in the Greek: [J]made themselves vile—[R]were blaspheming God [Gk: Heb *for themselves*] (1 Sam 3.13); [J]their glory—[R]the glory of God (Ps 106.20, lit. his glory, which is the reading of one major Greek manuscript).

Masoretic notes of another type refer to hundreds of places in the text where unusual forms or uses of words occur. The normal form or word is given with the Aramaic tag *s̀bīr* (i.e., expected or supposed). Whether these notes imply that the reading in the text is a mistake is uncertain, but that this was so in some cases can hardly be doubted.

In Judg 2.22 JR read with some Hebrew manuscripts and the Versions what the Masoretes note as *s̀bīr:* [J]keep the way of the

LORD to walk therein—[R]take care to walk in the way of the LORD (most of the manuscripts read "keep the way of the LORD to walk in them"; this cannot be correct, though possibly "way" should be "ways"). In Num 33.8, where R keeps to the Masoretic text, J follows manuscripts and Versions which agree with the *sbīr:* [J]from before Pihahiroth—[R]from before Hahiroth. Twice where J follows the standard text R adopts the *sbīr* with the support of two Versions in one case and of both manuscripts and Versions in the other: [J]A man that hath friends—[R]There are [Syr Tg; Heb *a man of*] friends (Prov 18.24); [J]my people—[R]peoples (Lam 3.14).

A few other Masoretic notations may be mentioned. In Judg 18.30 the name Manasseh is written with the *n* raised above the line, and a marginal note says "*n* suspended." Without this letter the Hebrew consonants would spell "Moses." This is the reading of some Greek and Latin manuscripts and fits the context; R therefore adopts it: [J]the son of Manasseh—[R]the son of Moses [Another reading is *Manasseh*].

Sometimes the scribes inadvertently copied words or letters twice. Where the Masoretes recognized that the repetition was a mistake, they kept it in the text but put dots above the letters that should be omitted. Twice in Ezekiel J translates words so marked; R omits them: [J]the wall of the temple—[R]the wall (41.20; v. 21 in the Hebrew begins with "the temple"); [J]these four corners [Heb. *cornered*]—[R]the four (Ezek 46.22; the word "corners" occurs earlier in the verse and was probably written here by a scribe whose eye wandered; some of the Versions omit it).

§ 130 Another category of textual changes adopted by R without footnotes rests on the fact that the vowels, with a few exceptions, were not indicated in the written text before the 7th century A.D., and were therefore more subject to change in earlier times than the consonants (§ 125). Where a clearer, more fitting, and more convincing reading can be had by changing the vowels without changing the consonants of a word, R assumes that such a change requires no footnote to explain it.

Many of the changes of this sort adopted by R are presupposed by one or more of the Versions (§ 135), but because only the vowels are altered R has no footnote. In Judg 5.5, for instance, the Masoretic text reads *nāzlū,* from the root *NZL* ([J]melted [Heb. *flowed*]). The Greek, Aramaic, and Syriac Versions read "quaked," presupposing *nāzōllū* in the Hebrew (from the root *ZLL*), and R so reads. In Is 64.1, [J]might flow down—[R]might quake, and v. 3, [J]flowed down—[R]quaked, the Masoretic text itself reads *nāzōllū;* here J follows the Greek and Vulgate, which presuppose *nāzlū.*

In many other places R assumes a vowel-pointing different from that of the Masoretic text but agreeing with one or more of the Versions and sometimes one or two Hebrew manuscripts;

e.g., [J]from thence is the shepherd—[R]by the name of the Shepherd (Gen 49.24); [J]her mother in law saw—[R]she showed her mother-in-law (Ruth 2.18); [J]Give a perfect lot [Or, *Shew the innocent*]—[R]give Thummim (1 Sam 14.41, cp § 140); [J]they helped them not—[R]he did not help them (1 Chron 12.19); [J]milk—[R]fat (Job 21.24); [J]Men—[R]the dying (24.12); [J]sealeth—[R]terrifies them (33.16); [J]whose belly thou fillest—[R]May their belly be filled (Ps 17.14); [J]before God—[R]the God of gods (84.7); [J]liars—[R]a vain hope (116.11, lit. a lie); [J]The way of the LORD is strength to the upright—[R]The LORD is a stronghold to him whose way is upright (Prov 10.29); [J]hath a servant—[R]works for himself (12.9, a considerable difference!); [J]ask it either in the depth [Or, *make thy petition deep*]—[R]let it be deep as Sheol (Is 7.11); [J]for ever and ever—[R]as a witness for ever (30.8; cp Zeph 3.8, [J]to the prey—[R]as a witness); [J]he said—[R]I said (Is 40.6); [J]Thy children—[R]Your builders (49.17); [J]from being a pastor—[R]to send evil (Jer 17.16); [J]unto them that despise me, the LORD hath said—[R]to those who despise the word of the LORD (23.17); [J]the mingled people—[R]Arabia (Ezek 30.5); [J]Aven—[R]On (30.17); [J]young lions—[R]villages (38.13); [J]arm—[R]offspring (Dan 11.6, lit. seed); [J]baker—[R]anger (Hos 7.6); [J]from the sea—[R]water (Nahum 3.8). Only very rarely does R have a footnote in such cases; e.g., [J]of the inhabitants—[R]of Tishbe [Gk: Heb *of the settlers*] (1 Kings 17.1); [J]Why are . . . swept away—[R]Why has Apis fled [Gk: Heb *Why was it swept away*] (Jer 46.15).

§131 In many other places R gains a more satisfactory meaning by repointing the consonantal text without any precedent in Versions or Hebrew manuscripts;

e.g., [J]Calneh—[R]all of them (Gen 10.10); [J]saw it—[R]were afraid (Ex 20.18; cp 1 Sam 23.15); [J]the sword [Or, *drought*]—[R]drought [Another reading is *sword*] (Deut 28.22); [J]Ain, Remmon—[R]En-rimmon (Josh 19.7); [J]the highways—[R]caravans (Judg 5.6; cp Job 6.19, [J]troops—[R]caravans); [J]for the necks of them that take the spoil—[R]for my neck as spoil (Judg 5.30); [J]even unto the great stone of Abel—[R]The great stone . . . is a witness (1 Sam 6.18; cp § 126); [J]linen yarn—[R]from Kue (1 Kings 10.28, twice); [J]Lay down now, put me in a surety—[R]Lay down a pledge for me (Job 17.3); [J]who hast set thy glory—[R]whose glory . . . is chanted (Ps 8.1; J's rendering is not justified by the Hebrew); [J]hinds—[R]oaks [Or . . . *hinds*] (29.9); [J]the haughty people [Heb. *the height of the people*]—[R]the heavens . . . together with (Is 24.4; cp Hos 9.8, [J]with my God —[R]the people of my God); [J]ships—[R]lamentations (Is 43.14); [J]fortress—[R]tester (Jer 6.27); [J]Moab is spoiled, and gone up out of her cities—[R]The destroyer of Moab and his cities has come up (48.15; cp v.18); [J]the rod—[R]injustice [Or *the rod*] (Ezek 7.10); [J]it contemneth—[R]You have despised (21.10; cp v. 13, [J]if the sword contemn even the rod—[R]if you despise the rod); [J]Their drink—[R]drunkards (Hos 4.18); [J]the revolters—[R]of Shittim (5.2); [J]a rebuker [Heb. *a correction*]—[R]will chastise (same v.); [J]the murderer—[R]slaughter (9.13); [J]the most High—[R]the yoke (11.7); [J]the morning—[R]blackness (Joel 2.2); [J]the tabernacle [Or, *Siccuth*]—[R]Sakkuth (Amos 5.26); [J]Chiun—[R]Kaiwan (same v., see § 45); [J]the sin of Samaria—[R]Ashimah of Samaria (8.14; see § 45); [J]Bozrah—[R]in a fold (Mic 2.12); [J]a burden—[R]so that you will not bear (Zeph 3.18, lit. from bearing); [J]governor—[R]clan (Zech 9.7; cp 12.6); [J]because of the army—[R]as a guard (9.8); [J]his neighbor's hand—[R]the hand of his shepherd (11.6); [J]for one covereth violence with his garment—[R]and covering one's garment with violence (Mal 2.16).

A special case is Prov 22.20, [J]excellent things—[R]thirty sayings. Here R accepts the *qrē* (§ 127), as J does, but gives it new vowels to make it read "thirty." This is suggested by the 30 chapters of an Egyptian document, the *Wisdom of Amen-em-opet,* to which this part of the book of Proverbs is very closely related.

In a few cases R's repointing involves a change not only in the vowels but also in the division or combination of words;

e.g., [J]a root of them—[R]they set out thither (Judg 5.14); [J]for Saul, and for his bloody house—[R]There is bloodguilt on Saul and on his house (2 Sam 21.1); [J]Shamer; Ahi, and—[R]Shemer his brother (1 Chron 7.34); [J]from their fathers, and have not hid it—[R]and their fathers have not hidden (Job 15.18, lit. hidden them); [J]there are no bands in their death—[R]they have no pangs; . . . sound (Ps 73.4); [J]in the outmost fruitful branches thereof—[R]on the branches of a fruit tree (Is 17.6);

[J]the company [Heb. *the daughter*] of the Ashurites [Or, *well trodden*]—[R]of pines (Ezek 27.6); [J]as an oven heated by the baker, who—[R]like a heated oven, whose baker (Hos 7.4); [J]will one plow there with oxen?—[R]Does one plow the sea with oxen? [MT *does one plow with oxen?*] (Amos 6.12); [J]the most upright is sharper than a thorn hedge—[R]the most upright of them a thorn hedge (understanding "is" or "is like" from the preceding line, Mic 7.4); [J]even you, O poor [Or, *verily the poor*] of the flock—[R]for those who trafficked in the sheep (Zech 11.7); [J]so the poor—[R]the traffickers (v. 11; cp 14.21, [J]the Canaanite—[R]a trader).

Perhaps the most notable instance of such a difference in pointing and word-division is the Hebrew word used in Ps 23.4: [JR]the valley of the shadow of death [R mg Or *the valley of deep darkness*]. The Masoretic text reads one word, *ṣlmwt,* but points as though it were two words, *ṣal māwet,* i.e., shadow of death. The way the same word is used elsewhere, however, together with the fact that even in the Masoretic text it is not divided into two words, indicates that it is derived from a root *ṢLM,* found in other Semitic languages with the meaning "become black" or "become dark." R, with its usual conservatism in very familiar passages, keeps the traditional rendering in Ps 23, with "deep darkness," in the margin. Everywhere else, however, R reads either "deep darkness" (Job 3.5; 10.21, cp v. 22 mg; 12.22; 16.16; 24.17 twice; 28.3; 34.22; 38.17; Ps 44.19; Is 9.2; Jer 2.6; Amos 5.8) or "gloom" (Ps 107.14; Jer 13.16).

In a few cases R's repointing involves not a change of vowels but the shift of a dot whose position distinguishes *s* from *š* (*sh*);

e.g., [J]there—[R]he has appointed [MT . . . *there*] (Eccles 3.17); cp 2 Chron 1.5, [J]he put—[R]there (here many manuscripts read "there"); [J]look—[R]Depart [Or *Look*] (Song 4.8).

Chapter XXIX

TEXTUAL CHANGES WITH FOOTNOTES

§132 In addition to such textual changes as those described in the preceding chapter, which are not indicated by footnotes, there are others that require more justification, because they involve changes in the consonants of the text with little or no support in Hebrew manuscripts. In most cases, though the difference in meaning may be considerable, the change in the Hebrew consonants is very slight, and the reading in the text can be explained by a natural mistake in copying.

At three places in the book of Jeremiah a name of the hostile Babylonian empire has been disguised by a peculiar rabbinical cipher. This consists of using the last letter of the Hebrew alphabet (*t*) for the first letter ('), the next to the last (*š* or *s*) for the second (*b*), etc.; hence the name "Atbash" (i.e., *'tbš*). In Jer 25.26 and 51.41 Babel, the common Hebrew name for both Babylon and Babylonia, becomes by this device Sheshach (*ššḥ* for *bbl*). J reads "Sheshach" in each place, with a note at 25.26, "According to ancient tradition a cypher for Babel." R reads "Babylon" with a note, "Heb. *Sheshach,* a cipher for Babylon." In 51.1 the Hebrew name Kasdim (i.e., Chaldea) becomes by "Atbash" Leb-qamai (*lbqmy* for *ksdym*). This time J translates the cipher, apparently not recognizing it as such; R proceeds as before: [J]the midst [Heb. *heart*] of them that rise up against me—[R]Chaldea [Heb *Leb-qamai,* a cipher for Chaldea].

§133 As has been noted in § 126, when R adopts a variant reading attested by only one or two Hebrew manuscripts, a footnote calls attention to the fact. In most of these cases there is support also in one or more of the Versions (see § 135);

e.g., [J]three—[R]thirty [Two Hebrew Mss Syr: MT *three*] (2 Sam 23.18); [J]I flee unto thee to hide me [Heb. *hide me with thee*]—[R]I have fled to thee for refuge [One Heb Ms Gk: Heb *to thee I have hidden*] (Ps 143.9). At the end of Ps 145.13 R adds two lines, with the note, "These two lines are supplied by one Hebrew Ms, Gk and Syr."

Sometimes a reading directly attested by only a single Hebrew manuscript is supported by parallel passages (cp § 134); e.g., [J]. . . and the arches thereof—[R]. . . and its vestibule were of the same size as the others [One Ms Compare verses 29 and 33: Heb. lacks *were of the same size as the others*] (Ezek 40.36, doubtless an instance of accidental omission in copying). In other cases R adopts a reading from one or two manuscripts simply on the basis of intrinsic suitability in the context; e.g., [J]Syria—[R]Edom [One Ms: Heb *Aram* (Syria)] (2 Chron 20.2); [J]by the Egyptians—[R]the Egyptians [Two Mss: Heb *from Egypt*] (Ezek 23.21).

The most notable instances of preferring a particular manuscript to all others are in Isaiah, where thirteen readings adopted by R were provided by the great complete scroll of that book found in 1947 in a cave near the Dead Sea. They are indicated in the footnotes as attested not merely by "One Ms" but by "One ancient Ms," since the scroll is more than a thousand years older than the oldest Hebrew manuscripts of OT books known before it was discovered. Since these readings have been discussed elsewhere in some detail [1] they need only be mentioned briefly here.

In seven instances the ancient scroll confirms readings attested by one or more of the Versions (14.30; 15.9; 45.2; 49.24; 51.19; 56.12; 60.19). In the other six places there was no such additional attestation (3.24; 14.4; 21.8; 23.2; 33.8; 45.8). The mere fact that such readings were interesting and often tempting was not, of course, the only reason for adopting them. Other notable readings of the scroll were examined by the Committee and rejected.[2]

Innumerable scrolls and fragments of scrolls of other OT books have been discovered in the caves near the Dead Sea since

[1] See *The Dead Sea Scrolls,* by Millar Burrows (N.Y., The Viking Press, 1955), pp. 305–310.

[2] Op. cit., pp. 310f; see also the author's *More Light On The Dead Sea Scrolls* (N.Y., The Viking Press, 1958), pp. 147–153.

1947, but none of them had been published when R was completed; most of them, indeed, had not yet been discovered. They are still in process of publication. As they appear, they will be carefully studied by the Committee to determine their value for any further revision of R.

§ 134 The fact that passages, sometimes of considerable extent, often appear in more than one place in the OT with more or less variation, affords another means of correcting the text in some places. It cannot be assumed, of course, that changes were not made intentionally when a passage was repeated or quoted; there was obviously some revision in many cases (cp the Ten Commandments, for example, in Ex 20.2–17 and Deut 5.6–21). R avoids harmonizing when such differences between parallel passages belong clearly or probably to the correct text. There are places, however, where faulty readings can be corrected from the parallels.

Sometimes there is support in the Versions (§ 135) for emending the text to agree with the parallel:

e.g., [J]on all manner of instruments made of fir wood—[R]with all their might, with songs [Gk 1 Chron 13.8; Heb *fir-trees*] (2 Sam 6.5); [J]shall not depart—[R]I will not take [Gk Syr Vg 1 Chron 17.13: Heb *shall not depart*] (2 Sam 7.15); [J]seven—[R]three [1 Chron 21.12 Gk: Heb *seven*] (2 Sam 24.13).

In other cases a correction is clearly called for even without such support;

e.g., [J]tribes—[R]judges [1 Chron 17.6: Heb *tribes*] (2 Sam 7.7); [J]they shall be afraid—[R]and came trembling [Ps 18.45: Heb *girded themselves*] (22.46; J harmonizes here without a note); [J]the armies—[R]the forces in the open country [With Jer 40.7: Heb lacks *in the open country*] (2 Kings 25.23); [J]oxen—[R]gourds [1 Kings 7.24; Heb *oxen*] (2 Chron 4.3, twice); [J]My goodness [Or, *my mercy*]—[R]my rock [With 18.2 2 Sam 22.2: Heb *my steadfast love*] (Ps 144.2; cp § 77).

Sometimes the context gives the clue for a correction of the text;

e.g., [J]unto Abel, and to Beth-maachah—[R]to Abel of Beth-maacah [With 20.15: Heb *and Beth-maacah*] (2 Sam 20.14); [J]on the outside—[R]from the court of the house of the LORD [With 7.12. Heb *from the outside*] (1 Kings 7.9); [J]the messenger—[R]the king [See 7.2: Heb *messenger*] (2 Kings 6.33); [J]the bones—[R]the logs [Compare verse 10: Heb *the bones*] (Ezek 24.5); [J]Helem—[R]Heldai [With verse 10: Heb *Helem*] (Zech 6.14); [J]Hen—[R]Josiah [With verse 10: Heb *Hen*] (same v.).

§135 In the foregoing sections reference has been made frequently to the ancient Versions. A brief account of these and their use in R is now in order.[3] From the third century before Christ and through the early centuries of our era the need for translations of the OT was felt, first by Jews who did not know Hebrew and later by Christians. Four major translations which were made to meet this need are used in R as aids in the establishment of a more correct Hebrew text. They are indicated in the footnotes by abbreviations, as follows:

(1) Gk, the ancient Greek Version or Septuagint, made in Egypt during the last three centuries before Christ, by far the oldest and most important of the Versions;

(2) Tg, the Aramaic Version or Targum, more exactly a series of translations of different books, made at different times from the first century A.D. and on into the Middle Ages;

(3) Syr, the Syriac Version or Peshitta, made by Jewish or Christian scholars in the second century A.D., if not earlier;

(4) Vg, the Latin Version or Vulgate, made in the late fourth or early fifth century A.D.

Commonly grouped with these, though it is not itself a Version, is

(5) Sam, the Samaritan Pentateuch, which preserves the Hebrew text of the five books of the Law in a form independent of the Masoretic revision (§ 125). Possibly pre-Christian in its present form, it reflects the tradition of the Samaritans from the time of their separation from the Jews.

There are also three other Greek Versions, later and less important than the Septuagint, and only partially preserved, but sometimes useful and occasionally cited in R's footnotes:

[3] For a somewhat fuller discussion see Introd RSVOT, Chap. IV.

(6) Aquila, a Jewish Version made early in the second century A.D., reproducing the Hebrew very literally and presenting Jewish interpretations as against what were regarded as Christian perversions in the Septuagint;

(7) Theodotion, a second-century revision, perhaps Christian, of an older Greek translation, used by R only in Daniel, where in most of the Greek manuscripts it replaces the text of the Septuagint;

(8) Symmachus, another translation from the late second century, couched in more idiomatic and elegant Greek than Aquila. This version, of which only fragments survive, is very rarely cited by R.

Two Latin Versions in addition to Vg (No. 4) are referred to by R in some places; they are much less important than Vg, being based on Gk instead of the original Hebrew:

(9) Old Latin, a translation (or several translations) from the second century A.D., of which only fragments have survived in manuscripts and quotations;

(10) Jerome, a translation of the Psalms by Jerome which is included in the Vulgate instead of the translation he made later from the Hebrew.

§ 136 From the number of footnotes citing the Versions in R, and the lack of such notes in J, it might be supposed that R followed the Versions much more freely than J did. The fact is that J has frequently substituted for the Hebrew text a reading from one or more of the Versions, without any note to show that this has been done. In the following places, for example, J's readings are those of Gk, Syr, and Vg, not those of the Hebrew, which R retains:

[J]Uncover not your heads—[R]Do not let the hair of your heads hang loose (Lev 10.6); [J]So the ark of the LORD compassed the city—[R]So he caused the ark of the LORD to compass the city (Josh 6.11); [J]even of all that have been before them—[R]he was over all of them (Eccles 4.16).

In some places J has a marginal note but does not mention the Versions; e.g., [J]What he did in the Red Sea [Or, *Vaheb in Suphah*]—[R]Waheb in Suphah (Num 21.14). In other places both J and R follow the Versions, but with different notes; e.g., [J]your dreamers [Heb. *dreams*]—[R]your dreamers [Gk Syr Vg: Heb *dreams*] (Jer 27.9). In still other places R has a note and J has none, as in Job 37.7 and Ps 22.16. Sometimes, where the reading of the Versions is merely a matter of assuming different vowels from those of the Masoretic text, neither J nor R has a note; so, e.g., Ps 68.30; Jer 51.2. In Hos 13.10 J follows the Hebrew but adds a very peculiar note: I will be thy king [Rather, *Where is thy king?* King Hoshea being then in prison, 2 Kings 17.4]. R follows the Versions: Where [Gk Syr Vg: Heb *I will be*] now is your king . . . ?

The treatment of the Versions was one of the points on which the nineteenth-century British and American committees differed most sharply (cp § 2). They agreed to follow the Hebrew text in their translation, with very few exceptions (e.g., 1 Sam 6.18); but E has many marginal notes citing variant readings from the Versions, whereas A declines to recognize them even in the margin. R's attitude is more free and at the same time more critical than that of J or that of either E or A. Readings of the Versions are adopted not only in the notes but in the text when they seem clearly better than those of the Hebrew; but the literal meaning of the Hebrew is given in the footnotes, and the Versions from which the adopted reading comes are specified.

§ 137 The importance of the Versions lies in the fact that they reflect an earlier stage in the history of the Hebrew text than the standardized form perpetuated by the Masoretes. It does not follow that where they differ from the Masoretic text their readings are necessarily better. The Hebrew manuscripts on which they were based may or may not have been better than those used by the Masoretes. Sometimes the readings of the Versions are undoubtedly older and more authentic than those of the Masoretic text, but very often they are demonstrably worse. Each Version had its own history, with its own mistakes and alterations in the process of copying manuscripts. In many cases, moreover, the Versions preserve an interpretation rather than a literal translation of the text before them. Every variant reading must therefore be judged on its own merits, and the mere fact that it seems clearer or more plausible than the Masoretic text is not sufficient reason to adopt it.

In general it may be said that the Versions have no authority.

They offer precedents and possibilities which are very important; but only if they point to a convincing reconstruction of the Hebrew text itself can they be accepted. Where R has a reading from the Versions, it is because a majority of the Committee has judged that the possibility indicated by the Versions is more probably correct than the reading of the Hebrew text. Most of these readings involve only a very slight correction of the Hebrew text.

In some cases the word "Compare" precedes the abbreviations for the Versions cited. This means that the restored Hebrew text as translated by R does not correspond exactly to the reading of the Versions but has been suggested by it.

§ 138 Since R's footnotes are so explicit, it is unnecessary to give here many examples of the use of the Versions. A few passages will show the nature of the readings adopted and those of the Masoretic text which they replace. R's notes, being unnecessary here, will be omitted in most instances.

The Samaritan text, which includes only the Pentateuch (§ 135), is followed in very few places, and in most of these there is also support in at least one of the Versions. In Gen 31.48f J reads with the Hebrew, "Therefore was the name of it called Galeed; And Mizpah," as though the heap had two names. Instead of Mizpah Sam has "the pillar." R combines these two readings and translates, "Therefore he named it Galeed, and the pillar [Compare Sam: Heb lacks *the pillar*] Mizpah."

Examples of readings from Sam with support from the Versions are the following:

[J]And Cain talked with Abel his brother—[R]Cain said to Abel his brother, "Let us go out to the field" [Sam Gk Syr Compare Vg: Heb lacks *Let us go out to the field*] (Gen 4.8); [J]the seven years, which were in the land of Egypt—[R]the seven years when there was plenty [Sam Gk: Heb *which were*] in the land of Egypt (41.48); [J]he removed them to cities—[R]he made slaves of them [Sam Gk Compare Vg: Heb *he removed them to the cities*] (47.21); [J]I thy father in law Jethro am come—[R]Lo, [Sam Gk Syr: Heb *I*] your father-in-law Jethro is coming (Ex 18.6; the Hebrew may mean "am coming" but not "am come," and v. 7 shows that Jethro had not yet arrived).

§139 The Septuagint (Gk), being the oldest and most important (§ 135, No. 1), has been followed, both alone and with others, far more often than any of the other Versions. The following are some of the most important of R's readings that are attested by the Septuagint only:

[J]the blessings of my progenitors unto the utmost bound of the everlasting hills—[R]the blessings of the eternal mountains, the bounties of the everlasting hills (Gen 49.26); [J]but it gave light by night—[R]and the night passed (Ex 14.20); [J]In that I command thee—[R]If you obey the commandments of the LORD your God which I command you (Deut 30.16; J connects with what precedes, R with what follows); [J]Gilgal—[R]Galilee (Josh 12.23); [J]. . . with the web. And she fastened it—[R]". . . with the web and make it tight with the pin, then I shall become weak, and be like any other man." So while he slept, Delilah took the seven locks of his head and wove them into the web. And she made them tight (Judg 16.13f; here fourteen or fifteen words which have dropped out of the Hebrew text are preserved in the Greek; see 1 Sam 10.1 for a similar instance); [J]Michal Saul's daughter loved him—[R]all Israel loved him (1 Sam 18.28); [J]The LORD said that he would dwell—[R]The LORD has set the sun in the heavens, but has said that he would dwell (1 Kings 8.12; the meter favors this addition from Gk); [J]thou shalt be built up—[R]and humble yourself (Job 22.23); [J]but let them not turn again to folly—[R]to those who turn to him in their hearts (Ps 85.8); [J]meddle not with them that are given to change—[R]do not disobey either of them (Prov 24.21); [J]found him not.—[R]found him not; I called him, but he gave no answer (Song 3.1; again the meter favors Gk); [J]I will bring you into the bond of the covenant—[R]I will let you go in by number (Ezek 20.37); [J]when I shall bring thy destruction—[R]when I carry you captive (32.9); [J]upright ones—[R]terms of peace (Dan 11.17); [J]shall sorrow [Or, *begin*]—[R]shall cease (Hos 8.10); [J]for joy—[R]Exult not (9.1); [J]Bethel—[R]house of Israel (10.15); [J]at Ashdod—[R]in Assyria (Amos 3.9); [J]in our palaces—[R]upon our soil (Mic 5.5); [J]Since those days were—[R]how did you fare? (Hag 2.16); [J]crowns—[R]a crown (Zech 6.11; see also v. 14).

Note also Lam 5.5, where R follows Symmachus (§ 135, No. 8), and Dan 8.24 and 10.13, where readings of Theodotion (§ 135, No. 7) with some support in Gk are adopted.

§ 140 Many of R's readings are supported not only by Gk but by as many as three of the other Versions. Instances of this have been noted already in § 130; a few more may be mentioned here:

[J]A greyhound [Or, *horse*. Heb. *girt in the loins*]—[R]the strutting cock [Gk Syr Tg Compare Vg: Heb obscure] (Prov 30.31); [J]hast consumed—[R]hast delivered [Gk Syr Old Latin Tg: Heb *melted*] (Is 64.7); [J]carry out—[R]go [Gk Syr Vg Tg: Heb *bring*] out (Ezek 12.5); the statutes of Omri are kept [Or, *he doth much keep the &c*]—[R]you have kept the statutes of Omri [Gk Syr Vg Tg: Heb *the statutes of Omri are kept*] (Mic 6.16). Cp [J]the light shall not be clear [Heb. *precious*]—[R]there shall be neither cold nor frost [Compare Gk Syr Vg Tg: Heb uncertain] (Zech 14.6); [J]unto me—[R]to him [Theodotion Gk Syr Vg: Heb *me*] (Dan 8.14).

In a great many places R is supported by Gk and two other Versions, most frequently Syr and Vg;

e.g., [J]Great men are not always wise—[R]It is not the old that are wise (Job 32.9); [J]to the good—[R]to the good and the evil (Eccles 9.2, cp the context); [J]the lips of those that are asleep—[R]lips and teeth (Song 7.9); [J]I will destroy—[R]I will watch over (Ezek 34.16); [J]will make thee sick—[R]I have begun (Mic 6.13); [J]the island of the innocent—[R]the innocent man (Job 22.30, cp § 71). In the Psalms R has a number of readings following Gk, Syr, and Jerome (§ 135, No. 10); e.g., [J]he passed away—[R]I passed by (37.36); [J]because of the truth—[R]from the bow (60.4); [J]bind—[R]instruct (105.22). R follows Symmachus, Syr, and Vg in Ezek 32.5; Gk, Syr, and Old Latin in 34.29; Gk, Vg, and Symmachus in 2 Sam 18.3; Aquila, Symmachus, Syr, and Vg in Job 5.5.

Other readings are attested by Gk, Syr, and Tg;

e.g., [J]he was taken up—[R]he was left hanging (2 Sam 18.9); [J]That thy foot may be dipped [Or, *red*]—[R]that you may bathe your feet (Ps 68.23); [J]to help him—[R]his helpers (Ezek 12.14).

Even more numerous are the places where a reading of Gk adopted by R is found also in one other Version, which is Syr in the largest number of instances;

e.g., [J]mine iniquity—[R]my misery (Ps 31.10); [J]Light is sown—[R]Light dawns (Ps 97.11); [J]in his death—[R]through his integrity (Prov 14.32);

[J]the men of thy kindred—[R]your fellow exiles (Ezek 11.15); [J]messengers . . . in ships—[R]swift messengers (30.9); [J]the calves of our lips—[R]the fruit of our lips (Hos 14.2).

R has also many readings based on Gk and Vg;

e.g., [J]out of the meadows of Gibeah—[R]west of Geba (Judg 20.33); [J]in Caleb-ephratah—[R]Caleb went in to Ephratah (1 Chron 2.24); [J]and seeth the place of stones—[R]he lives among the rocks (Job 8.17); [J]gotten by vanity—[R]hastily gotten (Prov 13.11); [J]rejoice—[R]swoon away (Jer 51.39); [J]desolation—[R]the raven (Zeph 2.14). Note also the following, where R's note reads "Vg Compare Gk": [J]Saul said unto the LORD God of Israel—[R]Saul said, O LORD God of Israel, why hast thou not answered thy servant this day? If this guilt is in me or in Jonathan my son, O LORD, God of Israel, give Urim (1 Sam 14.41, cp § 130); [J]and Jashubilehem—[R]and returned to Lehem (1 Chron 4.22). Cp [J]that she tarried a little in the house—[R]without resting even for a moment [Compare Gk Vg: the meaning of the Hebrew text is uncertain] (Ruth 2.7). In some places R's note cites Gk and Old Latin (Judg 19.2; Is 48.11; Jer 15.11; 30.8; Lam 1.4; Ezek 1.13; 25.8; 32.27; 34.31); in others Vg Old Latin Compare Gk (Judg 2.3), Gk Jerome (Ps 119.128), or Theodotion Symmachus Compare Vg (Job 35.15).

In only a few places Gk and Tg together attest R's readings;

e.g., [J]and goeth at—[R]and captain over (1 Sam 22.14); [J]the middle chamber—[R]the lowest story (1 Kings 6.8); cp [J]among the grass—[R]like grass amid waters [Gk Compare Tg] (Is 44.4).

§ 141 Syr alone is the basis of R's readings in many places;

e.g., [J]to be enlightened with—[R]that he may see (Job 33.30); [J]take counsel—[R]bear pain (Ps 13.2); [J]Make me to hear—[R]Fill me with (51.8); [J]wait upon thee—[R]sing praises to thee (59.9); [J]that they may dwell—[R]and his servants shall dwell (69.35); [J]we spend our years—[R]our years come to an end (90.9); [J]that I may plant—[R]stretching out (Is 51.16); [J]is cleansed—[R]is defiled (Ezek 44.26); [J]unto the potter—[R]into the treasury (Zech 11.13, twice). There are also several places where R mg reads Compare Syr (Job 23.9; Ezek 23.34; 47.8f, 18).

Sometimes Syr, Vg, and Tg have a reading adopted by R which is not in Gk;

e.g., [J]took a burnt offering—[R]offered a burnt offering (Ex 18.12); [JR]bitter (Job 23.2; here J too follows the Versions instead of the Hebrew); [J]I am broken—[R]I have broken (Ezek 6.9). Cp [J]To him that is afflicted [Heb. *to him that melteth*]—[R]He who withholds [Syr Vg Compare Tg: Heb obscure] (Job 6.14); [JR]that all men may know his work (Job 37.7 [R mg, Vg Compare Syr Tg: Heb *that all men whom he has made may know it*]); [J]In measure—[R]Measure by measure [Compare Syr Vg Tg: The meaning of the Hebrew word is unknown] (Is 27.8).

Syr and Vg, without Gk or Tg, are the source of R's readings in some places;

e.g., [J]come forth—[R]stay (1 Sam 22.3); [J]from one side of the floor to the other [Heb. *from floor to floor*]—[R]from floor to rafters (1 Kings 7.7); cp [J]began he to go up [Heb. *was the foundation of the going up*]—[R]he began to go up [Vg See Syr: Heb *that was the foundation of the going up*] (Ezra 7.9). Cp 1 Chron 7.1, R mg Syr Compare Vg; 2 Chron 15.8, R mg Compare Syr Vg; 1 Kings 9.8, R mg Syr Old Latin; Ps 77.6, R mg Syr Jerome.

Only rarely are Syr and Tg, without Gk or Vg, R's witnesses for its readings;

note, however, Ps 52.7; Prov 18.24 (see § 129) and Is 52.14. A much discussed passage, important in the history of the Messianic hope (§ 146), is Gen 49.10: [J]until Shiloh come—[R]until he comes to whom it belongs [Syr Compare Tg: Heb *until Shiloh comes* or *until he comes to Shiloh*]. Cp [J]it had gone down—[R]the sun [Syr See Is 38.8 and Tg: Heb lacks *the sun*] had declined (2 Kings 20.11).

R has taken a number of readings from Vg alone;

e.g., [J]a strange woman—[R]foreigners (Prov 27.13, cp 20.16); [J]when thou shalt make his soul an offering—[R]when he makes himself an offering (Is 53.10); [J]men—[R]mourners (Ezek 24.17, 22); [J]And it shall be unto them for an inheritance—[R]They shall have no inheritance (44.28). In Ruth 4.5 R follows the Old Latin and Vg: [J]thou must buy it also of Ruth—[R]you are also buying Ruth.

Tg is cited with Vg for R's reading in Ezek 27.32; Jerome and Tg are cited in Ps 16.2. Tg, being often very free, with considerable expansion, is on the whole less useful than the other Versions, except where it agrees with their readings and thus strengthens the evidence for a correction of the Hebrew text. Some good readings, however, are indicated by Tg alone;

e.g., [J]welfare—[R]sacrificial feasts (Ps 69.22); [J]the flesh of his own arm—[R]his neighbor's flesh (Is 9.20, with partial support in one manuscript of Gk); [J]he knew their desolate palaces—[R]he ravaged their strongholds (Ezek 19.7); [J]wrapped up—[R]polished (of a sword, 21.15).

§142 When the text has clearly suffered in the course of transmission, and cannot be restored by any of the means thus far reviewed, it is necessary to accept the best correction that the ingenuity and learning of scholars can devise. This is obviously a hazardous undertaking, requiring great caution. Rarely if ever can one be quite sure that the reading proposed is what originally stood in the text; one can be sure only that it is more probable than what now stands there. There was a period in the history of OT criticism when scholars indulged rather freely in emendations of the text, sometimes demonstrating only that their own knowledge of the Hebrew language was imperfect. A large body of proposed corrections was accumulated, however, and through a process of critical sifting many very impressive suggestions have emerged from the mass.

The present generation of scholars has a wholesome respect for the traditional text and views with suspicion all efforts to improve it. Alterations are accepted only as a last resort, and only when there is a substantial consensus of favorable judgment among competent scholars. To be convincing, a correction must require a minimum of change in the traditional text, and the latter must be explicable as a corruption of the adopted reading. There are several well-known kinds of scribal errors, remarkably like the mistakes made by typists and typesetters to this day.

Where corrections of this kind have been adopted by R, they are marked in footnotes with the abbreviation "Cn." There are more of them in some books than in others, because the text is not as well preserved in some books as it is in others. The Committee was conscientiously conservative in making such changes, and did so only when it seemed necessary. Many corrections proposed by members were decisively rejected by the majority. The nature of the ones adopted may be made clear by indicating in a few important instances how the adopted reading differs from the standard text. The consonants of the Masoretic text will be given with the abbreviation MT, those of the correction with the abbreviation Cn. It must be pointed out that the correction often resembles the standard text much more closely in the Hebrew script than it does in our transliteration.

Gen 16.13; [J]Have I also here looked after him that seeth me?—[R]Have I really seen God and remained alive after seeing him? MT *hgm hlm r'yty'ḥry r'y,* Cn *hgm 'lhym r'yty w'ḥy 'ḥry r'y.*

2 Sam 1.21: [J]fields of offerings—[R]upsurging of the deep. MT *sdy trwmt,* Cn *šrʻ thwmwt* (suggested by an expression in a Ugaritic text, cp § 38).

Is 35.7: [J]in the habitation of dragons, where each lay—[R]the haunt of jackals shall become a swamp. MT *bnwh tnym rbṣh,* Cn *nwh tnym lbṣh* (the verb is understood from the first line; cp §§ 46, 73 on [J]dragons—[R]jackals).

Ezek 27.17: [J]wheat of Minnith, and Pannag—[R]wheat, olives and early figs. MT *bḥṭy mnyt wpng,* Cn *ḥṭym zyt wpgg* (3 Hebrew manuscripts read *wpgg*).

Ezek 31.3; [J]the Assyrian was a cedar—[R]I will liken you to a cedar. MT *'šwr 'rz,* Cn *'šwk l'rz* (the chapter deals with Pharaoh, not Assyria).

Hos 5.13; 10.6: [J]king Jareb—[R]the great king. MT *mlk yrb,* Cn *mlk rb* (a title of the Assyrian emperor; no king named Jareb is known to history).

Hos 10.15: [J]in a morning—[R]In the storm. MT *bšḥr,* Cn *bsʻr.*

Hab 2.4: [J]is lifted up—[R]shall fail. MT *ʻplh,* Cn *ʻlp.*

Not all of R's corrections are as simple as these. One in particular calls for some explanation. The most elaborate textual reconstruction adopted by R without help from the Versions or manuscripts is the one in vv. 11 and 12 of Ps 2: [J]and rejoice with trembling. Kiss the Son—[R]with trembling kiss his feet. On this R mg says, "The Hebrew of 11b and 12a is uncertain." It is worse than that. J's interpretation and the text it represents are as old as the Syriac Version (§ 135, No. 2), but they can hardly be correct. Gk, Vg, and Tg read "Receive discipline" or the like instead of "Kiss the Son." The word translated "Son," in fact, is not the Hebrew word *bēn* (§ 52, No. 2), which has just been used in v. 7. As pointed by the Masoretes, it is *bar,* which means "son" in Aramaic but not in Hebrew, and even in Aramaic would mean not "the Son" but "a son." The correction adopted by R is not the only one that has been proposed, but it is the one now most widely accepted among scholars.

The consonantal text and the reconstruction are as follows:

MT	*wgylw*	*br'dh*	*nšqw*	*br*
Cn		*br'dh*	*nšqw*	*brglyw.*

This involves not only a redivision of words but the transposition of several consonants. Displacements of letters and words, however, are not uncommon in manuscripts. The corrected text not only makes sense but has the advantage also of fitting the metrical form of the Psalm much better than the Masoretic reading does.

CONCLUSION

The differences between J and R which have been recorded in the foregoing chapters are only a fraction of the total amount; even so they may create an impression that R departs from J much more than it does. The fact that only differences have been discussed, and the agreements largely ignored, may have magnified unduly the relative amount of change. In a sampling of ten passages scattered through the OT it has been found that only one out of every five words in J has been changed by R, and most of these changes are matters of wording rather than basic differences of meaning.

As was stated in the Introduction (§ 1), R is not a new translation. Many new translations, by individual scholars or by Protestant, Catholic, or Jewish groups, have been issued or projected in recent years. R is not one of them. It is a revision of a revision of J (§ 2), more thorough than the previous revision (EA) but by no means drastic or radical. Only such changes have been made as seemed to be demanded by the evolution of the English language since 1611, by better understanding of the original languages, and by the possibility of establishing a more correct text than was available to the seventeenth-century translators.

Readers of this volume may be inclined to feel that most of the differences between J and R are of little or no importance. Members of the Committee, including this writer, have often had that feeling, especially after long, weary hours of arduous toil on minute details of text and translation. The public press recently reported a discussion of the question whether the fruit eaten by Adam and Eve was an apple or an apricot, and many readers must have sympathized with the statement of a prominent churchman, "It doesn't make a hoot of difference to the world situation." The same thing may be said of a great many points considered in these pages. But again it must be said that there is no way to draw a line between what is important and what is not, once the importance of the whole project is admitted. If the Bible is important at all, it is important that it be translated correctly and worthily, even in fine points that of themselves may not be very significant. And, of course, many of the changes made by R are by no means unimportant.

Whether they are all improvements may be debatable. Many of them were very seriously and even warmly debated by the Committee. The decision was not always unanimous, and the minority was not always convinced. Not even the alterations already made in J by EA were necessarily retained; but every departure from A was approved by a majority of the Old Testament Section of the Committee, and it can hardly be questioned that the judgment of the majority was sounder, by and large, than that of individual members.

Since the Bible is not merely a collection of historical and literary documents but sacred Scripture, accepted throughout Christendom as a divinely inspired guide for faith and practice, even the exact wording of a familiar translation acquires emotional associations, and any new translation or revision is inevitably subject to the suspicion that it is an attack on the integrity and truth of the Bible. R, like other translations before and since, has been denounced as not a revision but a perversion of the Scriptures.

The author may repeat here what he wrote for Introd RSVOT (p. 61): "Readers who find a cherished meaning or association lost at one place or another may be tempted to accuse the translators of reading into the text their own beliefs or reading out of it something in which they did not believe. It may be solemnly and emphatically stated in all good faith and conscience that only one theological assumption has dominated the work of the Committee, and that is the firm conviction that taking seriously the belief in divine revelation makes it obligatory to seek only the real meaning of every word and sentence in the Scriptures, and to express just that meaning as exactly and adequately as it can be done in English."

In other words, the impelling motive of the Standard Bible Committee was the same as that of the men who gave us the King James Version. The oft-quoted words of their preface express the purpose of the Revised Standard Version also: "Truly, good Christian Reader, we never thought from the beginning that we should need to make a new translation, nor yet to make of a bad one a good one; . . . but to make a good one yet better . . ." This famous preface, "The Translators to the Reader," and the elaborate marginal notes of J (both unfortunately omitted from many current editions) are worth careful study. They show how fully the spirit and basic principles of the men who made the old and new versions, their attitudes to the original text, and their conceptions of the nature of their task are substantially the same.

The most casual reader of this book must have been convinced that translating the OT is not simple or easy. If much that is here presented seems obscure and confusing, it should at least give some idea of the maze of problems through which a translator must thread his way. How well the Standard Bible Committee accomplished its task is still a fair question. That the Revised Standard Version is the best of all English versions, as it has been called, is not for one of those who made it to say. Others may have done or may do better at one point or another. Certainly R is not perfect. It could be improved, and no doubt will be improved in due time as the Committee continues to review it in the light of new insights and knowledge. But one thing can be said. The Revised Standard Version was made by a group of mature, trained, and dedicated scholars who took their work seriously and did the very best they could. The star that led them all the way was the deep desire expressed in the last sentence of their preface: "It is our hope and our earnest prayer that this Revised Standard Version of the Bible may be used by God to speak to men in these momentous times, and to help them to understand and believe and obey His Word."

INDEX OF SUBJECTS

(N.B.—References are to sections.)

SUBJECT	SECTION
Accusative case	103f
Accuse, accuser, etc.	54
Acquit, etc.	57
Acrostic poems	5
Additions	20f
Advisory Board	2
Akkadian language	38
Ambiguity	74
American Standard Version	2
Anachronisms	40
Angels	47
Animals	73
Arabic language	39
Aramaic language	38f
Archaic forms	11
Archaic words	12
Archeology	37
Article	91
Assyrian language	38
Atbash	132
Atone, etc.	63
Birds	73
Body	48
Body, parts of	48f, 88
Capital letters	7
Chasten, etc.	56
Cleanse, etc.	64
Cognate languages	38f
Condensation	15
Context	134
Corrections (Cn)	142
Defend, Deliver, etc.	62
Deities, pagan	45
Demons	47
Division of Christian Education	2
English of the KJV	3
Ethnic units	51
Euphemisms	34
Evil, etc.	61
Exclamation point	6
Family relationships	52
Footnotes	8f, 20
Free translation	24–35
Gender	95
Genitive case	100–102
Geographical terms	42, 99
God, Hebrew words for	43
God, Son of	53
Grammatical structure	35
Greek Versions	135, 139f
Guilt, etc.	59
Hebrew sacred persons, places, and objects	66
Hyphen	6
Idioms, Hebrew	29–31
Idiomatic translation	23, 28
Imperative	118
Imperfect tense	111–113
Impersonal verbs	107
Infinitive	114–117
Inscriptions	38
Insects	73

SUBJECT	SECTION
Inserted words	18f
Instruments, musical	70
International Council of Religious Education	2
Interpretation	4, 21, 123
Italics	6
Jerome	135, 140f
Judge, etc.	55
King James Version	1 et passim
Languages	4
Literal translation	24–35
Manuscripts	4, 126, 133
Masoretes, Masoretic text	125
Masoretic notes	127–129
Meanings of words	36ff
Meanings, new	13
Meanings, overlapping	74
Meter	5, 122
Misleading words and expressions	14
Moabite language	38
Musical instruments	70
Mythological references	46
Name, the Sacred	44
Names	41f
Names inserted	18
National Council of Churches	2
Nominal sentences	108
Nominative case	99
Notes, Marginal	8f
Notes, Masoretic	127–129
Nouns inserted	18
Number	96–98
Obsolete forms	11
Obsolete words	12
Offense, etc.	60
Omissions	17
Order of words	22f
Pagan deities	45
Pagan sacred persons, places, and objects	65
Parallels	134
Parallelism	5
Paraphrase	35
Parentheses	6
Participles	119f
Particles	92f
Passive meaning	107
Perfect tense	109f
Person (grammatical)	94
Personal names	41f
Phoenician language	38
Physiological terms	48f
Place-names	41f
Plants	72
Poetry	5, 22
Pointing	130f
Pronouns, personal and demonstrative	89
Pronouns, relative	90
Proper names	41f
Psalm titles	69
Psychological terms	50
Punctuation	6
Questions	124
Quotation marks	6
Repetition	16
Reptiles	73
Revised Standard Version	1 et passim
Ritual acts	68
Sacred persons, places, and objects, Pagan	65
Sacred persons, etc., Hebrew	66
Sacred times and assemblies	67
Samaritan text	135, 138
Save, etc.	62
Septuagint	135, 139–140

SUBJECT	SECTION
Simplification	15
Sin, etc.	60
Social units	51
Son of man, Son of God	53
Spelling	10
Standard Bible Committee	2
Stanzas	5
Stems of verbs	105f
Stylistic variety	25
Symbolic names	42
Symmachus	135f, 139f
Syntax	121
Syriac language	39
Syriac Version	141
Targum	135, 140f
Temptation	58
Tetragrammaton	44
Text, Hebrew and Aramaic	4, 9, 125
Theodotion	135, 139f
Titles of Psalms	69
Trees	72
Ugaritic language	38
Verbs, Impersonal	107
Verbs inserted or repeated	19
Verbal Stems	105f
Verse-division	122
Versions	135–141
Vocative case	99
Vowels	125, 130f
Vulgate	135, 140f

INDEX OF OLD TESTAMENT REFERENCES

(N.B.—References are to sections.)

GENESIS

REFERENCE	SECTION	REFERENCE	SECTION
1.1–5	15	3.17	15
1.2	46, 50, 79	4.1	34
1.5, 8, 13, 19, 23, 31	24	4.2	27
1.10	35, 79	4.3	15
1.11	11, 23, 90, 96	4.8	25, 138
1.12	79, 90, 96	4.10	18
1.14f	97	4.14	15, 25
1.18	7	4.15	25
1.20	26, 50, 88, 103	4.18	34
1.21	50, 79, 103	4.19	17
1.24	26, 50, 96	4.20	123
1.25	26	4.22	27
1.26ff	42	4.23	5, 25, 100
1.26	11, 79	4.25	25
1.28	11	4.26	114
1.29	15	5.1	30, 42
1.30	21, 50	5.2	30
2–5	42	5.3	34
2f	44	5.29	84
2.2f, 7, 10f, 13, 15, 20	79	6.2, 4	53
2.7	50	6.3	39
2.17	30, 117	6.5	44
2.23	5	6.10	34
2.24	111	6.13	35
3.5	30	6.15	15
3.11	114	7.16	25
3.14–19	5	7.21	26
3.15	95	7.22	50

REFERENCE	SECTION	REFERENCE	SECTION
7.23	26	16.5	100
8.1	50	16.11	120
8.4	41	16.12	27, 102
8.9	23, 35	16.13	142
8.10	14	17.3	15
8.11	33	17.4, 9	89
8.12	14	17.11, 14, 24f	105
8.14	11	17.19	80
8.19	26	18.3	15
8.21	15, 27	18.4	93
8.22	79	18.6	17
9.2	11, 26	18.10	31
9.3	19, 26	18.11	29
9.11	111	18.17	120
9.14–16	79	18.18	105
9.26f	112	18.19	31, 81, 115
10	79	18.20	100
10.10	131	18.21	93
10.11	104	19.1	123
10.12	91	19.13	100
10.21	121	19.14	120
11.2	84	19.18	104
11.3	11, 16	19.19	77, 93
11.4	17	19.20	93
11.8	11	19.21	35
11.11	34	19.29	15
12.3	105	20.12	83
12.5f	123	20.13	77
12.13	93	20.23	77
12.19	28	22.1	12
13.8	23, 92f	22.11	7
14.17	25	22.14	14
14.19f	5	22.15	7
14.19, 22	119	22.17	117
14.24	19	23.4f, 7, 10	25
15.4	34	23.9	24
15.5	93	23.15	100
15.13	107	24.1	29
15.15	89	24.3	16
16.3	27	24.7	44

REFERENCE	SECTION	REFERENCE	SECTION
24.10	35	29.6	76
24.11, 13	86	29.27	89
24.12	77	30.1	16
24.13	86	30.2	11
24.16	75	30.3	12, 112
24.27	44, 78, 121	30.4, 9	11
24.43	75	30.11	128
24.48	48, 78	30.14	93
24.49	77	30.17, 19	91
24.55	30	30.24	112
24.60	99	30.26	103
25.17	6	30.27	35
25.23	16	30.33	94
26.1	23	30.37	11
26.5	11	30.38	80
26.6	17	31.19	109
26.9	21	31.29	43
26.13	25	31.46	86
26.14	16	31.48–50	23, 138
26.15	23	31.55	16, 52
26.17, 20–22, 25	26	32.10	97
26.28	110	32.25	17
27.2	93	32.32	49
27.6	12	33.13	86, 107
27.7	35	33.14	35, 93
27.8	15	34.2, 5	26
27.9	93	34.4	49
27.10	35	34.8, 12	28
27.11	23	34.25f	25
27.19, 21, 26	93	34.30	34
27.25	17	35.2, 4	14
27.37	15	36.2	52
27.39	84	36.16–43	16
27.40, 45	11	36.24	73
27.46	52	37.2	33, 100
28.14	105	37.3	74
29.2	107, 121	37.19	12
29.3	11, 18	37.20, 22, 24	25
29.4	23	37.23, 32	74
29.6f	12	37.29, 34	26

REFERENCE	SECTION	REFERENCE	SECTION
37.35	42	45.26	18
38.1	15	46.30	21
38.9	34	47.8	24
38.23	12	47.21	138
38.26	34	47.27	27
39.9	92	47.28	24
39.11	30	47.29	78
39.21	77	48.1f	107
40.1	109	48.6	34
40.14	77	48.7	86
41.16	76	48.15f	5
41.44	28	48.20	105
41.48	138	49.10	141
41.54, 56f	25	49.13	25
42.3	27	49.24	43, 130
42.23	35	49.26	139
42.27f	12	50.3	24
43.23	35	50.4	100
45.13	112	50.23	37

EXODUS

1.5	34	7.18	34
1.9	84	8.3	26
1.14	11	8.14	34
2.2	15	9.6	41
2.5	33	9.10	68
2.8	75	9.15	109, 113
2.22	14	10.15	25
2.23	35	12.35	109
3.2	16	13.3f	120
3.14	11	14.20	139
3.15, 18	44	14.27	83
3.19	31	15.13	77
4.4, 26	6	15.17	7
5.1	44	15.25	18
5.7f, 14, 16, 18f	11	16.4	29
5.13, 19	29	16.20, 24	34
5.21	34	17.15	44
6.3	44, 82, 105	18.6	138
7.1	43	18.12	141

REFERENCE	SECTION	REFERENCE	SECTION
18.19	112	28.8	84
18.21	78	28.9	11
19.5	14	29.36	68
20.7–17	134	30.2	84
20.18	131	30.7f, 35	68
21.6	43, 76	30.33	14
21.8	127	31.16	115
21.22	20	32.4	27
21.26f	18	32.17	11
21.29, 31f, 36	25	32.18	117
22.2	13	33.3	19
22.6	117	33.6	84
22.7	112	33.7–11	113
22.8f	43	34.6	44, 77f, 102
22.9	27	34.29	16, 116
22.16f	75	34.34f	113
22.28	43	35.5, 22	25
24.6	68	37.8, 17, 21f, 25	84
25.19, 31, 35f	84	37.9	11
25.30	7	37.14	83
25.35	16	38.2	84
25.40	119	38.7	17
26.30	109	39.5	84
27.8	109	39.6	11
27.14	18		

LEVITICUS

REFERENCE	SECTION	REFERENCE	SECTION
3.16	91	12.2	30
4.12	35	13.2, 6–8, 28	49
4.14	68	13.33	106
5.13	28	14.21f, 30, 32	48
6.5	68	14.56	49
6.16	99	15.16–18, 32	34
7.34	68, 84	16.7, 10, 26	47
8.36	88	16.27, 30	107
10.4	52	17.7	47
10.6	136	18.18	27
10.9	11	18.21	45
10.11	88	19.20	54
11.13–19, 29	73	20.3	115

REFERENCE	SECTION
20.17	13
21.1	105
21.3	6, 75, 105
21.10	66
21.13f	75
22.22	49
23.11	64
23.15	67
23.34	8, 67
23.37	29
24.8	85
24.11, 16	17
24.18	50
25.8	67
25.12	102
25.25	79
25.35	35
25.47, 50	105
26.1	65
26.6	119
26.30	37
27.8	84

NUMBERS

REFERENCE	SECTION
1.16	52, 128
3.18, 21	41
3.23–5, 29–32	113
3.46, 49	63
3.51	63, 128
5.19f	87
6.5	30
6.6, 11	50
6.9, 18	102
7.84	85
8.7	64
8.11, 13, 15	68
8.21	68, 106
9.6f, 9	50
9.20f	92
10.11	22
11.27	91
14.17	44
14.18	77, 102
14.19	77
16.30, 33	42
18.16	63
19.3, 5	107
19.11	50
20.14	10
20.16	12
20.18	17
21.1	100
21.6–9	73
21.14	136
21.20	104
21.23	16
21.25	52
21.27	122
22.22	54
22.36	102
23.9	106
23.24	111
24.2f	123
24.9	120
24.17	111
24.19	84
24.21	117
24.24	41
25.3, 5	45
26.3	104
26.4	20
26.63	104
27.17	11
31.3	27
31.6	101
31.12	104
33.1	80
33.8	129

REFERENCE	SECTION	REFERENCE	SECTION
33.50	104	34.5, 8f, 12	25
33.52	65	35.6	92
34.4	25, 84	35.8	99

DEUTERONOMY

REFERENCE	SECTION	REFERENCE	SECTION
1.1	41, 85	17.15	14
1.5	85	18.1	121
1.28	96	19.6, 11	50
3.20, 25	85	21.2	18
4.3	45	21.13	102
4.15f	19	21.23	106
4.20	35	22.5	91
4.25	34	22.7	30
4.26, 40	30	22.14f, 17, 19f, 23, 28	75
4.34	43	22.30	34
4.46f, 49	85	23.23	68
5.6–21	134	24.4	60
5.23	120	24.15	30
5.24	18	26.12	68
5.33	30	26.18	14
7.6	84	27.20	34
8.11	115	28.22	131
9.25	16	28.26	119
10.15	49	28.27	11, 49, 128
10.18	115	28.32	43
11.2	31	28.68	106
11.9	30	30.3	74
11.19	115	30.16	139
11.30	85	31.10	67
12.5	117	31.12	35
12.19	30	31.14	28
12.21	111	31.19	17
13.13	47	31.26	88
13.16	68	32.1	112
14.2	14, 84	32.4, 15, 30f, 37	43
14.11–18	73	32.17	47
16.13, 16	67	32.22	42
16.20	57	32.25	75
17.7	96	33.2	8
17.9, 18	35	33.3	120

REFERENCE	SECTION	REFERENCE	SECTION
33.9	127	33.21	104
33.13–15	25	33.23	71
33.13	9	33.24	84
33.19	101		

JOSHUA

REFERENCE	SECTION	REFERENCE	SECTION
3.16	127	15.3	84
5.1	85	15.4, 7, 11	35
6.8	116	15.13	18
6.11	136	15.45–62	52
7.3f	25	16.3, 7	35
8.11	91	17.5	85
9.1, 10	85	17.7	71
9.4	126	18.4, 16	88
9.23	35	18.17	84
10.2	101	18.28	41
12.1	85	19.7	41, 131
12.23	139	19.11	71
13.1	29	19.33	41
13.4	84	23.1f	29
13.8, 27, 32	85	23.10	111
15.2–11	111		

JUDGES

REFERENCE	SECTION	REFERENCE	SECTION
1.8	109	5.21	112
2.3	140	6.5	114
2.11	45	6.11, 22	91
2.22	129	6.24	44
3.4	88	6.31	87
3.7	45	8.11	35
3.24	34	8.16	56
4.3	21	8.30	34
4.5	74	9.15f, 19	78
5.2	116	11.2	14
5.5	130	11.10	81, 111
5.6	131	11.12	83
5.7	94	11.31	76
5.10	8, 55	12.9	13, 35
5.11	109, 111	12.14	52
5.14, 30	131	13.3, 16–21	91

REFERENCE	SECTION	REFERENCE	SECTION
14.3	96	18.29	52
14.8	67	18.30	129
14.11	18	19.2	140
14.17	13	19.22	47
15.3	84	20.13	47
16.2	19	20.16	60
16.13f	139	20.33	140
17.10	17	20.42	123
18.15	76	21.12	75

RUTH

REFERENCE	SECTION	REFERENCE	SECTION
1.1, 5	15	2.20	63, 77
1.8	77	3.10	77
2.7	140	4.5	141
2.14	123	4.6	63
2.18	130	4.11	74

1 SAMUEL

REFERENCE	SECTION	REFERENCE	SECTION
1.5	9	9.12f, 27	30
1.16	47	9.14	12
1.25	91	10.1	139
2.1, 10	31	10.19	119
2.9	128	10.27	47
2.12	47	11.7	96
2.23	85	13.1	20
2.24	60	13.4	34
2.25	43	13.21	8, 37
3.3	121	14.2	91
3.8	120	14.12	15
3.12	117	14.41	130, 140
3.13	111, 120, 129	14.43	111
4.4	74	15.12	120
4.7f	43	16.4	83
4.18	18	17.23	128
5.9	49	17.34f	79
5.12	49, 128	17.56	75
6.4f, 11, 17	49, 128	18.7	15
6.18	126, 131, 136	18.21	30
7.2	30	18.28	139
9.6	109	20.8	44

REFERENCE	SECTION	REFERENCE	SECTION
20.12	20	24.7	14
20.14f	77	24.15	55
20.15	8	25.7, 16	30
20.21	12, 76	25.17, 25	47
20.22	12, 75	25.22, 34	34
20.30	91	25.28	30
20.40	13	26.6	15
20.42	8, 111	26.7	12
21.1	83	26.23	111
22.3	141	27.11	30
22.4	30	27.12	34
22.12	12	28.13f	98
22.14	140	29.4	54
22.15	30	29.9	7
23.15	42, 131	30.5	33
23.18f	42	30.22	47
24.3	34		

2 SAMUEL

1.21	142	9.1, 3, 7	77
2.2	33	9.11	120
2.6	78	10.2	77
2.32	27	10.6	34
3.3	33	12.18	22
3.7	18	12.30	45
3.8	77, 91	12.31	21
5.6	100	13.2	35, 75
5.12	82	13.18	74, 75
6.2	74	13.19	27, 74
6.5	134	14.17, 20	7
6.7	9	15.1	98
6.13	98	15.2, 5	113
6.17	66	15.32	107
6.19	9	16.7	47
7.14	53, 116	16.17	77
7.15	134	17.16	128
7.26	111	17.17	91, 113
8.3	127	17.21	18
8.12	126	18.3, 9	140
8.18	27, 66	18.8	16

REFERENCE	SECTION
18.13	127
18.28f, 32	76
18.29	17
19.7	49
19.13	88
19.18	116
19.22	54
19.27	7
20.1	5
20.9	76
20.14	134
20.26	66
21.1	131
21.2	17
22.3	7
22.4	111
22.6	14
22.9	84
22.19	14
22.24	17
22.30	111
22.31	58, 91
22.33	91, 128
22.34	128
22.42	19
22.45	113
22.46	134
22.51	128
23.6	47
23.7	17
23.9	128
23.18	133
23.20	8, 30, 38
23.23	84
23.27	41
24.1	58
24.5	104
24.13	134
24.14	97
24.21	14

1 KINGS

REFERENCE	SECTION
1.1	29
1.9	42
1.51	30
1.52	35
2.2	120
2.7	77
2.11	16, 30
2.25	88
2.27	115
2.31	57
3.2	30
3.4	113
3.6	30, 77
3.11	16
3.17	87
4.2	66
4.33	11
5.4	54
5.18	41
6–8	66
6.7	116
6.8	140
7.7	141
7.9	134
7.36	11
7.40	126
8.9	80
8.12	139
8.50	60
8.59	29
9.5	101
9.8	141
10.28	131
10.29	18

REFERENCE	SECTION	REFERENCE	SECTION
11.1	14	17.18	83, 124
11.5	45	17.24	89
11.11	87	18.5	84
11.14, 23, 25	54	18.19	45
11.33	45	18.25–7	98
12.31	100	18.39	91
12.33	68	19.3	126
13.3	110	19.18	110
14.27	11	20.22, 26	31
15.13	45	20.38, 41	38
15.25, 33	19	21.4f, 7	25
16.13, 26	103	21.10, 13	25, 47
16.34	128	22.5	30
17.1	130	22.48	32
17.7	30		

2 KINGS

1.3, 6	85	13.25	88
2.1	116	15.25	8
3.2	65	16.6	126
4.10	101	16.12	68
4.17	31	17.6	41
4.25	12	17.30	45
5.15	15	17.33	123
5.20	12	18.17	38
6.33	134	18.19	103
8.26	52	18.20	121
9.2	13	18.31	118
9.18f	19	19.7	50
9.30	11	19.21–8	5
10.27	65	19.21	22, 75
10.29, 31	103	19.26	121
11.15	14	19.28	33
12.10	116	20.11	141
13.1	19	21.7	45
13.2	103	23.4	45
13.3	29	23.5	15, 17
13.10	19	23.7	13
13.23	87	23.21	102

REFERENCE	SECTION	REFERENCE	SECTION
24.16	121	25.23	134
24.20	123	25.30	29, 30
25.19	35		

1 CHRONICLES

REFERENCE	SECTION	REFERENCE	SECTION
1.51–4	16	16.5	120
2.18	34	16.29	74
2.21f	128	16.37	29
2.23	121	16.42	66
2.24	140	17.24	111
4.19	100	18.10	76
4.22	140	19.2	77
5.26	41	19.6	34
6.65	15	21.1	47, 58
6.78	85	21.22	14
7.1	141	22.1	89
7.34	131	22.3	37
11.22	30, 38	22.7	127
12.15	120	22.10	101
12.18	5	23.3	15
12.19	130	23.4f	120
13.6	74	23.28	86, 108
13.11	103	23.31	115
14.2	82	25.5	31
14.3	34	26.21	9
15.20	69, 75	26.30	85
15.21	69	27.12	41
15.24	108, 120	28.5	101
15.27	91		

2 CHRONICLES

REFERENCE	SECTION	REFERENCE	SECTION
1.1	106	6.42	97
1.5	131	7.16	29
1.8	77	7.19	8
2.7	11	8.13f	29
3–5	66	9.11	9
4.3	17, 134	10.16	5
5.9	126	11.4	85
5.12	66	11.15	47
5.13	115	12.10	11

REFERENCE	SECTION	REFERENCE	SECTION
13.7	47	25.21	15
13.19	128	25.23	126
14.5	37	26.11, 13	88
14.7	123	28.9	88
14.11	87	28.10	87
15.8	141	30.3	89
15.11	30	30.17	106
15.16	45	30.19	121
17.7	83	30.22	49
18.4	30	31.14	66
19.11	112	31.16	29
20.2	84, 133	31.20	78
20.21	74	32.1	78
20.25	126	32.32	77
20.26	8	34.6	9
20.37	110	34.9	128
22.6	126	34.11	37
23.13	12	34.13	66
23.14	14	34.15	15
23.18	88	35.5, 7, 12	13
23.20	101	36.16	120

EZRA

2.1	41	7.9	141
3.4	29, 67	7.16	41
3.7	41	9.8	8
3.11	5	9.9	8, 108
4.7	8, 17	9.13f	62
4.10, 16f, 20	85	9.15	117
5.3, 6	85	10.1	116
5.8	37	10.2	14f
6.4	37	10.10	14
6.6, 13	85	10.29	128
6.20	52		

NEHEMIAH

1.1	15	3.7	85
1.8, 11	93	5.2	93
2.7, 9	85	5.8	63
2.16	120	6.1, 6	41

REFERENCE	SECTION	REFERENCE	SECTION
6.9	43	9.19, 27f, 31	97
6.16	126	11.24	29
7.2	78, 84	11.31	98
7.59	41	12.38f	86
9.2	34	12.47	29
9.14	88	13.6	30
9.17	64, 102, 126	13.26	14

ESTHER

REFERENCE	SECTION	REFERENCE	SECTION
1.7	48, 117	3.14	115, 120
2.1	63	5.5	114
2.3f, 17, 19	75	8.10, 14	73
2.18	48	8.11	23
3.12	18	9.5	103
3.13	23		

JOB

REFERENCE	SECTION	REFERENCE	SECTION
1.4f	113	9.5	80
1.6	53	9.8	46
1.6f, 9, 12	47	9.9	14, 42
1.19	85	9.13	46
2.1	53	9.19	9
2.1–4, 6f	47	9.20	57
3.5	131	9.21	123
3.12	14	9.22	89
3.24	88	9.23	58
4.6	122	9.35	87
4.5	50	10.9	65
4.17	84	10.12	77
5.5	140	10.13	87
5.24	60	10.21f	131
6.14	77, 141	11.19	119
6.19	110, 131	11.20	50
6.20	110	12.6	8
7.4	15	12.10	50
7.7	50	12.14f	79
7.20	129	13.12	49
8.6	102	13.15	128
8.17	140	14.1	102
9.2	87, 121	14.11	33

REFERENCE	SECTION	REFERENCE	SECTION
14.14–17	113	24.24	14
15.9	87	25.4	87
15.18	131	26.4	50
15.28	112	26.6	46
16.4f	113	26.12	46, 109
16.15	31	26.13	46, 50
16.16	131	27.5	57
17.1	50	27.6	84
17.3	131	27.11	88
17.6	70	27.14	27
17.16	42	27.22	18, 117
18.12	49	28.3	96, 131
18.14	123	28.22	46
19.14f	122	30.1	22
19.17	50	30.4	86
19.24	11	30.8	61, 84
19.25	63	30.11	33, 128
19.26	8, 84, 107	30.15	50
20.11	75	30.17	49
20.14	4	30.27	14
20.23	18	30.30	19
21.19–21	96	31.1	75
21.19f	112	31.12	46
21.24	49, 100, 130	31.22	49
22.4	100	31.35	54
22.20	81	32.8	50
22.23–6	79	32.9	140
22.23	139	32.15	110
22.30	71, 140	33.6	88
23.2	86, 141	33.9	57
23.7	57	33.16	130
23.9	141	33.18, 22	7
24.2	110	33.19	128
24.7	105	33.23	47, 91
24.10	106, 121	33.25	75, 84, 110
24.12	130	33.28	128
24.17	96, 131	33.30	141
24.18	19	34.22	131
24.20	9	34.29	86
24.21	61	34.31	93

REFERENCE	SECTION	REFERENCE	SECTION
34.33	8	38.21	124
35.3	84	38.32	13f
35.14	111	38.36	49
35.15	140	38.37	14
36.4	102	39.4	39
36.5	49, 100	39.12	128
36.18	92	39.13	73
36.33	95	39.27–30	95
37.7	141	40.2	56
37.9	71	40.15	46, 87
37.12	106	40.16	49
37.13	77	41.1	46
37.15	116	41.8	92
37.16	102	41.11	8, 14
37.18	111	41.25	43, 64
38.7	53	41.30	87
38.14	101, 106	41.32	35
38.17	25, 131		

PSALMS

2.1	96	8.8	11
2.7	53	9 title	69, 75
2.11f	142	9.3	113
3 etc., titles	69, 83	9.4	109
3.2 etc.	69	9.7	74
4 etc., titles	70, 83	9.11	96
4.2	53	10.16	7
4.5	101	11.6	50
5 title	70	12 title	69
5.9	49	12.3	112
5.11	112	12.7	112, 126
6 title	69f	13.2	29, 141
6.5	33	14.2, 5	110
6.10	111	15.1	12, 66
7.4	15	15.3	110
7.9	99	16 title	69
8 title	69	16.2	9, 141
8.1	44, 131	17.5	117
8.4	91	17.7	62
8.5	47	17.10	48

REFERENCE	SECTION	REFERENCE	SECTION
17.11	114	29.2	74
17.13f	104	29.9	131
17.14	130	29.10	110
18.3	111	29.11	112
18.5, 18	14	30.1	106
18.23	17	30.3	128
18.26	59	31.4	107
18.29	111	31.6	110
18.30	58, 91	31.7	31
18.32f	128	31.10	140
18.32	91	31.14	110
18.41	19	32 title	69
18.44	113	32.9	115
18.50	128	33.2	70
19.3	82	33.5	77
19.13	91	33.7	120
20.8	110	33.15	119
20.9	7	35.7	8
21.3	14	35.15	12
21.9	48	35.19	122
22 title	69	36.5	19
22.3	74	36.6	43
22.12	25	37.21	111
22.16	25, 136	37.26	83
22.30	107	37.36	140
23.1	10	38 title	68
23.4	131	38.16	81
23.6	10, 30, 76f	39 title	69
24.7	112	39.2	84
25.6	77, 97	39.5	96
25.10	78	39.6	65
26.2	58	39.11	100
26.8	110	40.10	78
26.12	98	41.1	30
27.2	110	41.6	13
27.5f	66	42.3	29
27.8	11	42.4	21, 79
27.13	126	42.10	29
28.2	66	44.1	30
29.1	43, 53	44.2	23

REFERENCE	SECTION
44.8	29
44.12	113
44.19	131
45 title	69
45.6	19, 101, 102
45.8	70
45.14	75
46 title	69, 75
47.2, 6f	7
47.4	110
47.7	69
47.8	101
48.1f	101
48.1	122
48.3	31
48.10	19
49.5	30, 49
49.10	111
49.14	8
50.1	43
50.14	68
50.18	110
51.4	57, 81, 91, 116
51.6	112
51.8	141
51.18	112
51.19	101
52.1	29
52.5	80
52.7	141
53.2, 5	110
54 title	70, 87, 124
54.6	68
55 title	70
55.9	110
55.12	113
55.15	14, 127
55.18	87, 110
55.19	74
55.20	76

REFERENCE	SECTION
56 title	69
56.1	29, 119
56.2	29, 43
56.5	29
56.8	40, 109
56.9	30, 80
56.13	124
57–9 titles	69
57.3	110
58.1	53
58.11	92
59.6	111
59.7	12
59.9	99, 141
59.10	14, 127
59.14f	111
59.17	99, 100
60 title	69
60.4	140
60.5	127
61.3	83, 110
61.6	112
61.7	74
61.8	29, 114
62 title	69
62.7	19
62.9	53, 115
63.3	77
63.8	110
64.5	110
66.15	68
67 title	70
67.3	11, 96
67.6	109
68.4	44
68.5	55
68.6	51
68.8	21
68.15, 17	43
68.18	103

REFERENCE	SECTION	REFERENCE	SECTION
68.19	91	78.54	66, 102
68.20	62, 91	78.63	27
68.23	140	78.68	110
68.24	68	78.71	85
68.25	75	79.1	51
68.30	8, 136	79.5	33
68.35	99	79.6	110
69 title	69	79.8	14
69.4	124	80 title	69
69.13	78	80.1	74
69.22, 35	141	80.3	112
70 title	68	80.5	109
70.4	111	80.7	112
71.6	4	80.10	104
71.13	54	80.19	112
71.17	87	81 title	69
71.20	128	81.6–16	6
72.16	122	81.6	62, 94
73.4	131	81.7	94
73.8	39	81.12	112
73.9	96	81.13	120
73.12	76	81.14	113
73.15	109	82.1	43, 53
73.16	31	82.3	57
73.20	65	82.6	53
73.22f	87	82.7	80
74.2	51	83.7	41
74.4, 8	66	83.18	44
74.11	127	84 title	69
74.13	46	84.3	104
74.22	29	84.5	8
75 title	69	84.7	130
75.4f	31	84.9	122
75.8	15	84.10	66
76 title	70	85.1	128
77 title	69	85.8	139
77.1	112	85.10	110
77.6	141	86.3	29
77.19	31	86.15	102
78.25	47	87.1	19

REFERENCE	SECTION	REFERENCE	SECTION
87.4	46	101.1	77
88 title	69	102.6	73
88.6	7	102.12	74
88.9	29	102.13	11
88.11	46	102.24	19
88.13	14	103.3	98
88.17	29	103.8	102
89.1	97	104.3	94
89.6	43, 53	104.4	47, 50, 94, 123
89.8	44	104.5–9	94
89.10	46	104.10, 13	25, 94
89.17	31	104.14	94
89.22	52	104.15	112
89.24	31	104.19	94
89.27	83	104.25	89
89.45	75	104.32	90
89.49	97	105.6, 15	96
90.5	15	105.17	109
90.9	141	105.22	140
90.11	31	105.24, 37	18
90.17	44	105.43	96
91.7	111	106.4	100
92 title	67	106.7	97
92.3	69f, 86	106.20	129
92.7	115	106.21	7
92.10	31	106.28	45
93.1	106	106.34	90
94.7	44	106.37	47
94.18	81	106.45	97
94.19	49	107.8	78
95.3	7	107.14	131
95.8	42	107.15	77
95.9	80, 109	107.16ff	113
95.10	31	107.21	77
96.9	74	107.22	103
97.4, 8	110	107.31	77
97.7	111, 118	109.6	54
97.11	140	109.12	77
99.3, 5, 9	95	109.19	105
100.3	127	109.20	54

REFERENCE	SECTION	REFERENCE	SECTION
109.21	44	120.5	87, 110
109.29, 31	54	120.6	87
111.7	78	121.1	124
113.6	82	122.2	120
115.15	120	122.8f	83
116.11	130	123.1	74
117.2	77	124.3	14
118.13	114	125.3	51
118.19	112	126.4	128
118.21	80	127.1	11, 110
119.1	5, 102	128.5f	118
119.7	101, 102	129.8	110
119.9	115	130.6	44
119.12	120	130.7	118
119.23	110	131.3	118
119.41	97	132.1	83, 100
119.56	83	132.2, 5	43
119.57	99	132.6	42
119.62	101	132.11	78
119.76	77, 114	134.2	104
119.79	128	135.4	14
119.85	11	135.7	84
119.90	19	137.3	15
119.123	101	137.5	38
119.126	107	138.2	78
119.128	140	138.4	109
119.134	100, 112	139.19	81
119.136	110	140.7	44
119.142	78	141.5	77, 104
119.146	112	141.7	8
119.147	14	142.4	31
119.148	14, 110	142.6	84
119.151	78	143.9	133
119.152	84	144.2	134
119.157	110	144.3	31
119.160	78	144.7	14
119.173	114	144.9	70
119.175	112	144.11	14
120–134	69	144.12	90
120.1f	123	145.8	102

REFERENCE	SECTION	REFERENCE	SECTION
145.13	9, 133	146.6	78
145.14	119	149.6	96
146.3	91	150.3–5	70
146.4	50		

PROVERBS

REFERENCE	SECTION	REFERENCE	SECTION
1.2–4	114	8.31	53
1.14	111	8.36	60
1.33	84	10.9	31
2.4	95	10.24	100
2.8	115	10.25	116
3.3	78	10.27	30
3.5	33	10.28	19
3.14–18	95	10.29	130
3.16	30	10.17	77
3.18	96	10.20	102
3.21	8	10.21	34, 48
3.27	43	10.23	19
4.1	31	12.9	130
4.5, 8	8	12.12	8
4.9	101	12.16	30
4.22	97	12.20	76
4.26	111	13.2	19
5.6	81, 94	13.7	106
5.11	28	13.11	48, 140
5.14	67	14.4	19
5.16	124	14.17	102
5.20	14	14.22	78
5.22	23	14.28	74
6.3, 5	105	14.29	102
6.30	124	14.32	140
6.34	30	15.7	33
7.5	114	15.11	46
7.14	86	15.18	63, 102
7.18	97	16.1, 4	83
7.20	30	16.5	48
8.3	88	16.6	78
8.4	53	16.10	55
8.11	95	16.17	117
8.26	15	16.26	50

REFERENCE	SECTION	REFERENCE	SECTION
16.32	102	23.27	14
17.1	68	24.15	99
17.18	49	24.21	139
17.26	86	24.22	100
17.27	128	26.10	9
18.24	129, 141	27.13	141
19.2	60	27.20	46
19.22	77, 100	27.23	117
20.2	60	27.24	19
20.4	84	28.2	60
20.6	77	28.14	44
20.11	106	28.16	32
20.16	141	28.17	14
20.24	84	29.14	78
20.27	50	29.17, 19	4
20.28	78	30.1	8
21.6	126	30.2	84
21.8	39	30.8	14
21.12	107	30.15	73
21.14	63	30.18	31
21.15	117	30.19	75
21.21	77	30.31	8, 140
21.29	128	31.6	119
22.14	120	31.26	77
22.20	131	31.30	112
22.25	33		

ECCLESIASTES

1.2–11, 15, 18	5	3.16	104
1.14	50	3.17	131
1.16	12, 86	3.18	114
2.6	16	3.19	28
2.7	84	4.4	100
2.8	14, 53, 70	4.16	88, 136
2.21	92	5.1	117
2.24	50	5.6	47
2.25	84	5.14	34
3.2–9	5	6.10	90
3.11	76, 95	7.1–13	5
3.12	31	7.8	102

REFERENCE	SECTION	REFERENCE	SECTION
7.12	98	10.1–4, 8–20	5
7.15	30	10.1	101
7.21	107	10.4	63
8.1	5	10.11	81
8.2	43	11.1–4	5
8.8	16, 50	12.5	76
8.10	91, 113, 126	12.9	121
8.12	30, 80	12.10	64
8.13	80	12.11	7
9.2	140	12.12	121
9.3, 12	53	12.13	105

SONG OF SOLOMON

1.3	75	4.12	126
1.15	102	5.1	96
2.1	72	5.12	4
2.2f	52	6.5	84
2.5	14	6.7	49, 85
2.7	95	6.8	75
2.9	84	6.9	52
2.17	27	7.1	49, 52
3.1	9, 139	7.4	91
3.5f	95	7.8	93
3.7	90	7.9	140
3.10	8, 84	7.12	97
4.1	49, 84f, 102	8.1	107
4.3	85	8.4	95
4.8	131	8.6	44
4.9	49		

ISAIAH

1.25	64	3.24	133
2.2	91	4.1	118
2.3	84	4.4	64
2.12	83	4.5	29, 121
2.19	18	4.6	29
3.6	104	5.1	93
3.8	101	5.12	70
3.18	11	5.13	85
3.20	50	5.14	97

REFERENCE	SECTION	REFERENCE	SECTION
5.16	91	14.12	46
5.17, 24	104	14.19	84
5.26, 28–30	98	14.25	16
7.2	73, 95	14.30	133
6.6	73	14.31	120
6.8	12	15.9	98, 133
6.9	117	16.8	104
7.1	104	16.10	33
7.8	6	16.11	49
7.10	130	17.2	119
7.13	84	17.6	131
7.14	75, 91, 110, 120	17.7	37
7.15	31, 115	18.2	42
7.16	31, 121	18.4	72
7.24	23	19.5	42
8.1	83	19.10	50
8.4	31	19.14	59
8.7f	95	19.17	90
9.1	110, 121	19.20	54
9.2	131	19.21	103, 105
9.3	127	20.1	16
9.6	102	20.2	6, 109
9.10	11	20.5	84
9.12	71	21.2	100
9.13	109	21.3	116
9.20	141	21.5	117
10.18	44	21.8	44, 133
10.20	14	21.14	14, 99
10.22	120	22.3	84
10.23f	44	22.5	44, 83
11.1	72	22.7	109
11.2	7	22.16	11, 83, 99
12.2	44	22.17	103
12.5	120	22.18, 23	101
13.3	89	23.2	133
13.4, 14, 17	119	23.4	75, 109
13.21	47	23.5	80, 100
14.4	9, 133	23.12	75
14.10	124	23.13	8
14.11	70	23.16	70

REFERENCE	SECTION	REFERENCE	SECTION
24.1	111, 120	33.8	107, 133
24.4	131	33.10	106
24.11	86	33.14	111
24.14	71	33.15, 19	116
24.22	16	34.3	99
25.2	84	34.6, 8	83
25.3	96	34.7, 11, 15	73
25.4	50	34.14	47
25.10	87	34.16	13, 126
25.11	98	35.1f	122
26.4	44	35.7	142
26.9	50	35.8	101, 126
26.10	112	36.2	38
27.1	46	36.5	121
27.2	126	36.12	19
27.8	14, 50, 141	36.16	118
27.9	37, 117	37.7	50
28.5	101	37.21	44
28.9	124	37.22–9	5
28.11	32	37.22	75
28.18	46	37.29	33
28.24	29	38.5	30
28.28	124	38.9	83
29.10	123	38.11	87
29.13	11	38.20	70, 115
29.21	106	39.8	78
30.4f	110	40.2	49
30.6	73	40.3	122
30.7	46	40.4	33
30.8	130	40.6	77, 130
30.12	14	40.24	72, 80
30.20	7, 126	40.30	117
30.29	43	41.4	7
30.33	32, 45	41.10	101
31.1	14	41.21	105
32.10	30, 86	41.22	11
32.12	120	41.23	128
32.14	98	42.3	78
33.1	94	42.25	31
33.4	96	43.3, 10, 13f, 25	7

REFERENCE	SECTION	REFERENCE	SECTION
43.4	110	49.5	109, 127
43.6	98	49.6	84, 116
43.9	78	49.7	7, 117
43.13	30	49.8	64
43.14	131	49.16	11
43.19	31	49.17	130
44.4	140	49.19	84
44.6	7	49.23	33
44.8	43	49.24	133
44.11	84, 106	49.26	7
44.14	83	50.1	102, 105
44.15	80, 84	50.10	14
44.16	80	51.1	32
44.23	106	51.6	73
44.24	7, 128	51.9f	46
44.26, 28	94	51.13	80
45.2	133	51.14	7
45.3	100	51.16	141
45.8	106, 133	51.19	133
45.11	13, 53	52.3	105
45.12	89	52.6	12
45.15	7	52.8	116
45.17	76	52.11	64
45.20	119	52.14	141
45.21	7	53.5	76, 100
46.4	7	53.8	84, 92
46.6	119	53.9	96
46.7	95	53.10	68, 141
46.11	100	53.11	57
47.1	75, 92	54.4	75
47.4	7	54.5, 8	7
47.11	31	54.6	94
48.2	84, 105	54.10	77, 111
48.5	65	54.18	85
48.11	140	55.3	77, 97
48.12	7	56.2, 6	116
48.14	110	56.5	121
48.15	106	56.12	133
48.19	113	57.1	77
49.1	4	57.4	28

REFERENCE	SECTION	REFERENCE	SECTION
57.5	32, 65	63.15	101, 124
57.9	45	63.16	7
57.16	50	63.17	84
59.1	33	63.18	101
59.11	117	64.1, 3	130
59.19	50	64.4	76, 97
60.4	33	64.5	21
60.5	39	64.6	97
60.7	101	64.7	140
60.19	133	64.8	7
61.6	7	64.9	93
61.8	78	65.1	12
62.4	42	65.7	80
62.5	75	65.8	96, 115
62.12	107	65.11	45, 68
63.1	82	65.17	97
63.4	63, 102	65.20	84
63.7	77, 97	66.3	33
63.8	7	66.6	91
63.10	7, 89, 102	66.21	84
63.11	7, 102, 126	66.22	97
63.12	102		

JEREMIAH

1.10	91	4.10	76
1.18	89	4.12	84, 89
2.2	77	4.30	11, 99
2.3	95	5.1	31
2.6	131	5.7	15, 83
2.19	4, 117	5.9, 28f	106
2.20	94, 128	6.2	110
2.21	78	6.10	33
2.24	112	6.11	30, 118
2.33	32	6.16	118
2.34	57, 94	6.25	83
2.36	84	6.27	131
3.1	117	7.16	89
3.17	91, 107	7.17f	119
3.19	53, 85	7.18	114, 117
3.25	93	7.23f	25

REFERENCE	SECTION	REFERENCE	SECTION
7.25	29	15.14	126
7.26–8	25	15.19	84, 112
7.32	85	16.3	16
7.33	119	16.6f	97
8.3	15	17.1	11, 126
8.8	80	17.4	126
8.11	52	17.8	128
8.13	9	17.9	31
8.19	7, 12	17.15	93
8.21	49	17.16	130
9.7	31, 52	17.26	18
9.24	77	18.3	12
10.4	23	18.7, 9	115
10.7	91	18.13	75, 102
10.10	7, 91	18.23	16
10.11	8	19.1	84
10.12	120	19.4	57
10.14	84	19.6	7
10.16	51	19.11	85
11.12	111	20.4	120
11.15	83	20.7f	29
11.17	15, 83	20.10	100, 110
12.1	55	20.17	84
12.5	39, 76	21.2	81
12.8	110	21.14	95
12.9	93, 104	22.14	95
13.1	83	22.28	65
13.14	116	22.30	120
13.16	27, 131	23.5	72
14.2	18	23.6	42
14.4	110	23.9	101
14.6	50	23.17	76, 130
14.8	7	23.18	127
14.16	88	23.28	83
14.17	75	23.38	81
14.21	101	23.39	126
15.4	128	24.9	128
15.8	71, 84, 109	25.15	102
15.9	50	25.25	41
15.11	140	25.26	132

REFERENCE	SECTION	REFERENCE	SECTION
25.28	117	32.29	107
25.29	12	32.31	86, 114
25.38	141	32.43f	107
26.3	81	33.6	9, 78
26.17	67	33.15	72, 101
26.19	120	33.20	100
26.24	88, 114	33.22	66
27.1	126	33.25	100
27.5, 7	89	35.15	118
27.9	136	36.12	12
27.10, 15	81	36.16	117
28.8	126	37.2	88
28.15	93	37.7	120
29.6	118	37.16	16
29.10	115	37.21	32
29.18	128	38.4	93
29.22	84	38.5	15
29.26f	106	38.14	66
30.3	12	38.15	124
30.8	140	38.20	93
30.10	119	38.22	120
30.11	4, 117	38.28	20
30.13	39	39.3	20, 38
30.14	103	39.10	84
30.21	89	39.11	88
31.3	77	39.13f	16
31.4	75, 102	39.13	38
31.11	84	40.4	88
31.12	39	40.4f	14
31.13	75	40.7	84
31.20	53, 116	40.10	21
31.21	75, 102	40.14	109
31.23	101	41.1	16
32.3–5	6	41.4	115
32.11	37	41.12	32
32.14	30, 37	42.3	112
32.18	99	42.13	115
32.19	53	43.6	52
32.25	6	43.13	65f
32.28	96	44.22	88

REFERENCE	SECTION	REFERENCE	SECTION
44.25	103	49.33	53
46.6	92	50.7	101
46.9	41	50.9	12, 119
46.11	75	50.13	95
46.13	114f	50.45	86
46.15	45, 130	51.1	50, 132
46.25	45	51.2	136
46.27	119	51.8	81
46.28	4, 117	51.15	120
47.5	99	51.22	75
48.18f	52	51.27	38
48.18	131	51.32	39
48.27	116	51.34	64
48.35	98	51.39	140
48.39	109	51.41	132
49.1, 3	45	51.44	39
49.2	52	51.46	81
49.5	88	51.49	80, 115
49.9	124	51.55	96
49.12	117	51.56	97
49.15	120	51.58	117
49.16	100	52.25	35
49.20	86	52.33f	30
49.28	109	52.34	29

LAMENTATIONS

1–5	5	2.21	75
1.4	75, 140	3.5	10
1.7	67	3.13	32
1.10	31	3.14	129
1.14	28	3.19	118
1.15	75	3.22, 32	77, 97
1.16	32	3.48	32
1.17	95	3.49	33
1.18	75	3.53	7
2.3	31	3.56	9, 33
2.6	66	3.59	100
2.8	28	3.64–6	111
2.10, 13	75	4.1	33, 101
2.17	30, 31, 32	4.3	127

REFERENCE	SECTION	REFERENCE	SECTION
4.6	9, 14, 56	5.5	139
4.8	31	5.6	41
4.12	109, 111	5.11	75
4.16	48	5.18	32
4.18f	109	5.22	124

EZEKIEL

REFERENCE	SECTION	REFERENCE	SECTION
1.4	50	12.5, 14	140
1.5	25	13.6	106
1.13	140	13.10	12
1.15	12	13.18	83
1.20f	83, 96, 114, 126	13.22	114
1.25	86	14.10	56
1.27	95	14.11	106
2.1	53	14.17	94
2.6	74, 82	15.8	60
3.3	4	16.25	34
3.11	13	16.30	33
3.18	116	16.43	124
3.20	128	16.49	83
3.25	107	16.51	57
3.27	119	16.52	57, 116
4.2	96	16.54	116
6.4, 6	37	16.56	124
6.8	116	16.57	126
6.9	141	16.61	84
6.14	84	17.3	102
7.10	131	17.6	87, 102
7.19	4	17.7, 9f	33
8.2, 5	84	17.9	115
8.8	12	17.12	82
8.12	102	17.14	14
9.1	105	17.17	116
9.6	75	17.18	115
10.15, 17, 20	96	17.21	98
11.5	99	17.22	89
11.7	107	18.7, 16	103
11.13	116	18.22	16
11.15	140	18.24	128
12.3	81	19.1	89

REFERENCE	SECTION	REFERENCE	SECTION
19.2	124	26.2	32
19.7	141	26.11	65
20.7f	100	26.20	82
20.7	105	27.3	102
20.8	115	27.5	98
20.12	119	27.6	131
20.21	115	27.11	13, 42
20.29	8	27.16	126
20.30f	105	27.17	142
20.37	139	27.24	39
20.40	68	27.26	32
21.5	32, 110	27.27	102
21.10	99, 131	27.32	141
21.12	110	27.34	32f, 67
21.13	131	28.2	43
21.15	141	28.3	107
21.30	124	28.9	43
22.2	89	28.13	70
22.3	86, 119	28.16	99, 107
22.6, 9	114	28.18	109
22.7	107	28.22, 25	105
22.29	103	29.3	46
23.7	105	29.5	98
23.10	107	29.7	96
23.21	133	29.13	33
23.24	9	29.14f	14
23.30	105, 117	29.18	103
23.34	141	30.5	130
23.40	94	30.9	140
23.42	9, 128	30.17	130
23.49	65, 107	30.22	28
24.5	134	31.3	142
24.7f	100	31.4	95
24.13	109	31.14	15
24.16	120	31.15	14
24.17, 22	141	32.2	100
24.25	102	32.3	32
25.4	12	32.5	140
25.8	140	32.9	139
25.12	116	32.16	107

REFERENCE	SECTION	REFERENCE	SECTION
32.21	102	39.27	105
32.27	140	40–48	66
33.2	91	40.10	15
33.5	89, 109	40.18	83
33.6	89	40.24f	89
33.8	116	40.36	133
33.10	80	40.38	98, 107
33.12	20	40.39	115
33.13	16, 97, 116	40.41f	107
33.14, 18f	116	41	66
33.21	18	41.12	71
33.22	18, 116	41.20	129
33.32	102	42.7	83, 99
34.2	120	42.9	87
34.6	92	43.6	120
34.16	140	43.8	91, 98
34.19	112, 124	43.21f, 25, 27	107
34.28	96, 119	44.3	15
34.29, 31	140	44.26, 28	141
35.9	97, 128	45.5–7	83
35.14	116	45.7	68
36.11	28	45.17	86
36.20	109, 116	45.23	29
36.21	28	46.7	48
36.22	120	46.9	18
36.23	105	46.12	68, 107
37.5, 8–10	50	46.14	39
37.6	28	46.15	107
37.16	91	46.19	12
37.19	120	46.20	114
38.8	18	46.22	129
38.10	30	46.23	87
38.12f	103	47.3–5	16
38.13	130	47.3	116
38.23	105	47.6	15
39.7	106	47.7	12
39.11	107	47.8	33, 141
39.13	105	47.9	50, 141
39.17, 19	68, 103	47.12	15, 99
39.26	119, 127	47.18	141

REFERENCE	SECTION	REFERENCE	SECTION
48.1	21, 84	48.13, 21f	83
48.11	16	48.31ff	16
48.12, 18	68	48.35	30

DANIEL

REFERENCE	SECTION	REFERENCE	SECTION
1.3	84	4.29	101
1.7	15	4.30	15
1.9	77	4.32	84, 97, 107
1.12	107	4.33	30, 97
1.18	30, 107	5.1	83
2.2	107	5.2	107
2.4	8, 17	5.5	17, 30, 83
2.9	80	5.6, 9	49, 86
2.12f	107	5.10	49, 83, 86
2.16	114	5.13	41, 124
2.18	97	5.20	21, 107
2.21	31	5.21	97, 107
2.27	23	5.23	107
2.28	109	5.24	17
2.30	96, 107	5.25, 28	79
2.36	28	5.26	101
2.38	89	5.29	107
2.41	80	6.2	89
2.43	34, 80	6.4	88
2.45	91	6.7	43
2.46	68, 107	6.10	28
3.5, 7, 10, 15	70	6.16	107
3.6, 15	30	6.18	70
3.13, 19	107	6.22	57
3.15, 28f	43	6.23f	107
3.25	53, 91	7.1	97
4.6	107	7.4	98
4.7	120	7.5	107
4.15	95	7.9	7
4.17	14	7.13	7, 53, 107
4.19	30	7.22	7
4.23	95	7.23	99
4.24	89	7.25	87, 91, 98
4.25	84, 107	7.26	107
4.26	107	7.27	96

REFERENCE	SECTION	REFERENCE	SECTION
7.28	49, 86	11.5	86
8.4	97	11.6f	123
8.11	7, 84	11.6	33, 130
8.13	87, 91, 117	11.7	82
8.14	57, 140	11.8	84
8.19	100	11.9f	121
8.24	139	11.11	16
8.27	94	11.12	107
9.1	34	11.14	100
9.4	119	11.17	83, 87, 95, 114f, 139
9.11	117	11.18	83, 100
9.18	97	11.19	96
9.25	38, 99	11.21	101, 107
9.26	95	11.23	116
9.27	21, 119	11.25	107
10.5	91	11.27	99
10.10	23	11.30	39, 41
10.11	116	11.35	64
10.13	139	11.36	43
10.17	110	11.38	79
10.19	116, 126	11.39	87
11.1	99	11.45	97, 101
11.2	116	12.10	106

HOSEA

1f	42	5.15–6.3	21
1.10	53	5.15	59
2.13	30	6.4	77
2.15	30, 84	6.6	77, 110
2.19	77	7.1–3	25
2.22	42	7.1	32
3.2f	83	7.4	116, 131
4.1	77	7.5	105
4.2	117	7.6	130
4.14	89	7.10	88
4.16	111, 124	7.11	49
4.18	131	7.14	126
5.2	106, 131	8.1	60
5.7	14	8.5	57, 98
5.13	39, 142	8.7	81

REFERENCE	SECTION	REFERENCE	SECTION
8.10	139	10.15	139, 142
8.11	114	11.1	53, 83
8.14	66	11.2	113
9.1	14, 139	11.3	83, 89
9.6	12, 102	11.7	8, 107, 131
9.8	131	11.10	53
9.10	45	12.10	89f
9.11	48, 84	13.5	89
9.13	115, 131	13.10	136
9.15	110	13.13	14
10.3	110, 111	13.14	124
10.6	142	14.2	140
10.9	124	14.3	43
10.11	112	14.8	89
10.12	77, 83	14.9	124

JOEL

REFERENCE	SECTION	REFERENCE	SECTION
1.2	89	2.32	62
1.4	73	3.3	109
1.8	75	3.4	83
2.2	131	3.5	66
2.13	77, 102	3.6	13
2.18	109	3.13	11, 39
2.24	11	3.17	119

AMOS

REFERENCE	SECTION	REFERENCE	SECTION
1.3	116	5.2	75, 102
1.6	103, 116	5.4, 6	118
1.9	52, 103, 116	5.8	42, 131
1.11, 13	116	5.12	119
2.1, 4, 6	116	5.13	89
2.7	114	5.20	108
2.8	56, 121	5.23	70
2.13	106	5.26	45, 102, 131
3.3	111	6.1	121
3.9	139	6.5	70
4.2	12, 96	6.12	131
4.4	27, 104	7.1	120
4.5	68, 84	7.2	89
4.7	113	7.4	113, 120

REFERENCE	SECTION	REFERENCE	SECTION
7.5	89	8.5	114f
7.7	86, 120	8.9	30
7.13	66	8.13	75
7.14	72, 108	8.14	45, 131
7.15	85	9.1	86
8.1f	8	9.10	14

OBADIAH

1.1	14	1.6	97
1.2	15, 120	1.7	76
1.3	16	1.9	81
1.4	117	1.10	100
1.5	9	1.17	62

JONAH

1.5	109	3.3	21
1.6	43	3.9	111
1.10	89	4.2	77, 102
2.2	84	4.9	87
2.3	98	4.10	52
2.8	77		

MICAH

1.3	119	4.4	119
1.6	33	5.1	9
1.12	109	5.5	139
1.13	32	5.6	98
2.3	108	5.8	81, 92
2.6	97, 112	6.8	77, 117
2.11	50, 120	6.9	51
2.12	131	6.13	114, 140
3.2f	11	6.16	109, 140
3.6	84	7.1	110
3.8	80, 89	7.4	131
3.11	111	7.7	89
4.2	84	7.12, 16	96

NAHUM

1.2	119	1.8	104
1.3	102, 122	2.2	6, 123

REFERENCE	SECTION	REFERENCE	SECTION
2.3	100	3.8	130
2.7	39	3.10	107
2.8	119	3.11, 16	84
2.11	21, 119	3.17	38
2.12	120	3.18	119

HABAKKUK

1.3	106	2.16	84, 100
1.17	111	2.17	100
2.1	86, 100	2.18	11, 115
2.3	81	2.19	91, 124
2.4	142	3.1, 3, 9, 13, 19	69
2.6	38	3.2	100
2.7	97	3.16	87, 110
2.8	100	3.17	111
2.10	60	3.19	70

ZEPHANIAH

1.5	45	2.14	32, 73, 98, 140
1.6	85	2.15	31
1.8	14	3.2	110
1.9	98	3.6	85
1.11	42	3.7	94
1.12	119	3.8	130
2.4	107	3.13	119
2.5	85	3.15	126
2.6	40	3.16	99
2.13	91	3.18	131

HAGGAI

1.4	89	2.18	85
1.10	14	2.19	124
2.13	50	2.21f	111
2.16	11, 139	2.21	120

ZECHARIAH

1.8, 10f	120	3.3	120
2.7	104	3.7	119
2.8	109	3.8	72
3.1	47, 54	3.9	11, 99

REFERENCE	SECTION	REFERENCE	SECTION
4.6	15	10.5, 11	107
5.7	4, 89, 91	11.2	39
6.5	50, 104	11.4	100, 109
6.11	139	11.6f	131
6.12	72, 87	11.8	91
6.14	134, 139	11.9	120
7.5	89	11.11	131
7.7	92	11.13	141
7.9	77, 97, 103	11.15, 17	65
7.12	88	11.16	33
7.14	107	12.2	98, 120
8.8	78	12.6	131
8.9	119	12.11	41, 100
8.12	76	12.13	41
8.16	103	13.6	49
8.21	117	14.1	100
9.1	83	14.3	116
9.4	12	14.4	104
9.7	121, 131	14.6	140
9.8	84, 131	14.11	107
9.9	79	14.12	32
9.11	15	14.13, 15	100
9.15	98	14.16, 18f	67
9.17	75	14.20	7
10.2	110	14.21	13

MALACHI

REFERENCE	SECTION	REFERENCE	SECTION
1.2f	109	2.10	52
1.4	107, 111	2.11	110
1.5	86	2.13	85
1.7	116	2.14	102
1.9	84	2.16	131
1.11	108	2.17	116
1.13	129	3.3	64
2.5	102	3.11	15
2.6	78	4.2	100
2.9	14, 88	4.5	117

INDEX OF HEBREW AND ARAMAIC WORDS

(N.B.—Words are arranged according to the order of the Hebrew alphabet: *’ b g d h w z ḥ ṭ y k l m n s ‘ p ṣ q r ś š t.* For the system of transliteration used see Note on p. ix.

References are to sections. Where words are numbered within sections, the word-numbers are given in parentheses following the section-numbers; e.g., 81(3) means 81, No. 3.)

WORD	SECTION
’āb	52(1)
’ēb	72(43)
’baddōn	46(2)
’ābīr	43(5)
’abbīr	47(3), 73(3)
’bāl	80(6)
’ādām	53
’dāmāh	71(1)
’dōnāy	44
’ōhel	66(9)
’ūlay	81(2)
’ūlām	80(7)
’āwen	59(4)
’ōr	72(26)
’ōrah	72(27)
’azkārāh	68(38)
’āḥ	52(4)
’ōḥīm	47(8)
’ḥaštrān	73(7)
’īy	71(5), 73(13)
’ayyāh	73(21)
’ayil	65(6), 69(14), 72(13)
’ayyelet	69(13)
’ayin	92(2)
’īš	53
’ōkēl	73(50)
’ākēn	80(8)
’al	92(3)
’al tašḥēt	69(16)
’ēl	43(2), 65(6)
’el	82(1)
’ēlāh	72(12)
’lōhīm	43(1)
’alyāh	68(33)
’līl	65(5)
’elep	51(7)
’el-pnē	88(7)
’im	81(1)
’met	78
’nāqāh	73(32)
’ap	80(2)
’pēr, ’ēper	38(1)
’arbeh	73(46)
’rī’ēl	38(7)
’ereṣ	71(1)
’ēšel	72(14)
’āšām	59(2), 68(7)
’šer	80(4), 90
’šērah	45(3), 65(3)
’ēt	92(4)

WORD	SECTION
b-	82(2), 116
BGD	60(2)
bhēmōt	46(4)
BḤN	58(2)
byad	88(1)
bayit	51(9), 66(1)
bākā'	72(9)
bikkūr	72(45)
beker, bikrāh	73(9)
blī	82(3)
bliyya'l	47(11), 61(10)
bēn	52(2)
ben šānāh	68(28)
ba'būr	82(4)
b'ēber	85(2)
b'ēnē	88(12)
bipnē	88(6)
biqqōret	54(6)
brōš	72(5)
brōt	72(4)
BRR	64(6)
bat	52(3)
bat ya'nāh	73(23)
btūlāh, btūlīm	75
gā'ōn	71(3)
G'L	63(4)
gō'ēl	63(5)
g'ullāh	63(6)
gab	49(1)
gbūl	71(6)
gōb	73(49)
gōy	51(1)
gēzel	59(23)
gāzām	73(45)
geza'	72(46)
gillūl	65(11)
gam	80(1)
gōme'	72(18)
gittīt	69(18)

WORD	SECTION
da'āh	73(19)
dbīr	66(13)
dābār	55(13)
dūkīpat	73(30)
daḥwān	70(22)
dī	80(5)
dayyāh	73(22)
DYN, DŪN	55(6)
dīn	55(7)
dayyān	55(9)
deše'	72(25)
dāšēn	64(17)
h-	93(1)
-āh	93(2), 112
higgāyōn	69(2)
hadrat qōdeš	74(5)
hawwāh, hōwah	61(9)
hēkāl	66(12)
hēylēl	46(6)
hlīkah	68(39)
hpakpak	59(17)
w-	79, 109
wāzār	39
ZBḤ	68(1)
zebaḥ	68(2)
ZWR	39
zīw	49(8)
zīz	73(12)
ZKH	57(1)
zākū	57(2)
ZKR	68(37)
ZLL	130
ZQQ	64(9)
ZRQ	68(34)
ḥbaṣṣelet	72(31)
ḥag	67(5)

WORD	SECTION	WORD	SECTION
ḤGG	67(4)	*YŠR*	56(1)
ḤṬ'	60(3), 64(3), 68(35)	*ya'nāh*	73(23)
ḥṭā'āh, ḥaṭṭā'āh, ḥaṭṭā't	60(5), 64(4), 68(6)	*ya'ar*	42(8)
		yēš	92(1)
ḥay	50(1)	*YŠB*	74(1)
ḥayyāh	73(11)	*yšū'āh*	62(4)
ḥayil	74(2)	*YŠ'*	62(1)
ḥālīl	70(9)	*yēša'*	62(3)
ḤLṢ	62(7)	*yōteret*	68(31)
ḥammūq	49(3)		
ḥōmeṭ	73(34)	*k-*	116
ḥammān	37	*kābōd*	101(1)
ḥesed	77	*KBŠ*	64(5)
ḥsīdāh	73(29)	*kōhēn*	66(1)
ḥāsīl	73(48)	*kōaḥ*	73(33)
ḥap	57(6)	*kī*	80(3)
ḥēpeṣ	64(18)	*kīmāh*	42(9)
ḥārgōl	73(41)	*kālīl*	68(12)
ḥārūṣ	38(4)	*kāmār*	65(1)
ḥraṣ	49(4)	*kēn*	73(43)
ḥōreš	42(7)	*kinnōr*	70(3)
		kuššemet	72(22)
ṬHR	64(8)	*KPH*	63(12)
ṭuḥāh	49(11)	*kpī*	88(14)
ṭḥōr	49(18)	*KPR*	63(1)
ṭipšar	38(3)	*kōper*	63(2), 72(20)
		kippūr	63(3)
y'ōr	42(4)	*karkārāh*	73(10)
yabbelet	49(21)	*ktīb*	127
yād	88(1–4)	*ktōnet paššīm*	74(4)
ydūtūn	69(12)		
YHWH	44	*l-*	83(1), 114f
yōneqet	72(41)	*l'ōm*	51(3)
yōnat 'ēlem rḥōqīm	69(14)	*lbōnāh*	68(23)
YKḤ	54(5), 56(4)	*leb-qāmāy*	132
yeleq	73(47)	*lūz*	59(14), 72(11)
yām	42(5), 46(10)	*lēwī*	66(12)
yēm	73(6)	*liwyātān*	46(5)
yanšūp	73(25)	*lzūt*	59(13)
yiššōr	56(2)	*leḥem pānīm*	68(16)

WORD	SECTION	WORD	SECTION
leḥem maʻreket	68(17)	*MLṬ*	62(8)
lyad	88(2)	*MLK, melek, mōlek*	45(4)
liydūtūn	69(12)	*malkūt*	101(4)
llammēd	69(10)	*malkām, milkōm*	45(4)
lmin	85(4)	*millipnē*	88(10)
lamnaṣṣēaḥ	69(11)	*mamlākāh*	101(4)
lmaʻan	81(4), 83(2), 114	*mimśāk*	68(20)
lʻummat	72(8), 83(3)	*min*	84, 116
lʻēnē	88(13)	*minḥāh*	68(4)
lpī	88(15), 115	*mnaʻnaʻ*	70(12)
loqbēl	83(5)	*mnaṣṣēaḥ*	66(3), 69(11)
liqraʼt	83(4)	*maśśāh*	58(5)
		maśśēkāh	65(16)
mēʼḥar, mēʼaḥrē	85(5)	*māśōrāh*	125
mēʼēn	85(9)	*mēʻēber*	85(3)
mēʼēt	85(6)	*MʻL*	60(6)
mibblī	85(7)	*maʻal*	60(7)
mibbaʻad	85(8)	*mēʻal*	86
middīn	55(8)	*maʻlāh*	69(8)
mūśār	56(3)	*maʻan*	81(4), 83(2)
mōʻēd	66(8), 67(3)	*maʻsēr*	68(41)
mūq	39	*mipleṣet*	65(7)
mōqdāh	68(36)	*mippnē*	88(9)
mōšīaʻ	62(2)	*maṣṣēbāh*	65(4)
mōšāʻāh	62(5)	*miṣṣad*	88(5)
mūt labbēn	69(19)	*maṣōr*	42(11)
māzōr	39	*miqdāš*	66(7)
mizmōr	69(6)	*maqhēl*	67(10)
MZR	39	*miqrāʼ*	67(11)
MḤH	64(1)	*mārōm*	43(4)
moḥlat (lʻannōt)	69(22)	*masʼēt*	68(9)
maṭṭeh	51(4)	*maskīl*	69(3)
muṭṭeh	59(2)	*maskīt*	65(17)
maṭṭāʻ	72(22)	*mišbāt*	67(2)
miyyād	88(3)	*miškān*	66(10)
mikšōl	60(1)	*mišpāḥāh*	51(8)
miktām	69(4)	*mišpāṭ*	55(5)
malʼāk	47(1)	*mašrōqī*	70(17)
MLḤ	39	*mittaḥat*	87(3)

WORD	SECTION
-nā'	15, 93(3)
nēbel	70(4)
negeb	42(3)
ngīnāh	70(1)
ndābāh	68(15)
ndībāh	50(2)
neder	68(42)
NHG	39
nahlōl	72(29)
nāhār	42(6)
NWḤ	63(13)
NZL	130
nḥīlāh	70(2)
nāḥāš	73(40)
nṭīšāh	72(38)
neṭa'	72(33)
nīḥōaḥ	68(24)
nākā'	61(11)
Ns̀H	58(4)
Ns̀K	68(18)
nes̀ek	65(15), 68(19)
nepeš	50(1)
NṢḤ	66(3), 69(11)
neṣaḥ	43(6)
NṢL	62(9)
nēṣer	72(42)
neqeb	70(10)
NQH	57(3), 64(2)
nāqī	57(4)
niqqāyōn	57(5)
NS'	64(11)
nāšeh	49(15)
nšāmāh	50(3)
nešer	73(17)
ntīnīm	66(5)
s̀bīr	129
s̀abkā'	70(19)
s̀gōr	68(32)
s̀ūmpōnyāh	70(21)
s̀ūt	58(1)
s̀ukkāh	67(6)
s̀elāh	69(1)
S̀LḤ	64(12)
s̀allāḥ	64(13)
s̀līḥāh	64(14)
s̀als̀illāh	72(37)
S̀LP	59(21)
s̀elep	59(22)
s̀appaḥat	49(20)
'abṭīṭ	38(5)
'BR	60(8), 62(13)
'ēber	85(1–3)
'ad	87(1), 116
'ēdāh	67(8)
'ūgāb	70(8)
'WH	59(5)
'WL	59(8)
'āwel	59(10)
'awlah	59(11)
'awwāl	59(9)
'ōlām	76(2)
'āwōn	56(9), 59(7)
'aw'eh	59(6)
'zā'zēl	47(10)
'ṭīn	49(10)
'ayin	88(12f)
'īr	71(4)
'akšūb	73(37)
'al	69(15), 86, 116
'al-yad, 'al-ydē	88(4)
'LH	68(3)
'āleh	72(40)
'ōlāh	68(14)
'lūmīm	75
'lūqāh	73(42)
'elem	75

WORD	SECTION
'almāh, 'lāmōt	75
'almūt	69(19), 75
'al-pnē	88(11)
'am	51(2)
'im	87(2)
'ummāh	83(3)
'āmāl	59(12)
'NŠ	56(8)
'ōpel	49(17)
'eṣeb	65(10)
'ōṣeb	65(9)
'ṣārāh, 'ṣeret	67(7)
'āqēb	49(16)
'iqqēš	59(15)
'iqqšūt	59(16)
'rābāh	42(1)
'ārāh	72(19)
'ar'ār	72(28)
'armōn	72(10)
'ōrēq	49(5)
'eseb	72(24)
'āsōr	70(5)
'SR	68(40)
PDH	63(7)
pidyōn	63(8)
pī	88(14f)
pīm	37
pluggāh	51(6)
PLṬ	57(8), 62(10)
plēṭāh	62(12)
plīlāh	55(11)
plīliyyāh	55(12)
PLL	55(10)
pen	81(3)
pānīm	88(6–11)
paššīm	74(4)
pešaḥ	68(29)
pšīl	65(14)
pešel	65(13)
pšantērīn	70(20)
PṢH	62(12)
PQD	56(6)
pquddāh	56(7)
par	73(1)
pereš	73(18)
pārāš	73(4)
PŠ'	60(9)
peša'	60(10)
PTL	59(19)
ṣe'el	72(16)
ṣāb	73(31)
ṣad	88(5)
ṣaddīq	57(12)
ṣedeq	57(10), 101(5)
ṣdāqāh	57(11), 101(5)
ṣawwārōn	49(9)
ṣūr	43(3)
ṣelem	65(12)
ṣalmāwet	131
ṣēla'	49(14)
ṣammāh	49(6)
ṣemaḥ	72(42)
ṣepa'	73(38)
ṣip'ōnī	73(39)
ṣārebet	49(19)
ṢRP	58(6), 64(10)
qā'at	73(27)
qbēl	83(5)
qōdeš	66(6), 74(5), 101(3)
qāhāl	67(9)
QṬR	68(21)
qṭar	49(4)
qṭōret	68(22)
qīqāyōn	72(23)
qītrōš	70(18)
QNH	63(9)

WORD	SECTION	WORD	SECTION
qāneh	49(2)	*sa'īr*	47(7)
qèsem	55(14)	*sārūq*	72(34)
qeṣaḥ	72(21)	*sārāp*	47(5), 73(40)
qrē'	127	*š'ōl*	42(10), 46(1)
qereb	49	*šēbeṭ*	51(5)
qarnā'	70(16)	*šabbāt*	67(1)
qereṣ	73(44)	*šiggāyōn*	69(5)
		šigyōnōt	69(23)
rā'āh	73(20)	*šēd*	47(6)
r'ēm	73(16)	*šiddāh*	70(15)
rō'š	72(7)	*ŠWB*	59(24)
RBK	68(27)	*ŠWB šbūt*	74(3)
rūaḥ	47(2), 50(4), 59(6)	*šōpār*	70(11)
rāḥām	73(28)	*šōq*	68(30)
RYB	54(4)	*šōr*	73(2)
rīb	54(3)	*šōšannīm*	69(15)
rekeš	73(5)	*šūšan 'ēdūt*	69(21)
rammāk	73(8)	*ŠYZYB*	62(14)
RŠŠ	39	*šaḥap*	36, 73(24)
ra'	61(3)	*šaḥar*	46(6), 69(13)
rā'āh	61(4)	*šiṭṭāh*	72(17)
rōa'	61(5)	*šīr*	69(7)
R'H	61(2)	*šīr ma'lōt*	69(8)
R''	61(1)	*ŠKḤ*	38(6)
RṢH	64(15)	*ŠKK*	63(10)
rāṣōn	64(16)	*šālōm*	76(1)
raqqāh	49(7)	*šelaḥ*	72(36)
rōqaḥ	68(25)	*šālīš*	70(6)
RŠ'	55(15), 61(6)	*šlāmīm*	68(5)
reša'	61(8)	*šmīnīt*	69(17)
rāšā'	61(7)	*šemen*	68(26), 72(2)
rōtem	72(30)	*šānāh*	68(26)
		šō'ēr	66(4)
sabkā'	70(19)	*ŠPṬ*	55(1–3)
sādeh	71(2), 73(11f)	*šepeṭ*	55(4)
sōkāh	72(39)	*špēlāh*	42(2)
SṬN	54(2)	*šiqqūṣ*	45(2)
sāṭān	47(12), 54(1)	*ŠQṬ*	63(11)
sekwī	49(12)	*šāqām*	72(44)
smāmīt	73(36)	*šarīr*	49(13)

WORD	SECTION
šēšak	132
štīl	72(35)
t'ō, tō'	73(15)
t'aššūr	72(1)
tidhar	36, 72(3)
thōm	46(7)
tōkēḥāh, tōkaḥat	56(5)
taḥat	87(3)
tamīd	68(13)
tōmer	72(15)
tnūpāh	68(11)
tannīn	46(9), 73(14)
tanšemet	73(26, 35)
tōp	70(13)
tip'eret	101(2)
tpillāh	69(9)
tōpet	70(14)
tiqqūnē sōprīm	129
trūmāh	68(10)
tirzāh	72(6)
trāpīm	65(18)
tšū'āh	62(6)